CW01574899

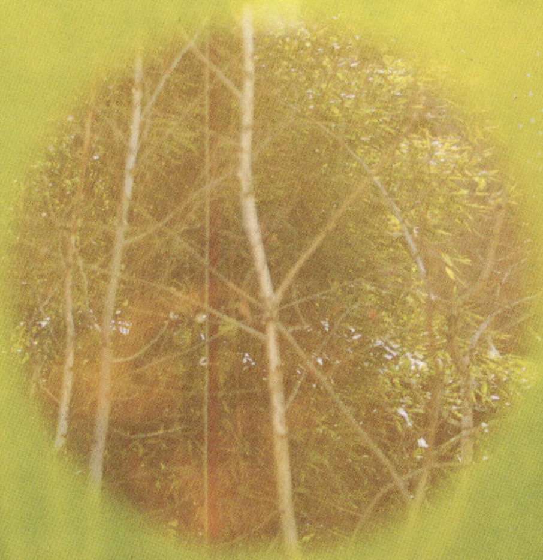

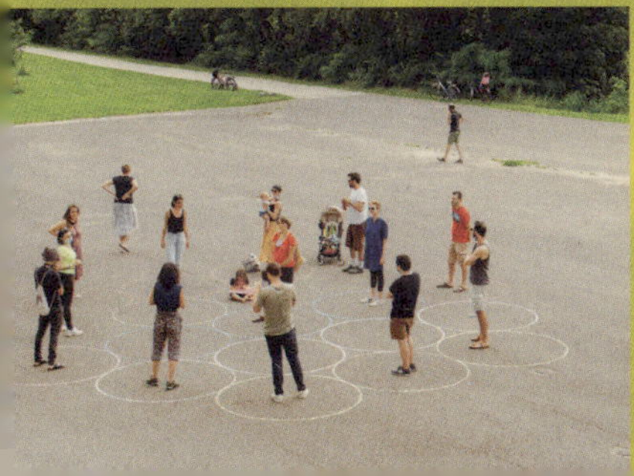

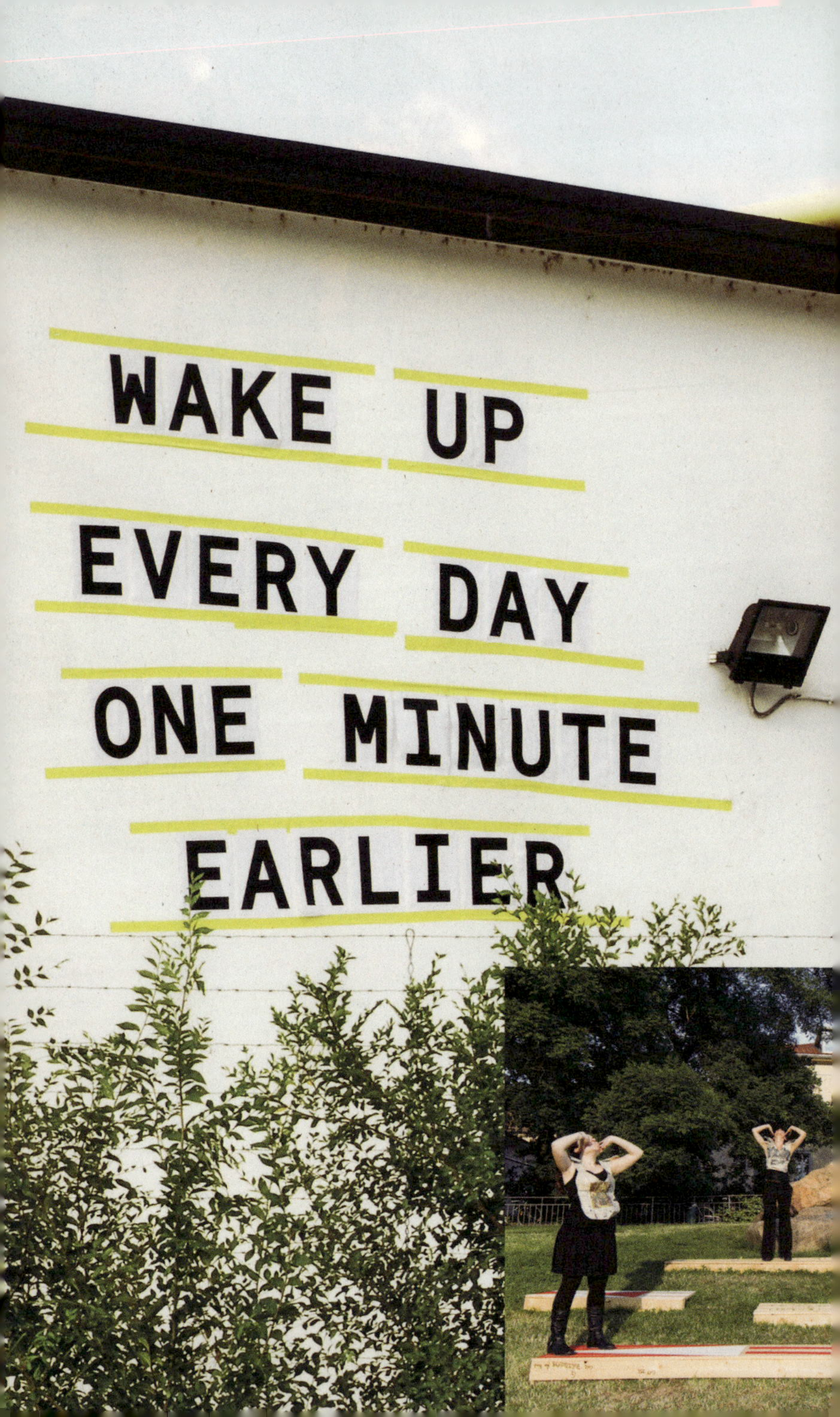
WAKE UP
EVERY DAY
ONE MINUTE
EARLIER

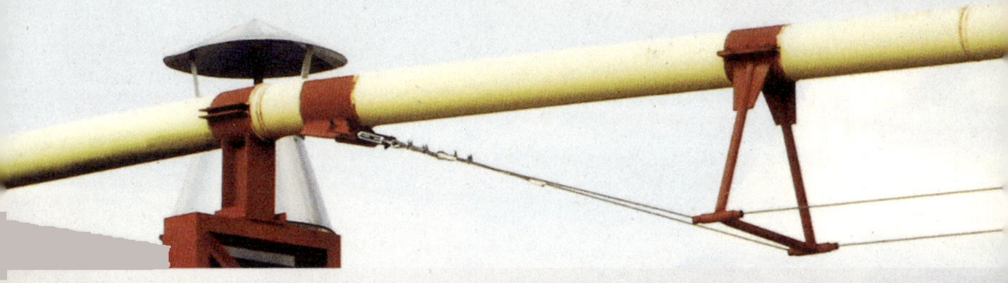

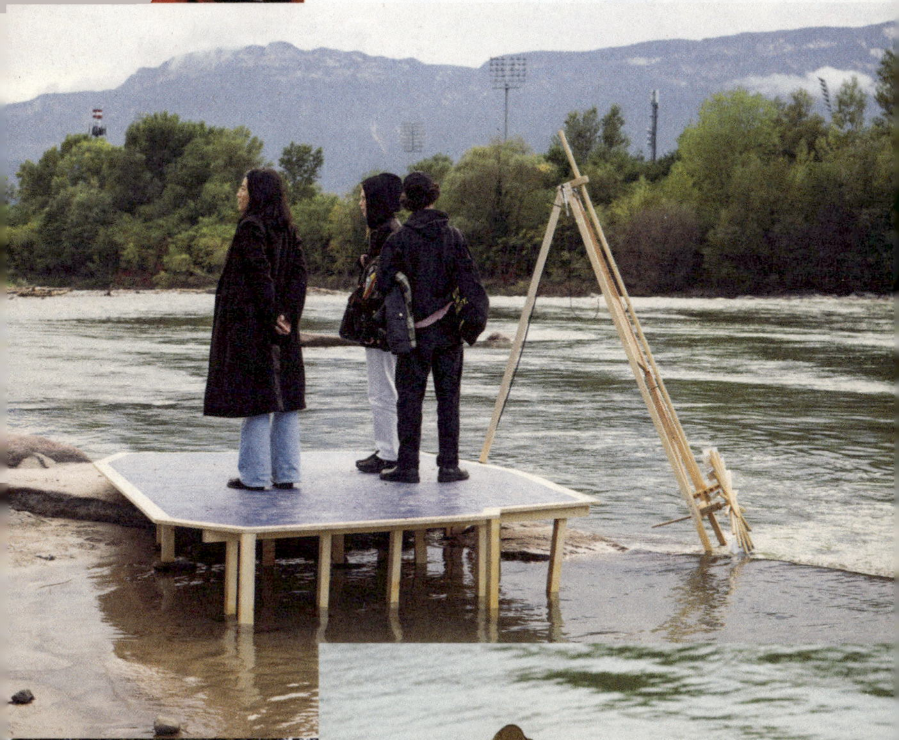

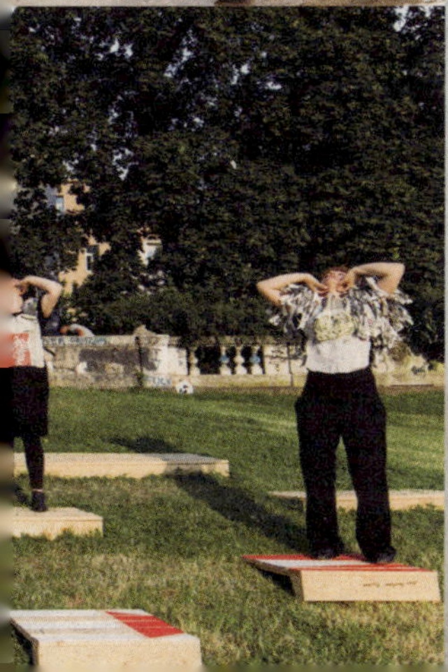

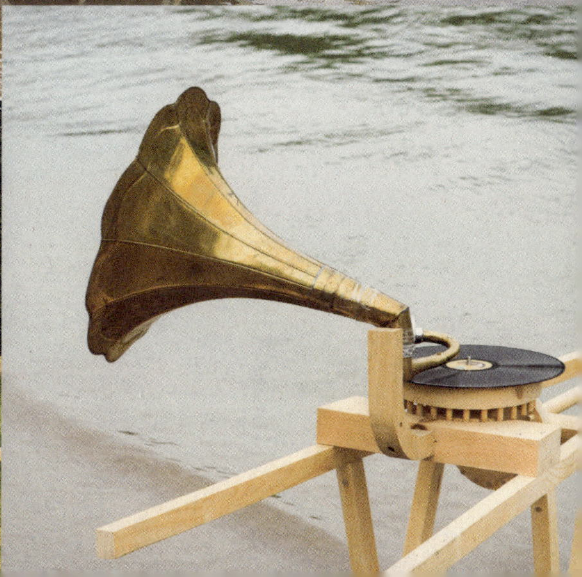

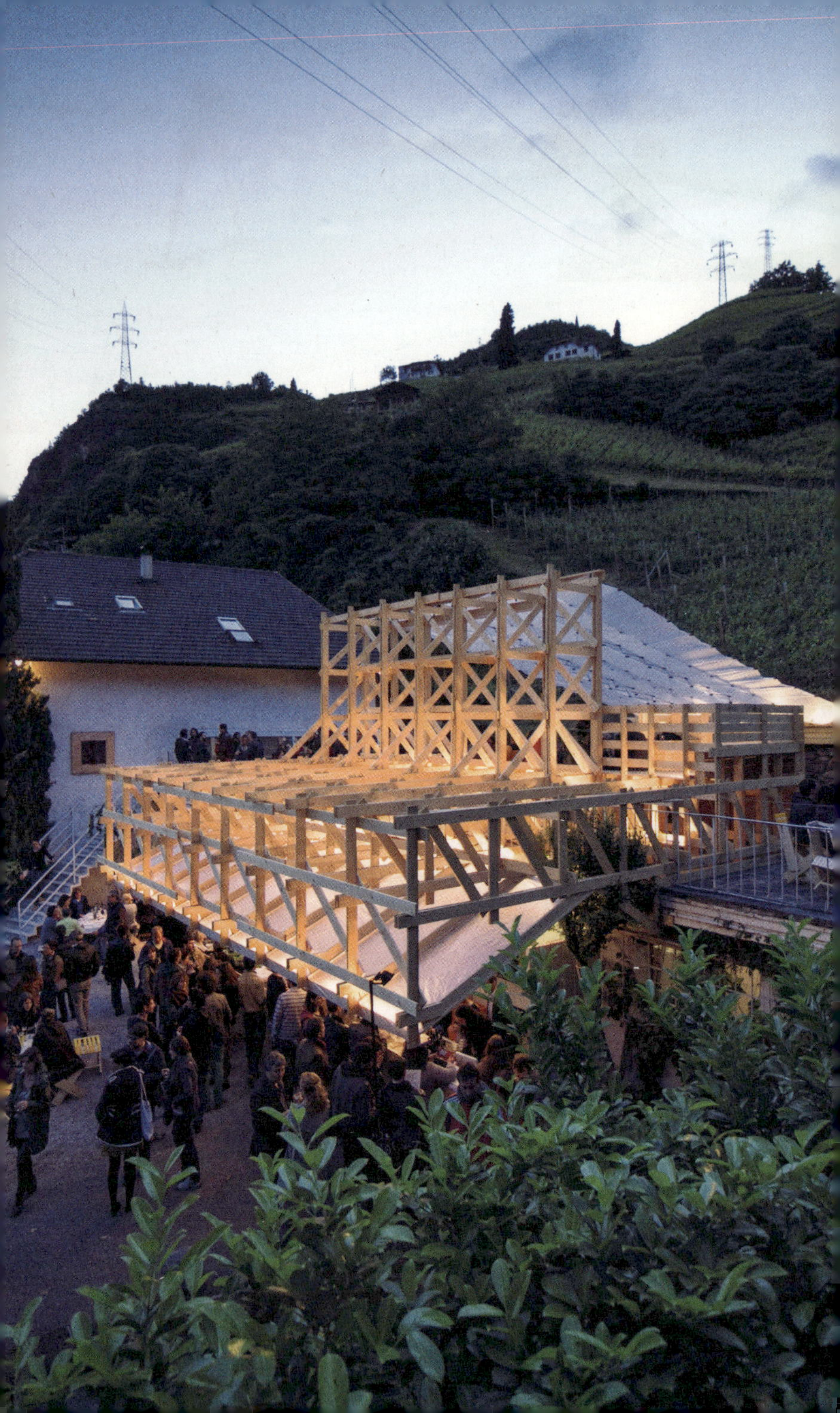

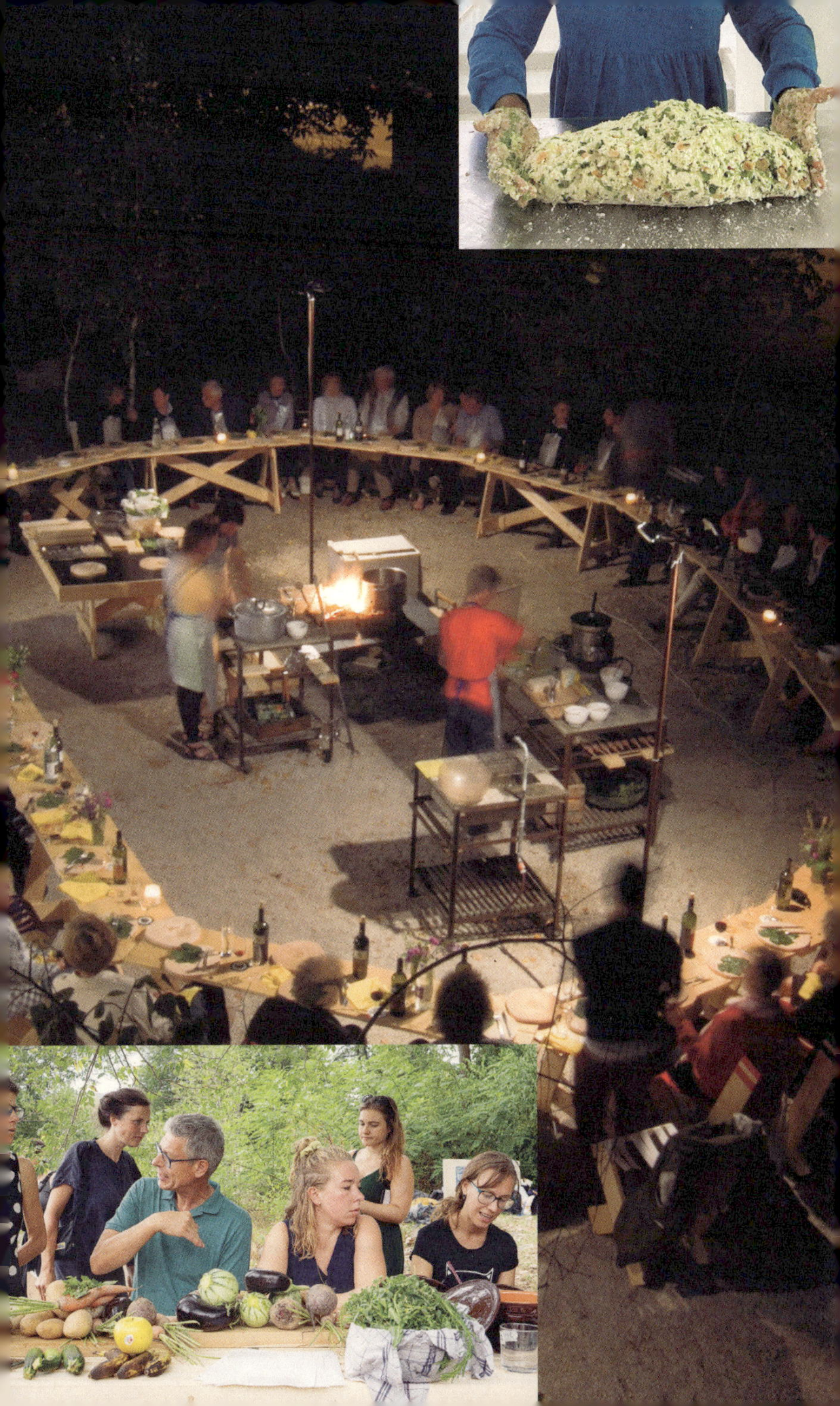

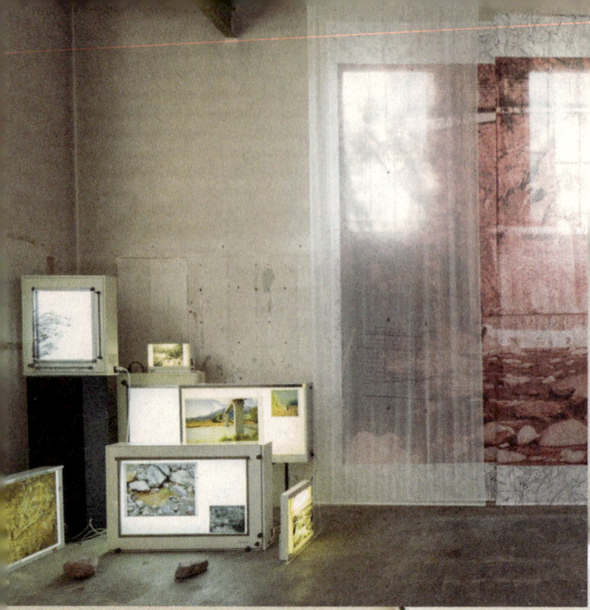

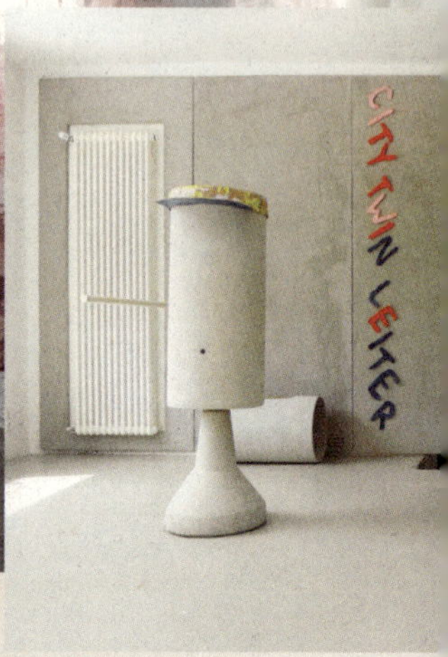
CITY TWIN LETTER

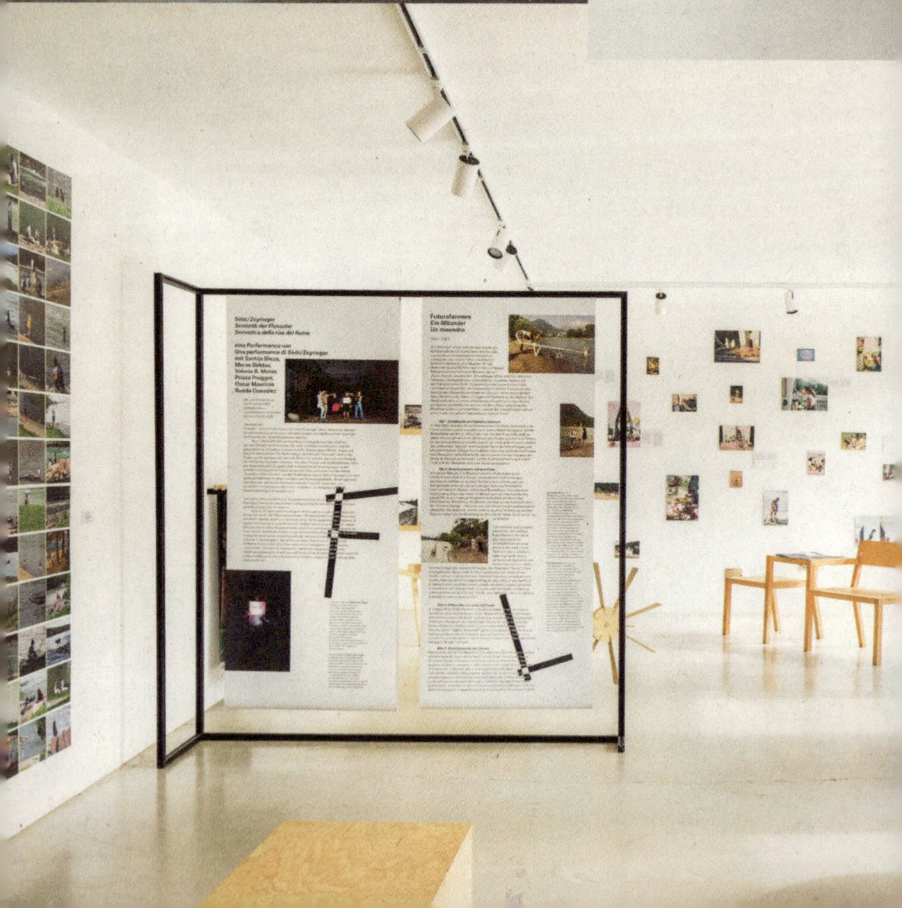
Futurefarmers
Ein Mäander
Un meandro

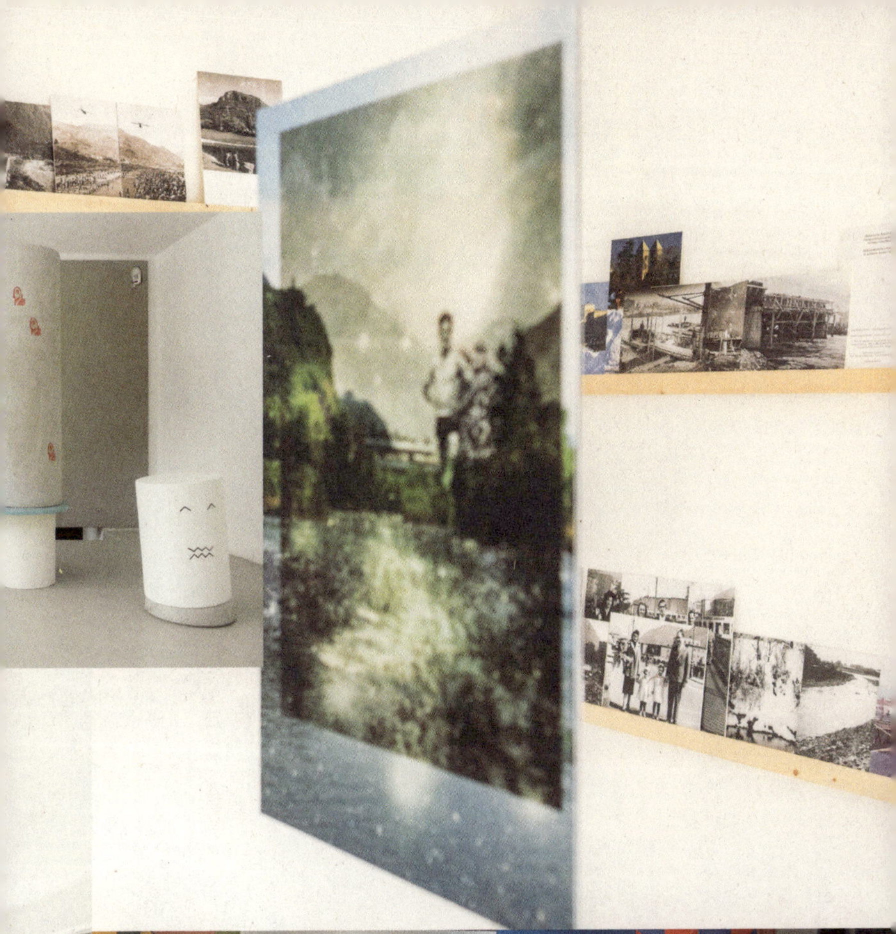

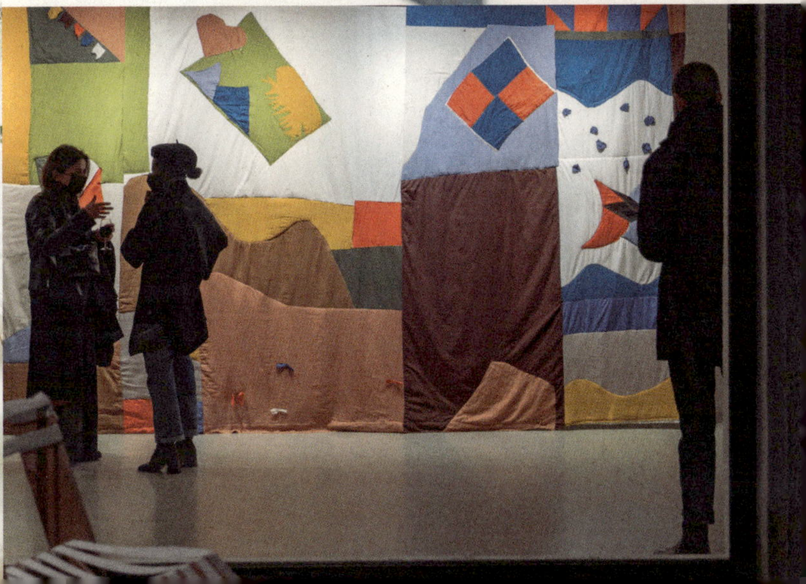

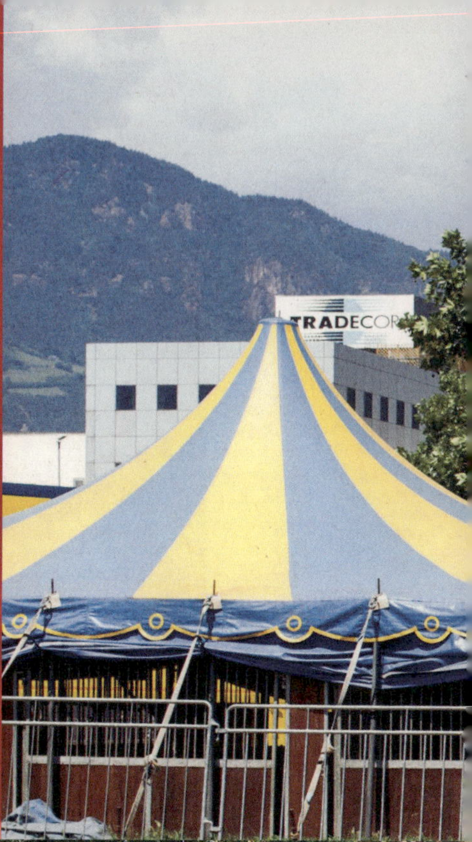
TRADECOR

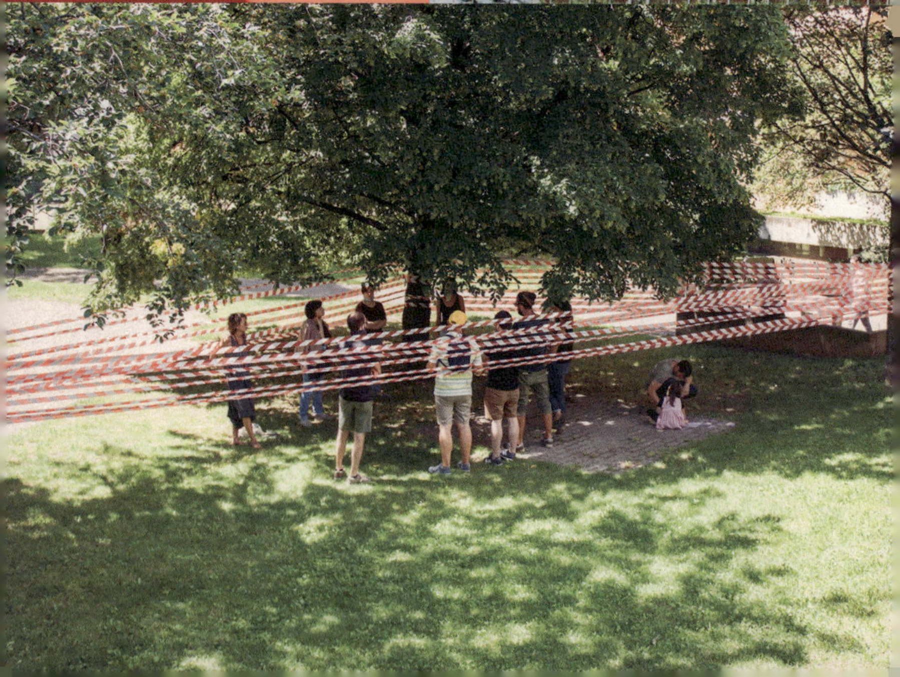

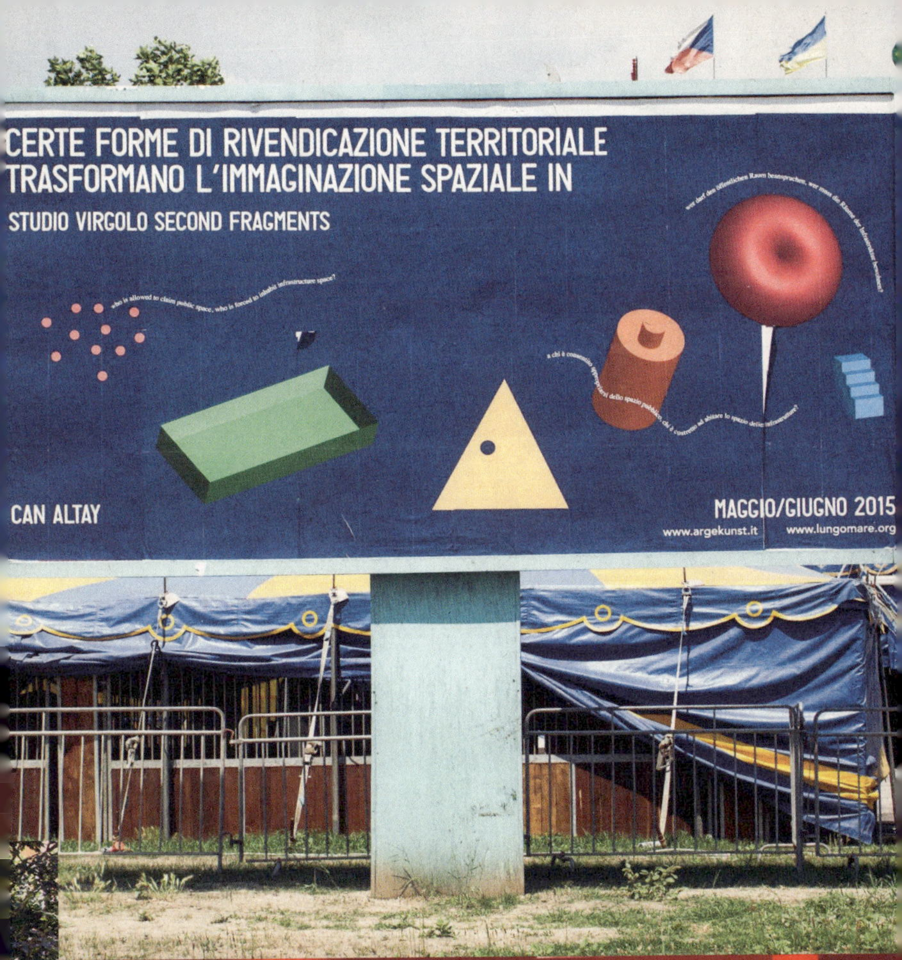

Entrance to the unfinished Virgolo Tunnel where a group had settled and lived inside for years.

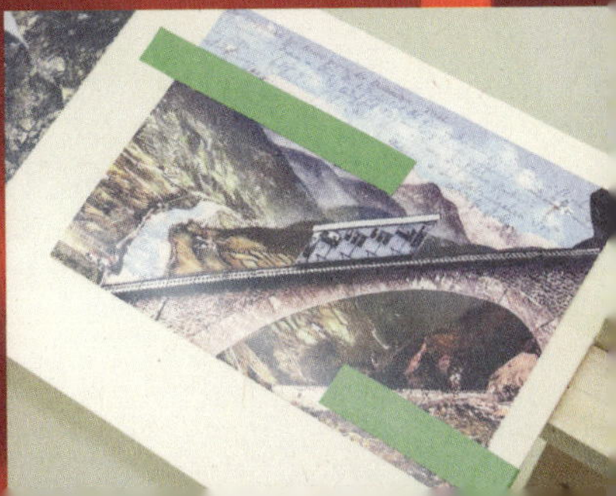

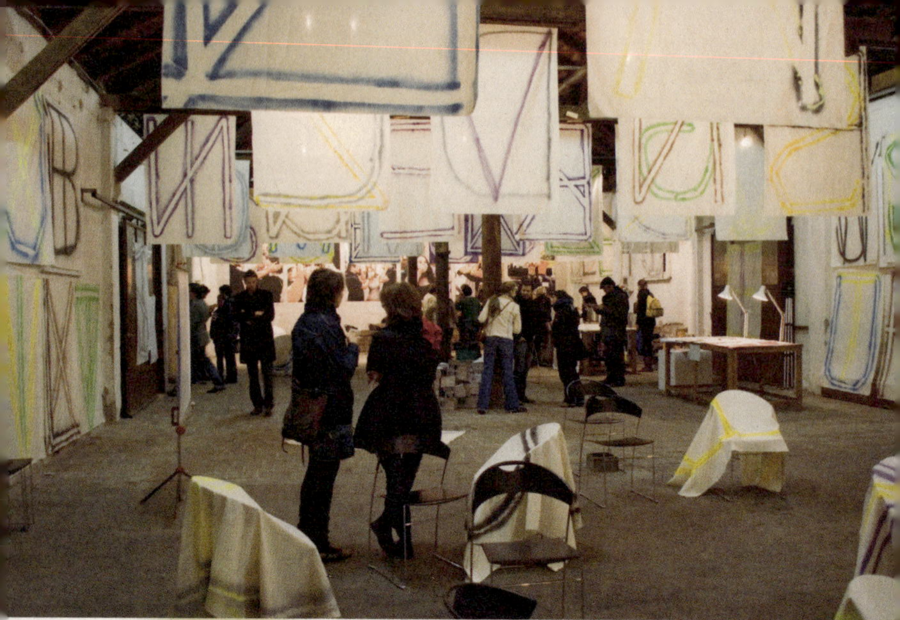

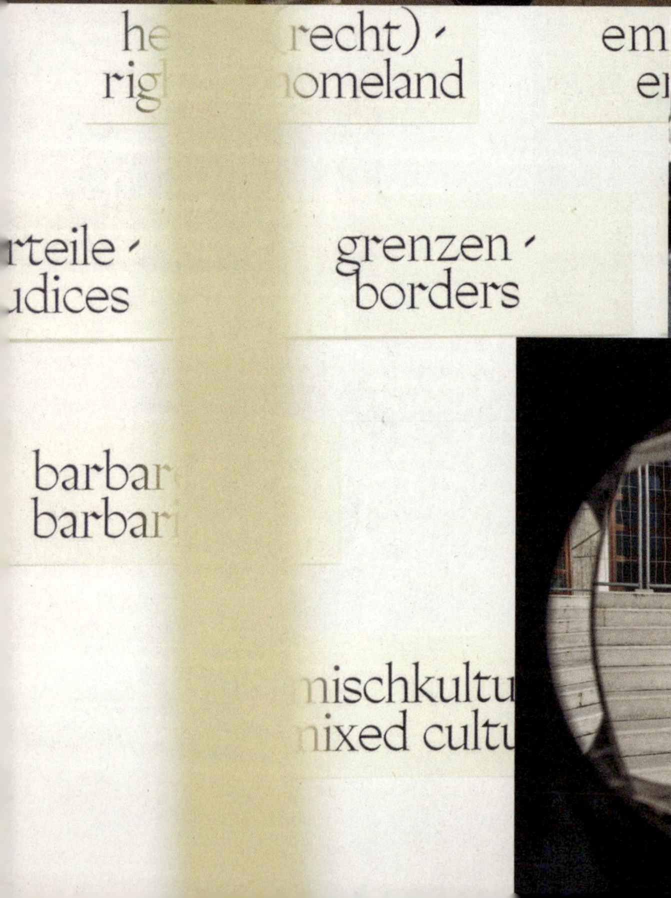
grenzen
borders

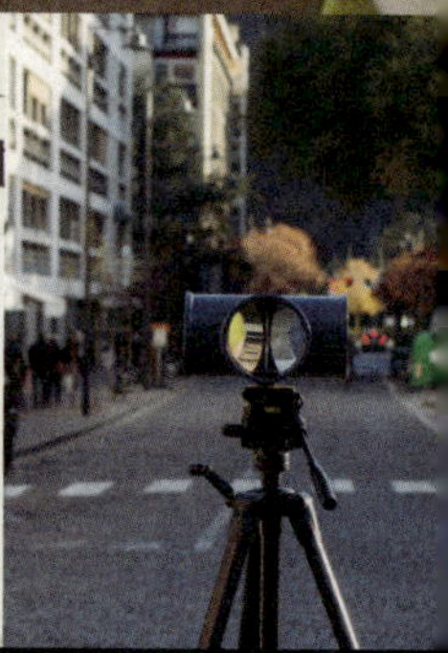

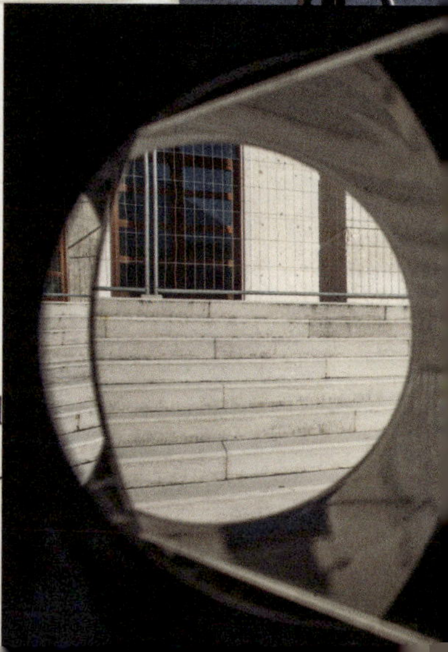

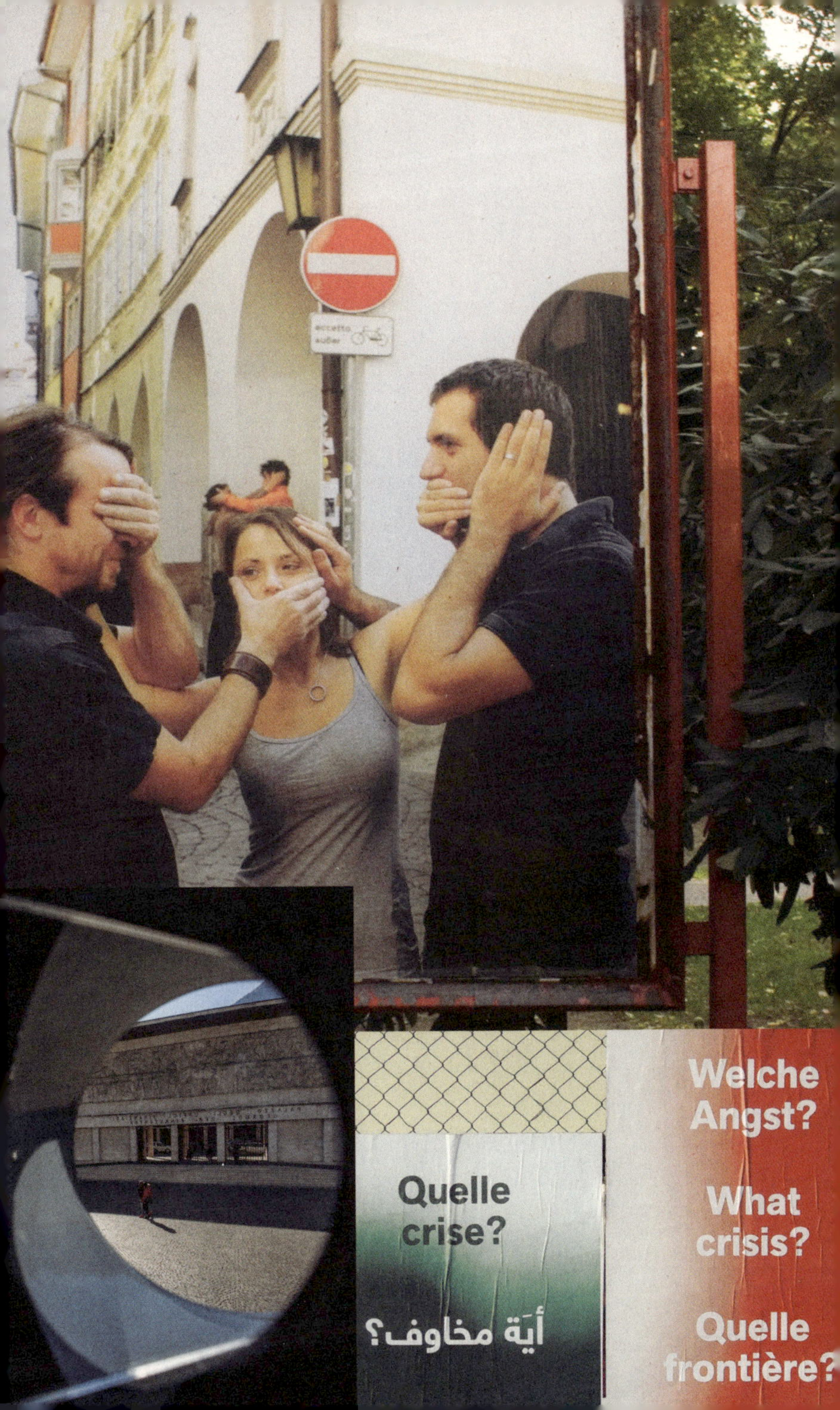

Welche Angst?
What crisis?
Quelle frontière?
Quelle crise?
أيَة مخاوف؟

AS IF

16 Dialogues about Sheep, Black Holes, and Movement

EDITED BY
Angelika Burtscher and Daniele Lupo

A LUNGOMARE READER

Spector Books

AS IF WE'RE ALWAYS IN MOVEMENT AND ALWAYS SEARCHING

↘ Angelika Burtscher AND Daniele Lupo

We walk, putting one foot in front of the other, searching for contact with the ground, looking back at the things that are behind us and forward to the things ahead. The horizon becomes fuzzy, we can make out outlines but can't get a clear picture. Nothing specific forms. Behind us lies a hilly landscape, not flat but full of sudden bends and crossing lines. We don't always remember where the paths go. It sometimes feels like we stop, turn around in circles, and suddenly are not able to tell what was behind us and what was in front. Everything blurs.

Who do we refer to when we say "we" in those lines? A "we" who comes together on the road, walking some of the way together? Or a "we" looking for the unembellished narrative of history, one that questions power dynamics and thinks them differently? Can we even talk about a "we" without thinking about "who" determines a "we" and for "whom"? When is a "we" a barrier, and when is it an opportunity?

"We" keep walking onward. We come across a number of people, exchange uncertain yet curious glances. Satisfied with how many pairs of eyes there are and how every glance conceals various experiences, histories, and layers, we continue moving ahead. What place does each history and each individual occupy, and what relationships arise as a result? We move ahead, balancing, the space narrows and balancers become tightrope walkers. We wriggle past one another, filled with the desire to weave a net from the rope to create space for coming into contact with the others. Perceiving what is around us, we seek the horizon. And quickly, we reach the "As If", thinking about possibilities and productive fiction.

Going, walking, perspectives, looking and being astonished, perceiving, uncertainty and fuzziness are closely linked with the name Lungomare. So is the debate around the *we* and the social relationships our work creates. Lungomare also describes the plurality that geographies and places contain. In almost every town beside the sea there are signs pointing to a Lungomare, a path running alongside the sea, perfect for strolling, meeting, and dreaming. The name becomes a metaphor for the movement, and describes a place where people meet with their ideas, wishes, proposals, and personal stories—they exchange views, linger, and make their arrangements for the following day.

In 2003 we[1] gave Lungomare in Bolzano, a precise place and context in the north of Italy on the border with Austria. There, geographies are laid one on top of the other, expanded, and clear boundaries are blurred to make space for new relationships and narratives. This Lungomare would also like to be a place of the "liminal, which unifies and separates, like a passage running underneath borders, removing all traces of occupancy and retaining the memory of a different type of clandestine activity—of occupation, resistance, and struggle. Not clandestine activity as some sort of stigma, but as an existential decision. The path along the sea shows the subversion of order, the challenging of the other and the elsewhere."[2]

Since Lungomare began its cultural and creative work, geographical points of reference and people's biographical histories have played a central role, constantly opening up spaces for possibilities, and inspiring Lungomare's projects from the very start. Thinking about the political and social space of the city and landscape, questioning the conditions in which it can be used, negotiating questions of distribution and prevailing power dynamics are all recurrent themes in the culture platform's work. We also want to share desires with one another, give it space, network, and allow the collective to become a tool and a process. Borrowing from the idea of a slow but attentive walk, in which the gaze is always fixed on the surroundings and the people within their contexts,

1 Lungomare was until 2020 a cultural association and was founded in 2003 by Patrizia Bertolini, Angelika Burtscher, Manuela Demattio, Roberto Gigliotti, Paulpeter Hofer, Brita Köhler, Daniele Lupo, and Josef Rainer. Angelika Burtscher and Daniele Lupo were joint artistic directors of the association until 2014; from 2014–2020 they co-curated Lungomare with Lisa Mazza and Roberto Gigliotti. The current Lungomare Cooperative was founded in 2021 by Angelika Burtscher, Frida Carazzato, Daniele Lupo, Eva Mair, and Georg Zeller. Angelika Burtscher and Daniele Lupo are the artistic directors.

2 Donatella Di Cesare, *Philosophie der Migration* (Berlin: Matthes & Seitz, 2021).

a situational, transdisciplinary, and transformative cultural practice has emerged.

Lungomare acts in this expanded practice, continually exchanging between different fields of work and disciplines, developing methods, languages, and experiences, and reacting to the interwoven relationships between places, people, and their histories. We learn from one another through exchange. There, the things we see and understand change, and we have the opportunity to rethink relationships between people, species, and spaces. Irit Rogoff underlines the potential of an expanded praxis, having exchanges with other forms and spheres of knowledge, and writes right at the start of her text "The Expanding Field": "We work in an expanding field, in which all definitions of practices, their supports and their institutional frameworks have shifted and blurred."[3] It's not about celebrating our own achievements, paradigms, knowledge, nor is it about building up competing interests; rather, it is about correlating missing knowledge.

"I'm not interested in asking 'what is art,' I'm more interested in asking 'where is art.' That means not asking about the origin and essence of art, or the fact art reflects itself, but it's about art in society and how it relates to the outside world."[4] This quote captures the working methods and the nature of Lungomare and the search for what resonance, sound bodies, and sound waves create art and design. Lungomare's artistic, cultural, and design practice engages with the world, questions assumptions, creates bridges, and negotiates commonalities and differences. The work becomes a process of developing an imaginative and responsible way of having a dialogue with society and one's surroundings.

3 Irit Rogoff, "The Expanding Field", Jean-Paul Martinon, *The Curatorial: A Philosophy of Curating* (London: Bloomsbury, 2015).

4 Transcript of a discussion between Philip Ursprung and Stéphane Verlet-Bottéro for the *OVERTIME PAPERS* project, published by Stéphane Verlet-Bottéro and Sophie Krier, curated and produced by Lungomare.

In 2023, after twenty years of Lungomare became active, this reader was created. To this end, we—the curators and editors—invited sixteen colleagues and artists, we have worked with to each initiate a dialogue. The reader *AS IF – 16 Dialogues on Sheep, Black Holes, and Movement* brings together a number of dialogues, trialogues, scenographies, letters, and glossaries from fifty-two authors, to assemble collected and new knowledge, and allow new connections between people and practices to emerge. With our colleagues and the artists, over the last few years we've created a number of projects and shared methods, needs, wishes, and joint struggles. At the end of each chapter, four accomplices we currently work with and have worked with in the past share closing remarks with their thoughts, woven into their experiences of working with Lungomare.

The four chapters of the book reflect Lungomare's practice: The activation of a context, and the multi-layered reading of this context; the public space as an anchor point and the possibility and potential for a common space which becomes a place of negotiation; sharing knowledge, and with it, the multi-voice transdisciplinary development of content; the question of belonging and the reflection on what borders, border crossings, origins, identities, and practices of radical hospitality mean.

AS IF – 16 Dialogues on Sheep, Black Holes, and Movement continues this walk and opens up questions about our present and future. This reader was born of a wish to bring different realities, perspectives, and ideas into dialogue, learn from one another, and experience something new. As part of this, all of the authors are united in their desire to radically reconsider the future and correlate history, (cultural) geographies, people, and nature. The book circles around places which cannot be considered in isolation, but exist in context and mutual dependency; around a "here" which makes "there" an offshoot. The authors reflect about the imminent, urgent need for changes to our cities, their architecture, the landscape, and living together in this complex system of interdependencies. They reflect about how cities and villages, the mountain and the valley, are interwoven. They place us humans in a new relationship with nature, and reflect on both ecological and human crises. What role do trees, branches, heterogeneity, listening, and dancing play when we think about commonalities? In their dialogues the authors also consider the perspective from which we view words, language, and entire realities, and call for us to take responsibility to create space for a varied society and for all species. On the one hand there are people, their histories, dreams, ideas, languages, and projects; on the other hand there are often answers which marginalize people, categorize them, and silence them.

The dialogues promote a radical openness and radical reconsideration, and see the potential of artistic processes creating resonance, and acting and being in a way which unites, heals, opens, and inspires people to social visions. Together, the authors set off on a search—the search for one another and the search for new relationships, languages, understandings of history, and ways of acting. In this book, differences and barriers should become bridges, and movements should become possibilities. As Audre Lorde says: "It is within our differences that we are both most powerful and most vulnerable, and some of the most difficult tasks of our lives are the claiming of differences and learning to use those differences for bridges rather than as barriers between us."[5]

And we keep walking ahead, across as many bridges as possible, carrying new experiences in our luggage, our vision getting sharper, recognizing the outlines ahead of us. What we see are countless connections, and ahead of us lies a horizon which makes it possible to perceive things no longer in isolation, but more comprehensively. And the net keeps being woven, by many hands, more and more finely. It's as if it isn't possible to fall through the gaps any more.

5 Audre Lorde, *Difference and Survival: An Address at Hunter College* (Tacoma: Blue Cactus Press, 2023).

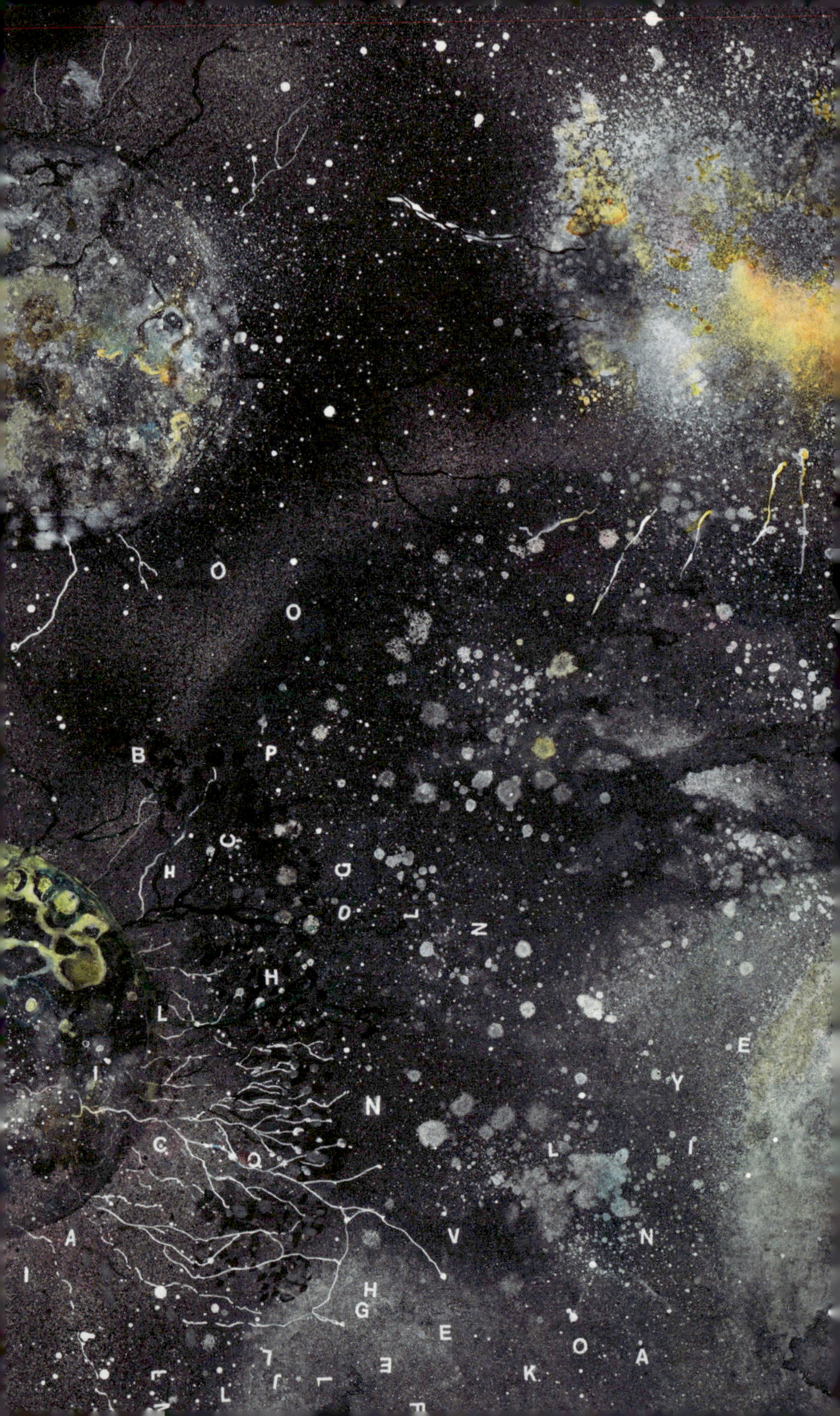

CHAPTER 1

ACTIVATING CONTEXTUAL PRACTICES

DIALOGUES

↘ Luigi Coppola
IN CONVERSATION WITH Pelin Tan

↘ Futurefarmers
IN CONVERSATION WITH Peter Galison

↘ Kolar Aparna AND Beatrice Catanzaro
IN CONVERSATION WITH Saba Hamzah
AND Linda Armano

↘ Barbara Holub
IN CONVERSATION WITH Grant Kester

NOTES OF AN ACCOMPLICE
↘ Lisa Mazza

ON LAND, EXTRACTION, COMMUNALITY

↘ Luigi Coppola
IN CONVERSATION WITH Pelin Tan

Saluzzo, Northern Italy, 23 March 2022

Dear Pelin,

I'm writing to you from Saluzzo, in Northern Italy, where my dear friend and colleague Marzia Migliora and I are putting the finishing touches to a project we're calling *In Erranza (While Wandering)*.[1] It brought to mind our wanderings in Basilicata,[2] going from town to town and getting lost in those varied landscapes, not a care in the world. In this new wandering, though, there are quite a lot of cares. Marzia and I, and the people close to us while we've been doing this project, are mourning the loss of loved ones. But we can't stop wandering. It's that spark of life, pushing us to go beyond the familiar, pushed ahead by our demons and by our weaknesses.

This time, the wandering was sorely needed. One of the first things we saw here behind the splendid façades of the town was a huge camp where seasonal migrant workers live. Thousands come every year to pick fruit. All around us, orchards, trees standing tall in straight lines stretching out as far as the eye can see. Head up the hill a little, and all you can see is a huge gray plastic sheet, part of the anti-hail measures covering the landscape. The trees should really be in bloom

1 *In Erranza* (2022) is a project by Luigi Coppola and Marzia Migliora, for Saluzzo Rural Happening, curated by Rebecca De Marchi. It is the end result of an artistic and research process, comprising a map inviting viewers to come up with creative alternative agroecologically sustainable travel routes from Saluzzo to the Po Valley and Varaita Valley.

2 Since 2019 Pelin Tan and Luigi Coppola have taken part in joint research and projects. They are both currently senior researchers at CAD+SR, Boston, USA. Pelin Tan, curator of *Gardentopia: Cosmos of Ecologies*, for Matera Capital of Culture 2019, invited Luigi to get involved with three projects relating to Basilicata and its communities.

just now, it should be stunning—we should be able to see the pink, the white, all the shades in between, of the peaches and pears, apples and kiwis. Instead, all we see is gray. It strikes me, not for the first time, how myopic it is of us to grow our food in such a senseless way. All the raw materials—seedlings, poles, nets, fertilizers, pesticides—even the seasonal labor, all of it imported from across the globe without a second thought for the disastrous environmental and humanitarian knock-on effects. None of this is economically viable without the European funds that back it all up, consolidating the disaster. There's no good outcome. However, these mountains... they show what's possible. They're full of history—partisans and antifascists once camped out here during the civil war—from which we draw strength. This is what guides us. We're meeting so many wonderful people, all of them creating change, children growing into the tools to shape our future.

When standard queues
production order
the logic of time
rootless fruits
the migrant's rib
the gray plastic sky
monoculture minds

give way

to boundlessness
to chestnut tree shade
to steep paths
to the partisan's flower

we wander.

Delving into the mountains
without digging trenches
tapping birch
growing food from change
carving new paths
swerving promised development
waking with wolves.

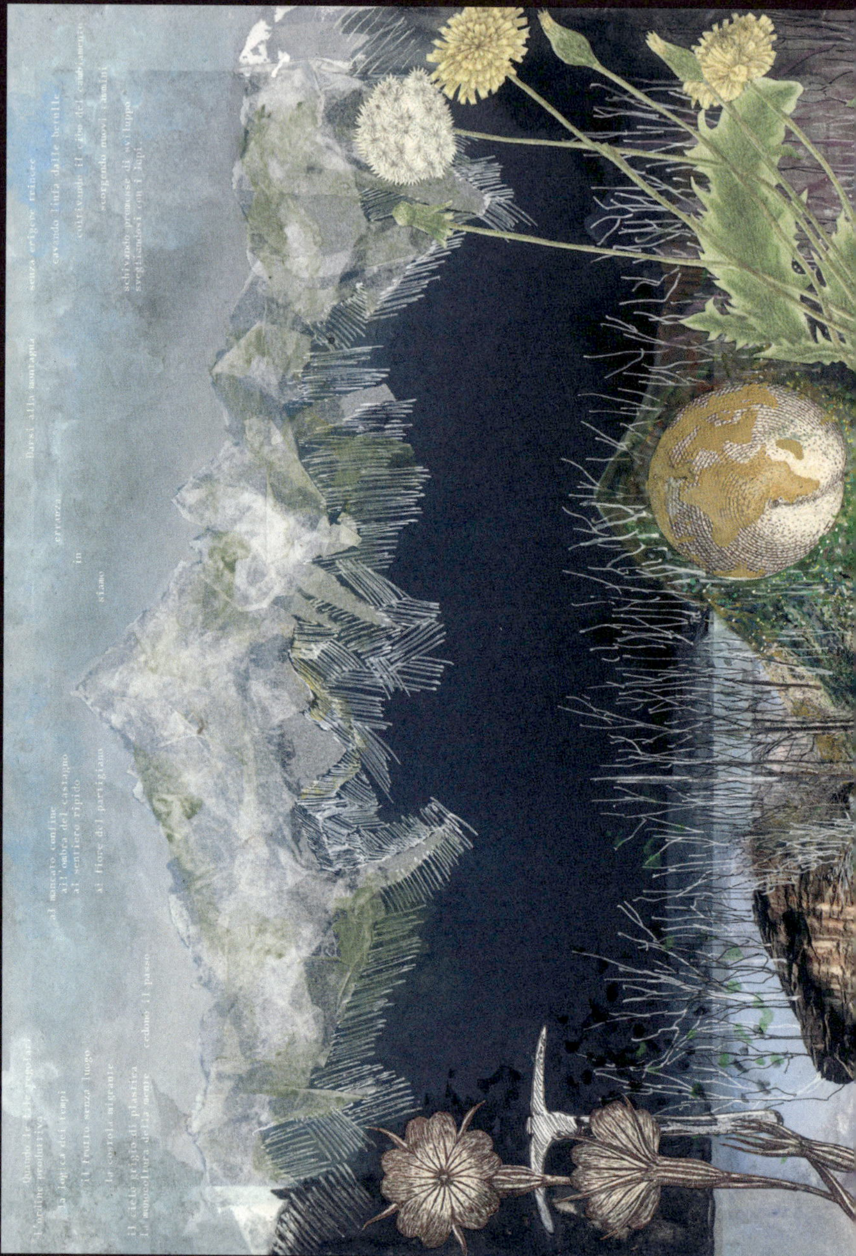

Marzia Migliora and Luigi Coppola, *In Erranza,* produced for Saluzzo Rural Happening, 2021–2022. Courtesy of the artist.

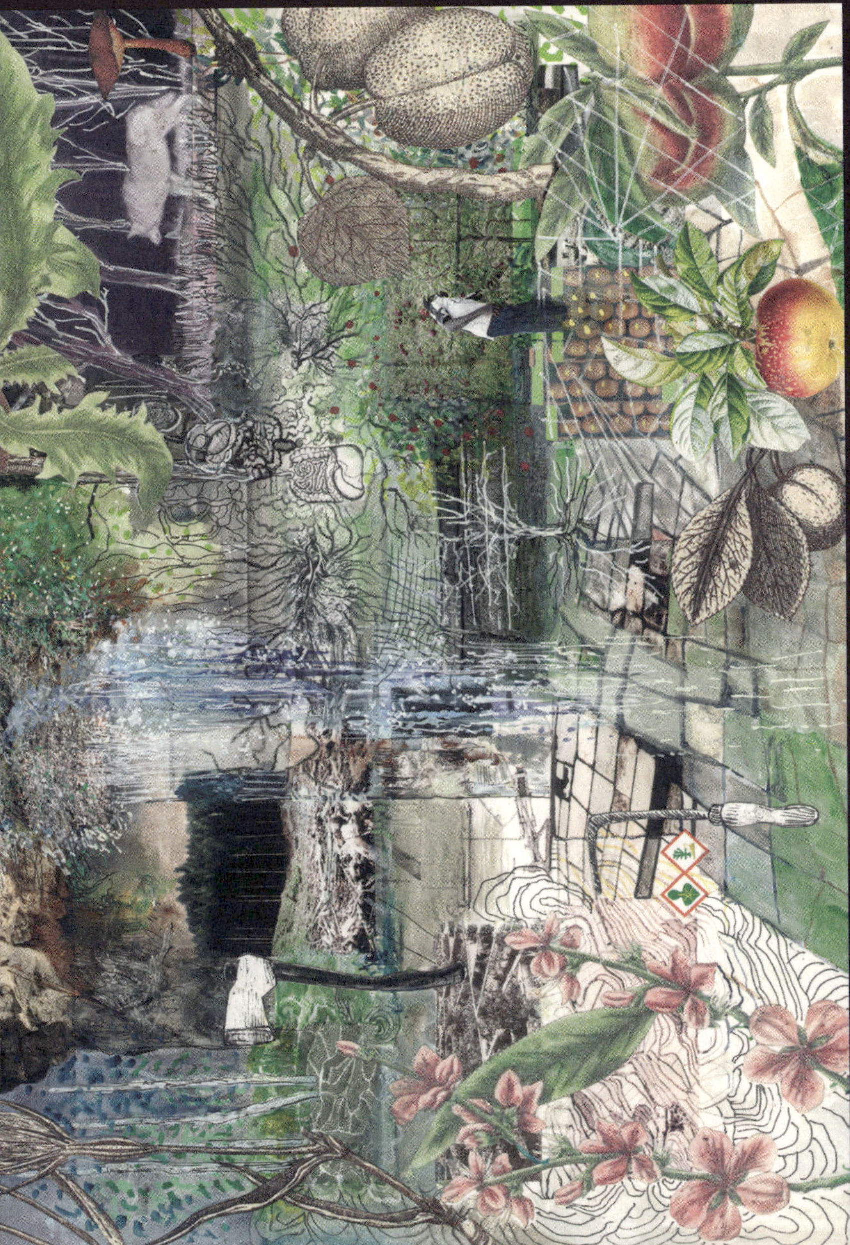

Antioch, Turkey, 19 May 2022

Dear Luigi,

I am standing near a refugee camp facing the Syrian city of Idlib, on the far side of the border from Antioch. Surrounding me is an ancient region that still produces large amounts of olives and olive oil. Fields of grain and olive trees covering the region used to be one of the most important parts of the Levant area. Nestled among olive tree fields, Boynuyoğun Refugee Camp hosts some eight thousand five hundred Syrian refugees, most of whom work as day laborers in the agricultural fields. Established as a tent camp in June 2011, it was transformed into a container camp in 2016. Between six in the morning and eleven at night, refugees are allowed outside of the camp to work. James C. Scott writes: "Hominids have, after all, been shaping the plant world—largely with fire—since before Homo sapiens." Later he writes: "In a grain state, one or two cereal grains provided the main food starch, the unit of taxation in kind, and the basis for a hegemonic agrarian calendar."[3] On the current borderlines of Turkey and Syria, state-making is entangled with the realities of Syrian refugees working as day laborers, and with harmful, state-led agricultural policies in the region—a region that used to be famous for bountiful, high-quality olives, olive oil, and wheat. My friends Apo and Shiraz, who are farmers and olive oil producers in Antioch—they are from Tokatlı, the only remaining Christian Arab village there—explain that one field in the Antioch region used to produce two tons of freekeh (frik) bulgur a day.

3 James C. Scott, *Against the Grain: A Deep History of Earliest States* (New Haven: Yale University Press, 2017).

I would like to mention again the impact of historical as well as recent colonization processes on the lands, more-than-human life cycles, and labor by referring to your first letters to me. The colonization and standardization of landscapes is always rooted in controlling the cultivation and erasure of localities. James C. Scott has pointed out how the cultivation and dissemination of grains and a variety of crops contributed to the formation of states, institutions of human slavery,

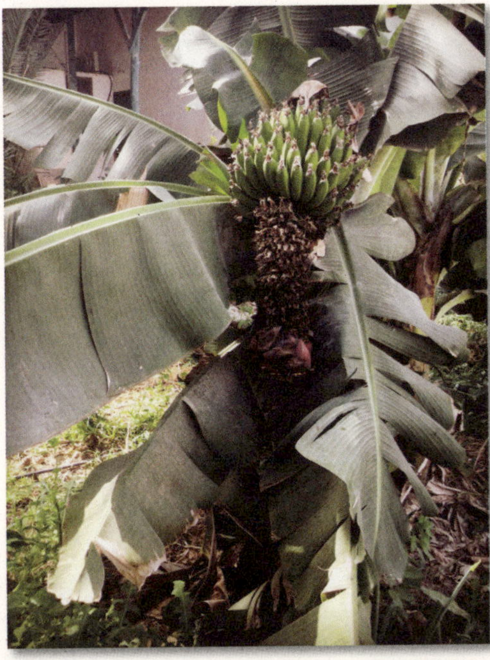

Banana tree at Musa Alami Farm, Jericho, Palestine, 2019, photo by Pelin Tan.

and administrative governance in ancient Mesopotamia and across the Mediterranean region thousands of years ago.[4] Today, the same region is inundated with wars and oppressions that destroy not only biodiversity but also the intangible

4 Ibid.

heritage of ingredients and their narratives across our earth. "Survival-with" and "through" is something of an entangled kinship that can be described as migrating ingredients, refugee seeds, and exiled foods. The scale of ethical responsibility also includes protection of the entangled relationship between nonhuman entities such as seeds, soil, and insects. Furthermore, as seed and soil represent heritage, they are the most important elements in a nomadic life of forced eviction or displacement due to war or colonial oppression. In our contemporary times, thinking of species as seeds is also a metaphor for survival during the Anthropocene, where humans are the main decision-makers—through neoliberal global companies and states—involved in extracting resources from the landscape and other parts of the earth. The idea of protecting the species as a seed for human needs must transform into an approach that questions how we might coexist together. How do we show solidarity with seeds? How might we create an entangled kinship with seeds? How might we create a collective empathy for this kinship? As the effect of the Anthropocene creates catastrophe and near-future dystopias, we must act in solidarity with other species for our collective survival.

Lubumbashi, Democratic Republic of Congo,
29 September 2022

Dear Pelin,

I arrived in Lubumbashi a few weeks ago to round off the first phase of *Ex Situ,*[5] the project I've been talking about so much the last few months. The Biennial will open in a few days and we're in the throes of some creative chaos just now! But I've carved out some time to write to you. It matters to me.

I'm writing from Picha's workshop in a district called Makomeno, just a few hundred meters from what was once the beating heart of the city's economy: the former Gécamines factory (former Union Minière of Haut Katanga). They were built in colonial times to process minerals, firstly copper, later cobalt. The city grew from nothing at the behest of Belgian colonizers looking to exploit the huge wealth of the Katanga region. Every day on my way here I pass a huge black hill of discarded by-products from mineral processing built up over decades. They call it Terril, and it's not just a landmark but has also become a symbol of the city itself. It's at once disturbing and fascinating. It's nothing but countless specks of dust, yet it persists, representing the strength and damnation of this city and those who live here.

I've told you already how this project has made me question things more than any other I've done. I spent half my

5 *Ex-Situ* is a long term research, community building, artistic and editorial production project led by Lugi Coppola and curated by Lucrezia Cippitelli. The project was site-specifically conceived and developed in the frame of Ateliers Picha, the permanent educational platform of Lubumbashi-based artist's collective Picha (Democratic Republic of Congo), and was part of the program of the 7th Lubumbashi Biennale (October 2022).

life in Belgium, so I've always been very aware of the Congo —mostly, it has to be said, as a fiery, divisive political issue. When I was invited to build a meaningful project here, I was equal parts scared and excited. I threw myself into it like crazy, reading all sorts of scientific articles about post-extraction environmental conditions, the country's history, everything from botany to sociology. Then I got here and realized: I know nothing. The way I was thinking and learning about the place was skewed both by a sense of guilt and by the post-colonial worldview we're drenched in. What I see now, though, is a continuum of events. There's no post-anything. Everything exists in the present, every historic choice this place has been subject to is a layer in how it's built, just like the Terril.

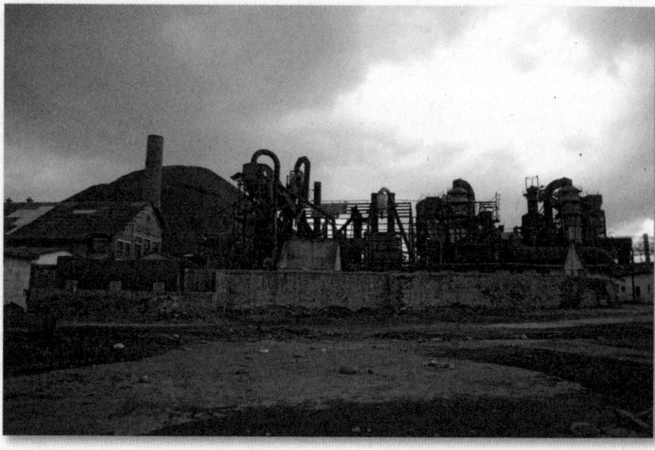

View of the Terril of Lubumbashi for *Ex Situ* by Luigi Coppola, 2022, photo by Kevin Kabambi.

When I got here I'd already built quite a lot of the project. Working with friends from Lungomare, I'd already created a free press which I brought copies of with me in heavy bags. It was a summary of the research on phytoremediation I'd done, involving a lot of back-and-forth with Congolese scientists and the group of workers involved in the project. I was proud of the outcome but still found it so hard to pull copies out of my cases and share them. The arguments I touch on are so complex and touch on the lives of people whose day-to-day existence is spent in the toxic waste of Western capitalism.

Using plants to discuss and create imagery was my way of feeling like I had adapted to this complexity. It's a language that has to be built, but one that always opens doors and gives rise to novel thoughts.

I used Lubumbashi soil as a pigment. We started out analyzing their fertility and toxicity. The data were concerning, more than I'd imagined. In the tapestries I'm painting, the roots of healing plants delve deep into the toxic earth. Doing this work is a healing process for me too. I see more and more of my mother in myself, hands never stopping, finding new ways to embroider and to turn raw ingredients into food, making enough to last decades.

To my mind, having this complexity sediment in a book is crucial.[6] There are so many people I want to involve, especially Congolese people, who are contributing to this project passionately and generously.

6 The book *Ex Situ: compatible avec la vie* is conceived as a theoretical and pragmatic tool, which explores the site-specific case of Lubumbashi, reflecting at the same time on topics related with the side effects of global neocapitalist extractivism in specific areas of the global south. Edited by Lucrezia Cippitelli and CAD+SR (Milan: Kunstverein Publishing, 2023).

Ramallah, Palestine, 21 February 2023

Dear Luigi,

I met and listened to Omar Tesdell, a Palestinian geographer who created the *Palestinian Wild Food Plants Archive* over the last few years, which aims to collect and preserve knowledge of the plants of Palestine, which is facing the violence of Israeli colonial settlers' attempts to grab and extract agricultural lands. Omar Tesdell tells us that landscapes move in slow, deep time, and that all wild plants, seeds, and healthy soil are our heritages. These heritages will not only support our precarious societies but may create an ethical, responsible entanglement of resilient coexistences for our collective future. Practices of collecting and archiving heirloom seeds are a form of solidarity and resistance against extractive capitalism and industrialized agriculture. Such projects protect and aim to restore natural habitats and biodiversity. They are critical of dominant monocultural approaches and embrace interspecies hybridization and circulation. Last year, I visited Vivien Sansour's Palestinian Heirloom Seed Library in the village of Battir in the West Bank, where in 2014 Sansour established her archive to preserve ancient seed varieties and traditional farming practices in collaboration with the villagers. Battir has Roman garden terraces that have been used for cultivating food for over two thousand years. It is also one of the many cultural landscapes in Palestine threatened by Israel's plans to build a separation wall through the area.

Sansour's library consists of heirloom seeds from the villages of the West Bank as well as from Gaza and other local communities. Palestinian farmers work under great strain as irrigation and water access are controlled by the Israeli government. Saving and sharing seeds for cultivation has impact beyond feeding human-centric needs; it also works toward preserving biodiversity and ancestral heritages that are under threat from colonial and structural violence. The West Bank is divided into three areas—A, B, and C—and Palestinians cultivate land in Area C. Israeli satellite housing projects occupy the lands, destroying Palestinian villages and farmland. Sansour's and the villagers' efforts toward uncovering and preserving seed stories is also about creating an infrastructure of seeds that is a form of decolonization. This work

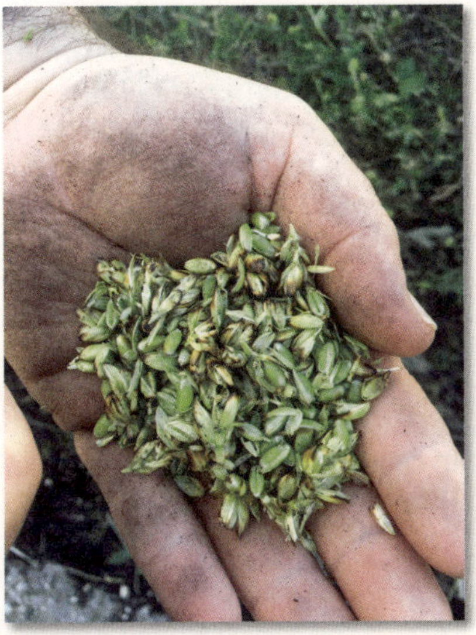

Freekeh Bulgur produced by Aşkın Demir, Antioch, Turkey, 2022, photo by Pelin Tan.

fights against the ongoing settler colonialism that continuously destroys and erases the ancestral knowledge of the Indigenous communities tied to that natural landscape. There is a collective called Sakiya in a village close to Ramallah that was attacked last year by colonial settlers. Sakiya collective convenes workshops and residencies that host artists, researchers, and curators who are interested in the research of a more-than-human world. Running an artist-led collective and residency in the landscape of a village by restoring an old building and setting agroecology practices, composting, and archive in a constrained territory is a hard practice that needs a constant collective effort and practices of solidarity.

In the last years I conducted field and archival research on Musa Alami Farm, which was established by Musa Alami in 1946 as an agricultural school, and ran until 1967. I am becoming more interested in how the history of Palestinian modernism, Israeli occupation of Palestinian lands, and the struggle for freedom and rights come together in a utopic agricultural school. I produced a short documentary film called *Landscapes as Archives*,[7] where I draw a narrative of how the transformation and extraction of landscape relates historically to colonialism and how a decolonial practice is possible; how landscapes are archives of our past and future about the memory of space and belonging.

Collective learning and the creation of decolonial methodologies against slow violence, extraction, and forced eviction/migration lead to pedagogies of the commons. Following insurgent plants through narratives, infrastructures, forgotten languages, and entangled exiles is not a metaphor. As artist Jumana Manna writes, we strive toward "imagining alternative/affirmative care structures that remain, within and beyond the current reality, aligned towards plant and human life alike."[8] Navigating through migrating ingredients, refugee seeds, and exiled foods, we witness and learn about extractive strategies, state-making, and slow violence. Non-extractivist practices are about dispossessed and cohabited landscapes and are about "survival-with" and "through" foraging, composting, preserving, landscaping, and burning ingredients, which together create relational phenomenologies.

7 *Landscapes as Archives*, a film produced by Pelin Tan for the Instant Modernism exhibition of Qattan Foundation, Ramallah (May—December 2023). 2023, 18', English/Arabic.

8 Jumana Manna, "Where Nature Ends and Settlements Begin", *e-flux journal*, n. 113, (2020).

Diso, Italy, 17 April 2023

Dear Pelin,

I hope you're well. Thank you for telling me about Palestine. I want to come visit soon. I can't wait to travel and do research together in Palestine, and in Sakiya, after talking about it for so long. We were supposed to go when COVID-19 happened. I had the tickets, but we all know what happened next. In the meantime, keep telling me things, so that when I get there everything will be less unfamiliar.

When people talk about how slowly things move in the south and in rural areas, Pelin, I get so pissed off. Here we do everything quickly, at a constant fast rhythm, never pausing to catch breath. Casa delle Agriculture[9] is an endless whirlpool of intentions becoming reality in daily life. It's increasingly about the starting point rather than the point you return to.

> *One needs a town, if only for the pleasure of leaving it. A town means not being alone, knowing that in the people, the trees, the soil, there is something of yourself, that even when you're not there it stays and waits for you.*[10]

9 Luigi Coppola is part of the collective Casa delle Agriculture, a community of practice established in 2011 in Castiglione d'Otranto, in the Southern Puglia (Italy), with the goals to revive abandoned lands, repopulate the countryside, generate solidarity-based economies, and strengthen the bonds of the community by building a new agroecological, cultural, social, and economic model of living together.

10 Cesare Pavese, *The Moon and the Bonfires* (Dublin: Penguin Books, 2021).

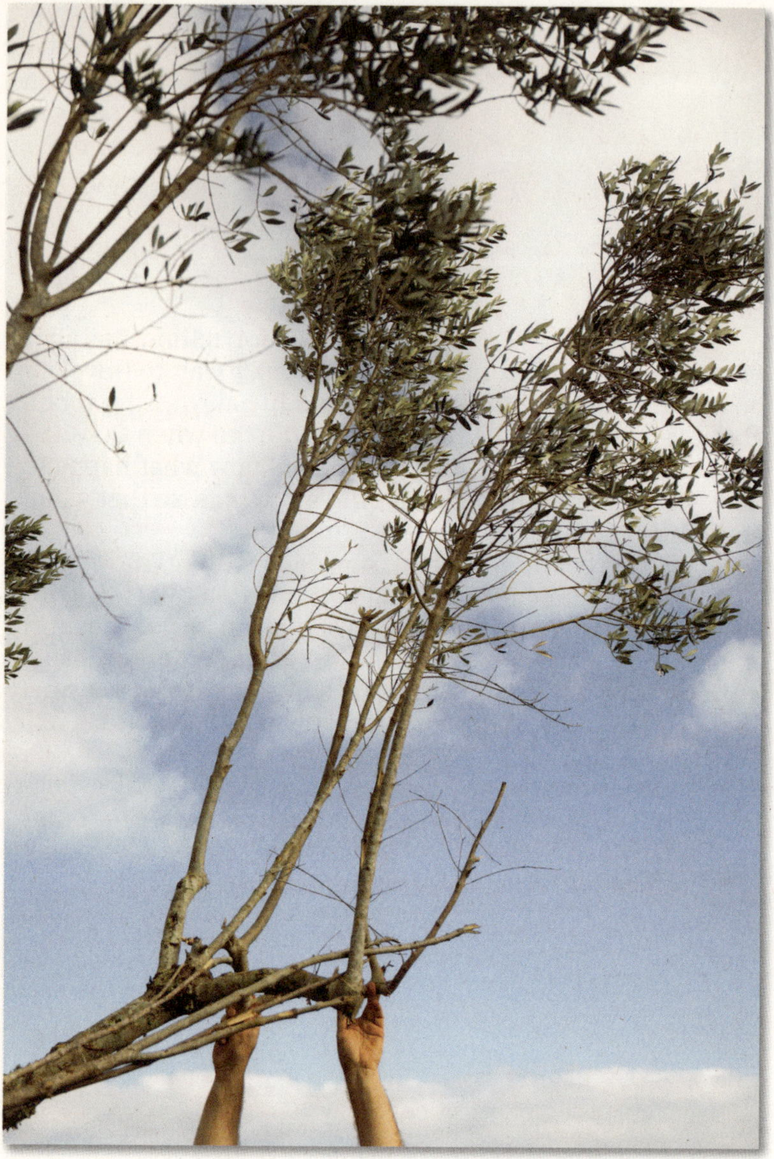

Luigi Coppola, *Vinculum*, 2021-ongoing, photo by Alessia Rollo.

This little passage is from Cesare Pavese's *The Moon and the Bonfires,* and it's engraved on a plaque we've installed on the piazza di Castiglione d'Otranto, where we work with the collectivc. I feel more and more attached to it. Often while there I feel like I'm at the center of the world—purely because we're trying to create a new one. This world, luckily, is not an island, and seeks to stay connected with other worlds and influence them. Many people are always coming to see us, and I'm overjoyed that we'll soon have a shared hospitality and welcome venue. I hope you'll come and enjoy it.

I'll say goodbye for now and get back to the garden (I can't tell you how happy the work I'm doing restoring the olive groves makes me.[11] It's almost like sculpting or agroecology. Learning and living all at once). Every morning, when I wake up, I wonder what little changes have taken place, and I want to go out and see how every little healing gesture returns to embrace us.

11 For over a decade, Salento has been undergoing one of history's biggest environmental disasters, as millions of olive trees attacked by the *xylella fastidiosa* bacterium are rapidly drying out.

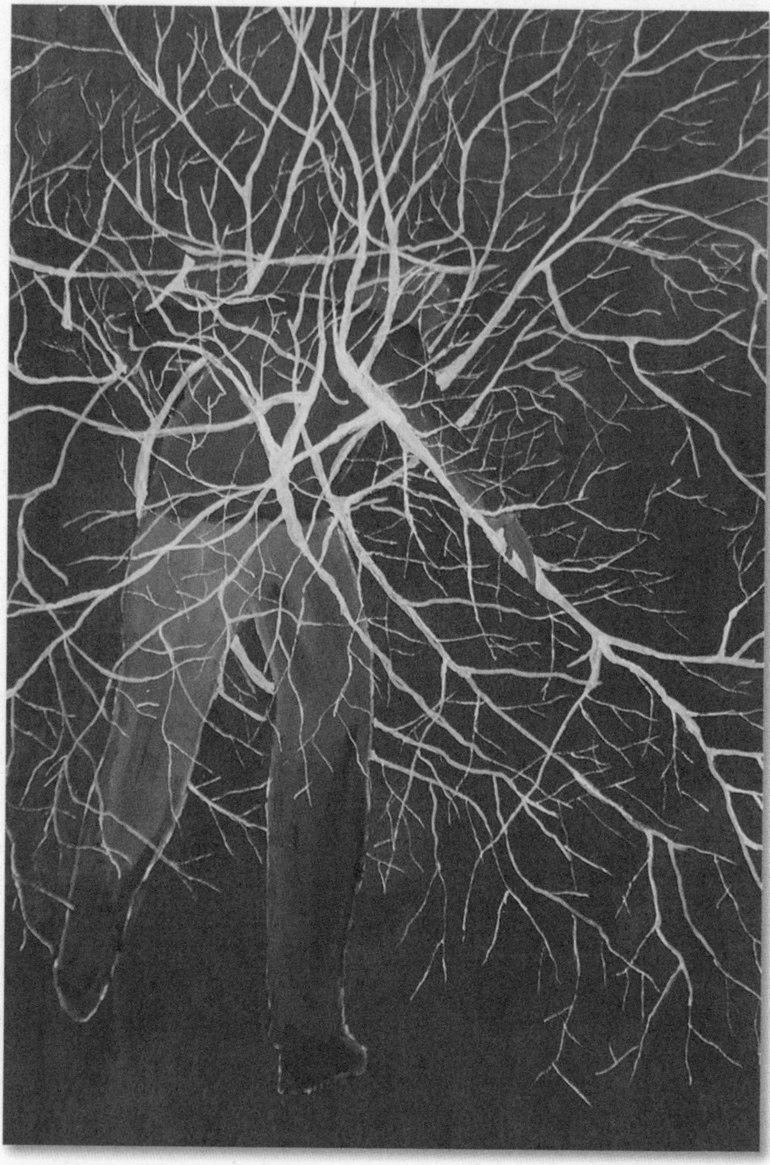

Luigi Coppola, *Vinculum*, painting on fabric, 2023. Courtesy of the artist.

↘Luigi Coppola

is an artist and agroecologist. He is a senior research fellow of the Center for Arts, Design, and Social Research in Boston, USA. Coppola is part of the collective Casa delle Agriculture, a project in Castiglione d'Otranto, Southern Italy, which seeks to revive abandoned land, repopulate the countryside, generate a sustainable economy, and strengthen community cohesion. He developed public art projects, performances, installations, and exhibitions in international contexts, including the 7th Lubumbashi Biennale (Democratic Republic of Congo); 5th Istanbul Design Biennale, 2020; *Gardentopia*, Matera European Capital of Culture (2019); Fondazione Merz Turin (2018); BAK Utrecht (2018). Luigi was joint Artistic Director with Michelangelo Pistoletto of the Urban Art Biennale *Art for an urban re-evolution* in Bordeaux, France. In 2023, he published the book *Ex-Situ: compatible avec la vie* (Kunstverein Publishing Milano).

↘Pelin Tan

is a professor at the Faculty of Fine Arts, University of Batman, Turkey. She is a senior research fellow of the Center for Arts, Design, and Social Research in Boston, USA. Her work is focused on urban and territorial conflicts, commons, labor conditions, and alternative pedagogies. Tan coordinates Arazi Collective's research on non-extractive practices of landscapes in Turkey, Palestine, Lebanon, and other geographies. In 2019, she was awarded the Keith Haring Fellowship of Art&Activism. In collaboration with the artist Anton Vidokle, Tan produces films about the future of art and society. She contributed to several publications such as *Climates: Architecture and the Planetary Imaginary* (Columbia University, 2017), *Refugee Heritage* (Art and Theory Publishing, 2021), and *Radical Pedagogies* (MIT Press, 2022). In 2019, Tan curated *Gardentopia* for Matera European Capital of Culture.

RELATIONAL FORCES

↘ Futurefarmers (Amy Franceschini AND Lode Vranken)
IN CONVERSATION WITH Peter Galison EDITED BY Elizabeth Thomas

AMY FRANCESCHINI Over the years we've had many conversations with you, and you have this incredible ability to travel with us through ambiguous, nascent moments of thought formation. For this publication, we would like to talk about tools, gravity, collaboration, the ungraspable, physics, and metaphysics.

PETER GALISON Oh, good. Metaphysical tools...

AF Imagine a whistling tea kettle atop a 14' makeshift tripod carried across open vistas, deeply forested enclaves, into dark caverns of astronomical research laboratories and set up in plazas in front of various departments amid the University of California at Santa Cruz campus. This whistling tea kettle was a central figure in *Fog Inquiry,* a research residency at the University of California, Santa Cruz, aimed at fostering connections between different aspects of a dispersed university setting. This "relational object" was used to prepare tea and to create a visual (and sonic) cue for an otherwise invisible project. In conceiving of the project, we used the regional physical phenomenon of fog as a framework to engage various fields of inquiry within the university setting; fog as a state of being whereby hierarchies get troubled, perspectives shift, and new modes of thinking (and making) can emerge.

Our first engagement was with Anna Friz, transmission artist/professor of film and digital media in a plaza in front of her department. We arrived with the tea kettle, not knowing how it was going to stand up or where exactly we would situate it. Without discussion, students began to gather and find rocks to hold the tripod upright, a passerby gave us a tea bag from her backpack and walked on, fellow faculty, staff and even a squirrel came by. This first meeting revealed an interest in "sonic" interference which led to a next meeting with astronomer/astrophysicist Alexie Leauthaud working with "visual" interference. As we moved to various locations on campus, the whistling kettle became a foggy site of exchange, and the surroundings became emergent scenographies which moved people to act, intermingle, and form new lines of inquiry.

PG I was struck by the size of the tripod—in its more upright position, it lifted the tea kettle out of reach. The sound calls people to it, but it's not graspable; I thought that was very evocative. And, of course, tripods are used all the time

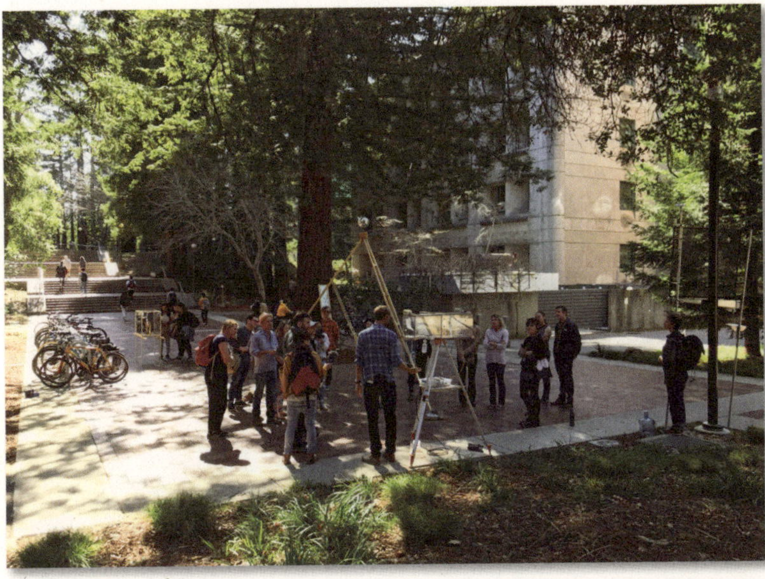

Futurefarmers, *Wandering Seminar Whistling Tea Kettle*, University of California, Santa Cruz, 2020, photo by Futurefarmers.

for telescopes, for photography, and for lighting, and so for someone like me who both makes films and studies astronomy, all those meanings come to mind. Like the optical quality of the mirror-coated kettle—it's the opposite of what a telescope mirror does, which is concentrate light and focus it down to a small point. What the spherical mirror gives you is an image of the whole space. Both are trying to capture the world, to make a miniature version of the larger world.

Science, in a way, takes a wider world or a smaller world and brings it into the graspable world, the world of images, equations, statistics—into something we can engage with. I work on black holes. There are two that are big enough for us to imagine. One, M87*, is fiftyfive million light years away; it's several times larger than the solar system. At some level, we have no grasp of it at all—we can't experiment on it or interact with it in any way. But suddenly we have the image, and we can begin to measure it and say what its mass is and say something about its other properties. There's a great richness there.

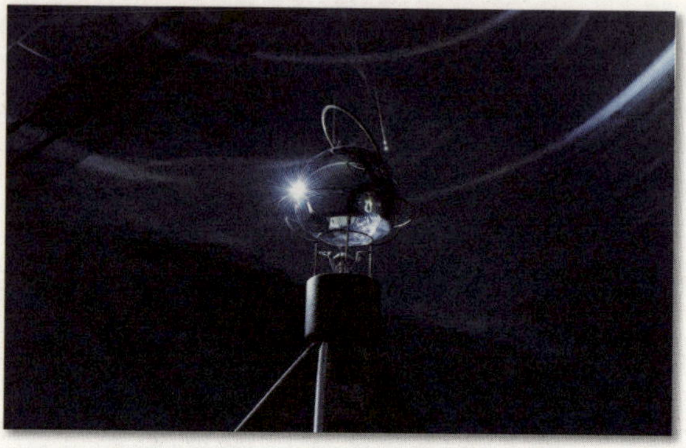

Futurefarmers, *Wandering Seminar Whistling Tea Kettle*, University of California, Santa Cruz, 2020, photo by Futurefarmers.

AF Let's go further into optics with our visit to Alexie Leauthaud who works on light moving around the universe—light being bent by a very foggy entity both conceptually and in reality called Dark Matter—one of the main components of the universe. Alexie took us to her "adaptive optics" lab where they design mirrors to correct "fogging"—the phenomena of interference in the reception of light as it enters the earth's atmosphere. The particular mirrors in this lab were being made for the largest telescope in the world which is arranged in a large array atop Mauna Kea in Hawaii to receive light from deep space.

During our exchange with the optics team, we asked if they could coat round surfaces, like a tea kettle. Their eyes lit up and before we knew it, we co-designed the next iteration of our kettle—a blown glass sphere coated with the most advanced mirroring surface on the planet. For the rest of our residency, we carried this reflective kettle—literally a materialization of encounters on campus—a beautiful object that is singular and rare, but at the same time functional tea kettle.

During our residency, there was a group of people protesting this new telescope because of its proposed site on a sacred mountain. This tension brought us into conversation with the physical site of the telescope and the complexity of interests at play. Because the mountain approaches the heavens, it is a singular and rare place. It has been kept untouched so there's no light pollution. Those very qualities make it the ideal place to experience nature under a wide-open sky, in one of the darkest places on earth. In practical terms it is the perfect location for scientific research. So there is this experience of nature in the present tense but at the same time there is the experience of something deeper, of how the overwhelming sky we see at night is not just natural but becomes spiritual also in past tenses, and how it also becomes about knowledge for the future. So, we have three kinds seeing and sensing and experiencing that intermingle there at that point that creates tension between seeing in a natural way, seeing in a religious way, and seeing in a scientific way. For us this small gesture of the specially mirrored kettle brought us into this more contentious conversation, and to larger questions about different forms of experience and knowing.

The relational object operates like a gravitational force that attracts people—together—to act. Is there a way to talk about gravity in a relational or social way?

PG Maybe that's the only way to talk about gravity—I mean, gravity is all about relations. There's a wonderful saying by John Wheeler that "objects teach space how to bend and space tells objects how to move."[1] That's a good formulation of what general relativity tells us about the wider world. Even in Newton, gravity is exactly that which tells you the spatial relationship of objects to what forces they'll feel. Every object in the Newtonian universe is attracted to every other object in the Newtonian universe. Every grain of sand, every planet, every galaxy, is related to every other through this magical formula that says the

1 From wikiquote, Wheeler traces the expression in this form in *A Journey into Gravity and Spacetime* (New York: Scientific American Library, 1999).

force attracting the two objects is inversely proportional to the distance squared between them and times the product of their masses. It's a very simple formula that became a model for science, and also for human understanding. The idea of natural law was associated with this universality. Newton's new science becomes a model for political discourse through Locke and through Locke to the foundational documents of the United States.

With Einstein's work, one is talking about objects bending space, or bending spacetime. And that bending of space then determines how every other object moves in it. So there's a mutuality there—as in Newton's theory, only now every grain of sand slightly bends the fabric of space and time. And other objects then have their patterns of motion determined. They follow the shortest line connecting two points in that now bent world of space. So yes, gravity is all about these relationships. In Einstein's theory, the complexity is that all the objects are bending space. So calculating what that straight line is, the shortest line between two points, becomes a complicated matter. But the law of motion is still very simple. An object travels in the straightest, shortest path. So yes, I think gravity—in both its force-organized form in Newtonian physics, or in its spacetime-bending form in Einstein—is very much about relationships or relational aspects of objects and their connections.

LODE VRANKEN I was quite enchanted by the moment in your movie, *The Edge of all We Know*[2] where all of the scientists are in a room and this thing is happening—the first ever picture emerging of a black hole—and there is an excitement that is indescribable like, oh, what are we doing here? Slow down, guys, slow down... Leibniz at a certain point says like physics, I can't reach, it blocks me. And then I go to metaphysics. In one of your articles you quote Einstein saying something similar, that if you get at the edge of your knowledge

2 Peter Galison, *Black Holes: The Edge of All We Know*. A documentary film following the quest to understand the most mysterious objects in the universe. https://www.blackholefilm.com

you meet God. Not that I'm a very religious person, but the tension between the religious ungraspable and the cognitive ungraspable that you meet in this scientific context—for me the similarities are very interesting.

PG I'll address this in a couple of ways. First about that moment and the work on imaging a black hole and what that meant, then a little bit about what was special about a black hole and then about the limits or edge of knowledge and its relationship to metaphysics.

There is a sociality in science that's really very fundamental to it, and sometimes that sociality is more hidden, and sometimes it's more explicit. Sometimes it involves the sharing of results and sending papers back and forth, or presenting results in other ways. It's very interconnected in that sense. But in a scientific collaboration like the Event Horizon Telescope, it's quite on the surface because you can't even begin to describe the experiment or the observation without understanding the relationship among a group of telescopes. One telescope by itself tells you nothing about the black hole. It's only the combination of these telescopes that provide the baselines. You could imagine the telescopes as if they had rubber bands between them, each one tuned to a different frequency, stretched to a different amount. So each combination of telescopes picks out a different visual frequency of the sky, and the combination of all visual frequencies is what can be used to create an image.

Right from the beginning, this concept of Very Long Baseline Interferometry (VLBI) only works with a collection of telescopes. And the more telescopes and the better distributed they are, the better the image you can form. It turns out that on broad and general principles, it was clear early on that we would need telescopes distributed around the whole Earth to be able to give the kind of simulation of a single Earth-sized telescope able to pick out this black hole against the night sky. You had to essentially transform the Earth into a kind of instrument. The Earth itself becomes part of the telescope.

Without any of those elements, there's nothing. But that means, because it's combining all these different things, people all over the world are involved. In the case of making that first image of the black hole, over many continents it took more than two hundred scientists working for years, the possibility of producing these images, gathering the data, combining them in a supercomputer, using that data with various computational algorithms, to make an image. And that moment that you described: where we're all sitting, waiting for the image, each of us trying to see it, see whether we get the same image. That was an extraordinary moment, a moment when something that had been unvisualizable, invisible to us, even thought to be speculative for many, many decades, suddenly became real. We had all made simulations of black holes but somehow looking at that dark shadow in the midst of this ring and there's a black hole, that meant something quite extraordinary. I think it was very emotional for all of us. No amount of prior calculation or simulation could quite prepare for the sudden hit of first seeing that image.

Some aspects of that might have been true even if we had been trying to capture an image of some other remarkable astrophysical effect. But because it was a black hole, you're looking at something which is in a very real sense an edge of the universe. When you pass through the horizon of a black hole, you are no longer able to communicate with the rest of reality. You are actually, in a mathematical, causal, and profound sense, outside the connected universe as we know it. So being able to see that, to see that shadow, to look at that and say there is an edge of the universe that is the black hole that we're looking at, there was something moving, terrifying, wondrous that was not just seeing another very interesting astrophysical effect. And because black holes are this membrane that you can pass through going in one direction but not in the other, they are redolent of and remind us always of death. We all are going to pass from life to death, but we're (under ordinary circumstances) not coming back. I think that that's why novelists, science fiction writers, physicists and astrophysicists, and people in everyday life use it as a metaphor, see black holes as somehow deathlike.

There is a way in which these become evocative of all sorts of other questions, not just in the popular culture, but for the scientists to work on it as well. And it's perhaps there that we come to the third part of your question in saying that it can provoke a sense of metaphysical wonder for some people that may seem to echo religious experience. There's one colleague we have, Heino Falcke, a theorist who is a lay minister in Germany. He thinks about the edge of the black hole, in effect, as the limit of science and in some ways to think much beyond that plunges him into religious reflection. But I think whether you see it as religious or whether it evokes other forms of metaphysical reflection, black holes are as provocative of thought about the edge not just of what we happen to know now, but of what we can know. And I think that is a tremendously, endlessly fascinating circumstance.

AMY FRANCESCHINI

What are your thoughts on this force (gravity) as a collaborator—a force that we all share—that is all around us?

PG Well, gravity does have a peculiar feature, which is that it's universal. No particle of the universe is immune to it, which is different than, say, electricity and magnetism. If you don't happen to carry a charge, you don't know about electricity or electrical forces—a neutral particle doesn't care about that. But no particle, even a neutral particle, is immune to the blandishments of gravity because it's universal. It is possible to think about it in a very different way already.

When Galileo dropped objects off of the leaning tower of Pisa, the heavy object and the light object hit the ground at the same time, not taking into account wind resistance. This led Newton to think that there are actually two different aspects of mass, that there's how hard it is to get something going and how attracted something is by gravity. Einstein took that thought and said, you know what? Gravity is such that every object in some ways responds to it the same way. You let go of both the big rock and the little marble, and they come down to the ground at the same time. They accelerate. The same way that you could think of gravity as not a force, but a change in the way the world is. Einstein realized that we could say: gravity changes the structure of space and time—and then "all" objects simply fall in the same way. You could stop talking about force altogether and just talk about the structure of space and time.

So gravity is special; it is universal. Even Newton's law was called his universal law of gravity, and it, along with his laws of motion, became the model for universality; Newton's laws of nature were shaped into a broader idea of law and then into the founding documents of the United States including the Declaration of Independence.

The aspiration for generation after generation of scientists was to be able to create in other domains of human activity something as universal as gravity, as force pulling two masses together equals the product of the two divided by the distance squared, something so simple to write down, and yet so absolutely ubiquitous, so all-affecting. So I think that there is a way in which gravity, which we can think about all the time or not think about at all; why we can walk on the ground and not float away; why the moon goes around the Earth and Earth goes around the sun; why stars form into galaxies, and why galaxies form into clusters. It's an organizing principle for our world in the broadest sense, but it has this feature of not being local in the sense of just working over short distances. It works. A grain of sand on Earth affects what goes on Alpha Centauri. Every object affects every other object in the universe. And every pair of objects is pulled together does so according to the same rule law.

AF Can you elaborate on this idea of "gravity as an organizing principle for the world," and the "constitutional" meanings of it?

PETER GALISON The different levels of order, the formation of planets, the formation of gas going around into planets and planets into planets going around the sun, the formation of stars: And then the formation of stars into galaxies and galaxies into clusters of galaxies. At every level, there's a different kind of order produced by gravity, and in a way, that's amazing,

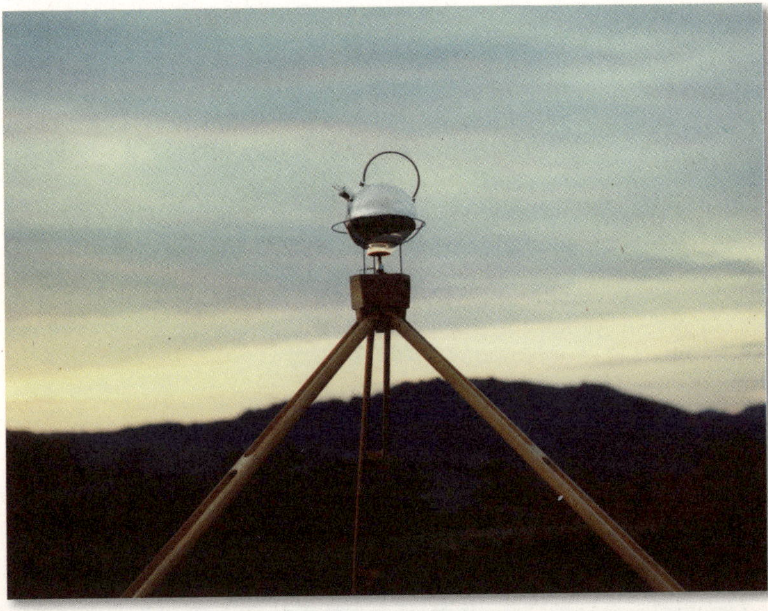

Futurefarmers, *Wandering Seminar Whistling Tea Kettle*, University of California, Santa Cruz, 2020, photo by Futurefarmers.

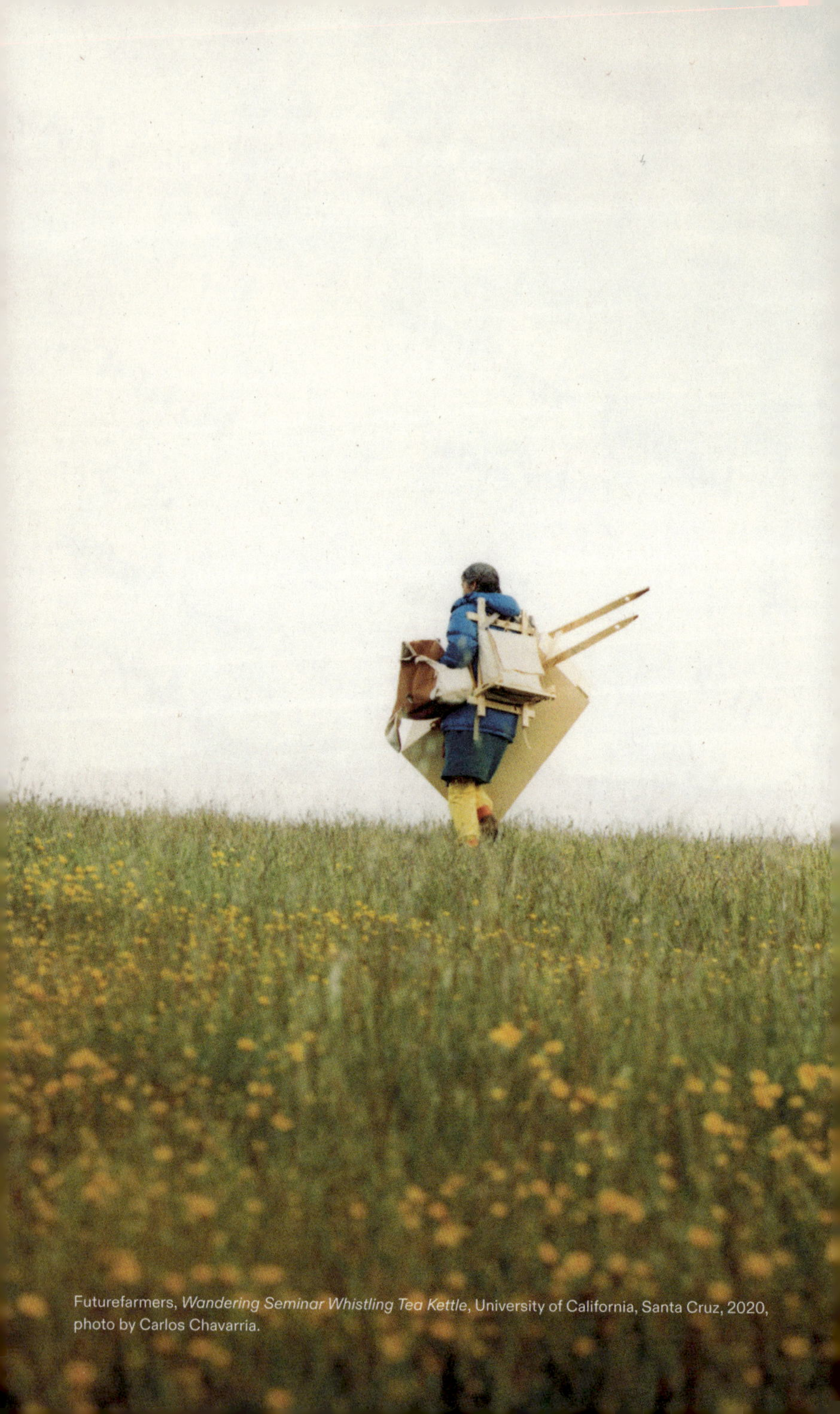

Futurefarmers, *Wandering Seminar Whistling Tea Kettle*, University of California, Santa Cruz, 2020, photo by Carlos Chavarria.

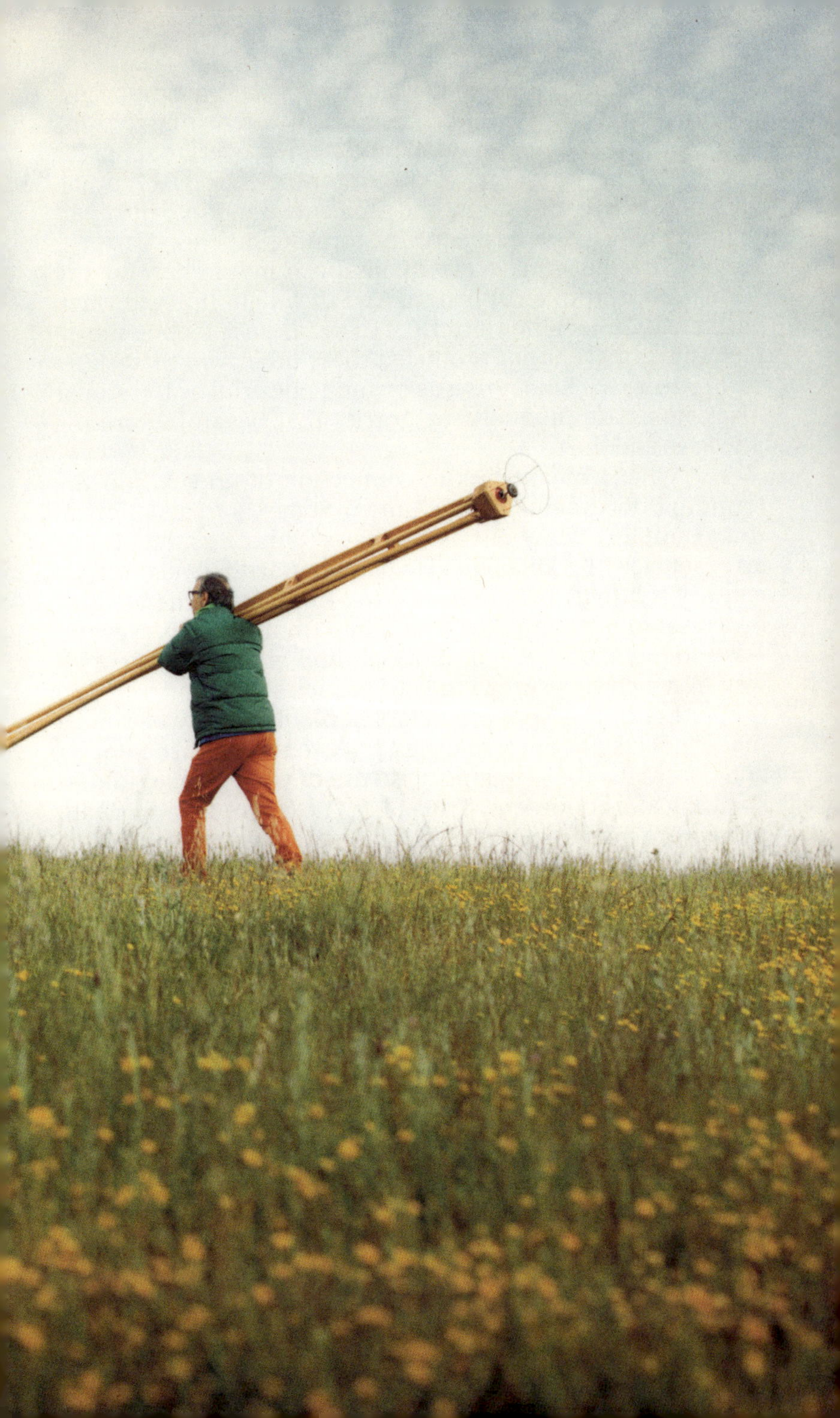

all from this simply stated law. So that's what I meant by giving order to the world. I find it endlessly interesting to think that there are these primordial particles left over from the Big Bang. And they form into what? Protons, electrons, eventually they coalesce into atoms and molecules, and into dust particles that are gathered by gravity, forming spheres.

And the spheres eventually push in and become hot enough to start nuclear fusion. And they light up. And when we look for or feel the warmth of the sun, we're feeling the effect of gravity that has produced these orbs. And that's kind of amazing that something as big and powerful as the sun or black holes are produced by gravity that began by forming particles and dust.

What I meant by the connection of gravity and the founding documents of the United States is this: Jefferson (for example) talks about natural laws (plural), as the historian of science I.B. Cohen liked to point out. In these eighteenth century writings, they're borrowing from Locke the ideas of universal and natural law that come from Newton. Newton was talking about laws of motion—and gravity. So there's a way in which this simple idea of particles being attracted to each other in this very predictable, calculable way became a model not just for other sciences, but even for social compacts and contracts, they became a picture of what human understanding and action was. True, in the next century and a half, there were many new ways in which theories emerged—like quantum mechanics—that were even more astonishing in the strangeness of their metaphysical underpinning. But what gravity has done is set a framework for the very idea of natural law, a framework that altered our very idea of the human ability to grasp the universal regularity of the world around us.

↘ Futurefarmers

is an international working group founded in 1995 in San Francisco. They are artists, designers, architects, programmers, anthropologists, writers, and farmers with a common interest in creating frameworks for exchange and production that invoke various media to call into question the context in which they work.Futurefarmers often engage the sciences to find synergies or trouble the brackets of scientific inquiry. Their work was exhibited at the Whitney Museum of American Art; the Museum of Modern Art; the Solomon R. Guggenheim Museum; MAXXI; the Sharjah Biennial 13 and the Carpenter Center for the Visual Arts of Harvard University. They are currently the lead artists for the public artwork *S(tree) twork*, which takes the form of a permanent workshop in an arboretum, where fallen trees are sculpted into musical instruments to summon the future forest aligned with the city of Philadelphia's strategic plan to forest underserved neighbourhoods.

↘ Peter Galison

is the Pellegrino University Professor of the History of Science and Physics at Harvard University, USA. His current research is on the history and philosophy of black holes and the changing relation of technology to the self. Among his seminal books are *How Experiments End* (1987) and *Objectivity* (with Lorraine Daston, 2007). Galison collaborated with William Kentridge, a South African artist, on the installation *The Refusal of Time* (2012) and an associated chamber opera, *Refuse the Hour*. He co-directs Critical Media Practice, a training program for a new generation of PhD students focused on digital media, and the Film Study Center at Harvard. Galison is a co-founder of the Black Hole Initiative, an interdisciplinary center for the study of black holes.

NARRATOLOGY OF PARADOXES

↘ Kolar Aparna AND Beatrice Catanzaro
IN CONVERSATION WITH Saba Hamzah AND Linda Armano

The most urgent question for us to explore through creating this text has been: How can we build capacities for other modes of listening and imagining? We have been honing our abilities to listen to that which "haunts". This listening occurs within the paradoxes that emerge from relations of extraction, silencing, erasure, and moulding and where the plural dimensions and complexities of beings are framed into fixed identities and categorized into already-given taxonomies.

What forms do we adopt in order to listen to that which haunts? How do we listen to what has been silenced for too long in and through our bodies? How do we initiate a process of listening without forcing agency onto silence or fixing it as a singular object/subject? How do we inhabit paradoxes of biographies for the sake of relating?

We played, searching for a language that would allow us to set in conversation relations emerging from paradoxes of a specific social phenomenon. We embraced the impossibility of mediating conflictual positions, instead making space for the multiplicity of inner/outer voices through relations of haunting.

Have you listened to a gem? When a diamond is taken from the earth, it unfolds as an assemblage of elements of multiple stone cohabitations. Each is the subject and witness of relations and encounters across immemorial time and space. Their histories and memories characterize the complexity of heterogeneous realities. The gem returns its biography in a convoluted gathering of multiple materialities as a silent reminder of relatedness.

The eye of the extractor sees harmful "impurities" that need to be erased by cleaning and carving processes in order to extract the gem's "purity." But who decides what is pure and what is not? A stable identity is constructed through cleaning and carving—gestures that symbolically evoke a mixture of "being a rough stone" and "becoming a carved and tradable diamond."

One seeks purity at the cost of unclarity, opaqueness, and dirt. The paradox of conflicting relations is resolved in the materiality of the rough diamond by a purifying process—by domesticating the diamond, any trace of coexisting conflictual realities disappears from sight, reiterating the illusion of purity as the original state of things.

The rough stone whispers that the cohabitation of paradoxical narratives is pre-existent or fundamental to any claim to identity. "Paradox" is the condition in which complexity expresses itself in the multivocality of simultaneous and often contradicting life experiences. The image of the rough gem narrates ways the stone includes multiplicity for the sake of complexity—suggesting that any attempt at its domestication will allow only a fragmented part to emerge while that which is erased continues to haunt. And yet, in these relations of purifying, the paradoxes that emerge from the impossibility of fully erasing the cohabitating other elements remain carried in all of our bodies. We have attempted to stage possible scenarios that consciously follow the threads of paradoxes.

We invite the reader to adopt a form of listening we have practiced. We present three scenarios that activate conversations following that which haunts—an imaginal absence-presence. The scenarios are based on stories that are not fully told to us and stories that also hide, remaining in our bodies across generations.

What does one have to give up in order to be seen or heard? Or, instead, how do we shift the modes of listening and sensing that which haunts? Our biographies and other biographies that emerge in partial stories, silenced histories, haunting life experiences, and dreams became a source of inspiration to search for settings and actors.

The diamond, the statue, the scorpion, the snake hill, the professor, the pilgrim, and the disguised companion, are actors that emerged as symbolic of the paradoxes of conflicting, entangled, merging realities of modernity and mythology, trauma and history, purity and impurity, perpetrator and victim, patriarchy and silence, object and agent, and so on. The reflective voice or the choir is the classroom, an unnamed figure, and the stone. They serve as witnesses, figures of doubt, holding the stick of intention to remain with the paradoxes towards a radical openness.[1] The drawings serve as a third space for context, a place that travels in the imaginal realm and becomes the location or setting for the story to land as part of the paradoxes within the reader's biography—inner and outer.

We invite you to journey through the three scenarios we present in the following pages as pathways to a sensorial journey, like sensing a poem.

1 bell hooks, "Choosing The Margin as a Space of Radical Openness", *Framework: The Journal of Cinema and Media*, n. 36, (1989).

SCENARIO 1
PILGRIM, HAVE YOU LISTENED TO THE GEM?

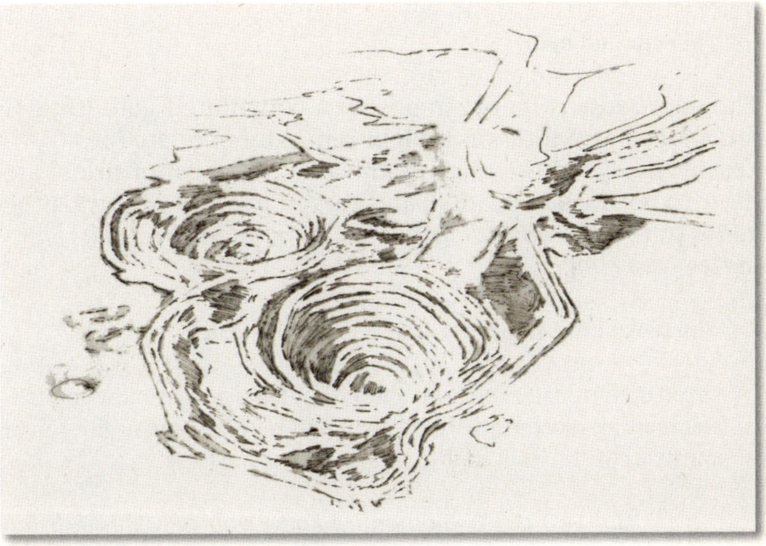

Have you listened to a gem? When a diamond is taken from the earth, it unfolds as an assemblage of multiple stone inclusion elements. Each is the subject and witness of relations and encounters across immemorial time and space.

In which ways can I encounter you, diamond?
domesticating?
controlling?
cleansing?
moulding?
extorting?
purging?

I, the diamond, am the memory of heterogeneous realities across time and space.

I carry fragments of telluric mysteries I encounter across the initiation to become what I am.

I am one and many.

The gem returns its biography in a convoluted gathering of multiple materialities as a silent reminder of relatedness. Yet, in the eye of the pilgrim, those harmful "impurities" are there to be erased, cleaned, and carved in order to extract the gem's purity: *a stable identity must be moulded through cleaning and carving*.

You seek purity at the cost of unclarity, opaqueness, and dirt.

If you domesticate me, the diamond, any trace of coexisting conflictual realities disappears from your sight, reiterating your illusion of purity as the original state of things.

But you are a diamond. I know you only through the partial shape of sparkling purity and desirability.
This is who you are to me.

While the rough stone, with its inclusions, whispers:

In me, the cohabitation of paradoxical narratives is pre-existent to any claim to identity. I am all this at once. Through a whack, my voice will remain unheard.

"Paradox" is the condition in which complexity expresses itself in the multivocality of simultaneous and often contradicting life experiences.

Pilgrim, which stories are you made of?

The rough diamond is an outer reminder of our internal world, suggesting that any attempt at domestication will allow only a fragmented story to emerge.

> I am a pilgrim. This is what they call me.
> I am a pilgrim. Before that, I cannot remember.

> How can I trust you if you do not remember the stories that made you who you are?

> I was domesticated, controlled, cleaned, moulded, extorted, and purged myself.

Blinding the sight towards that inner magmatic field turns the world into an inert matter to conquer, extract, and shape, uprooting its complex living narrative.

SCENARIO 2
THE PROFESSOR AND THE SNAKE HILL

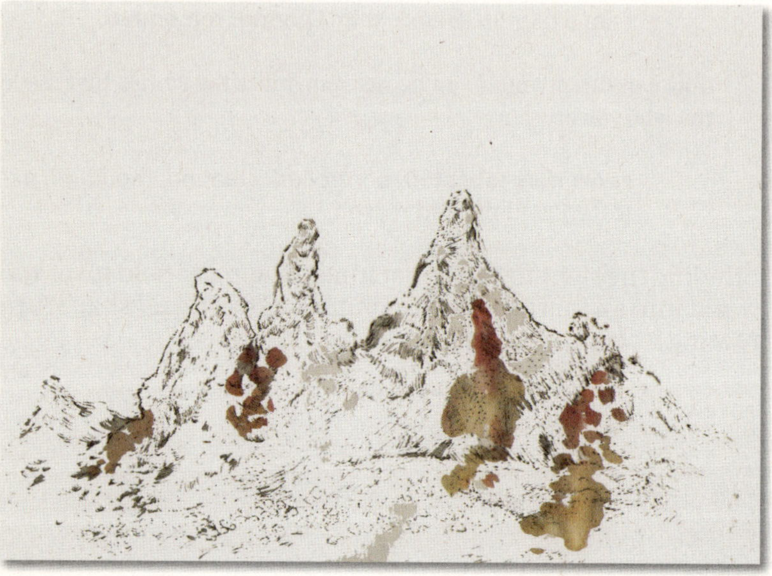

Do you hear the restless stone refusing to flow with the waves of the Baltic Sea.

She journeyed here from the land of peanuts

THE PROFESSOR
The snake hill is an impediment to industrial progress, and yet, I go to her when no one understands me.

THE SNAKE HILL
I wake up each day to the screams of their raging guts, whose bodies carry stories of beating drums. I too have written books that are buried in these lands. The snakes crawling in my veins seem to have forgotten to sense these buried herstories.

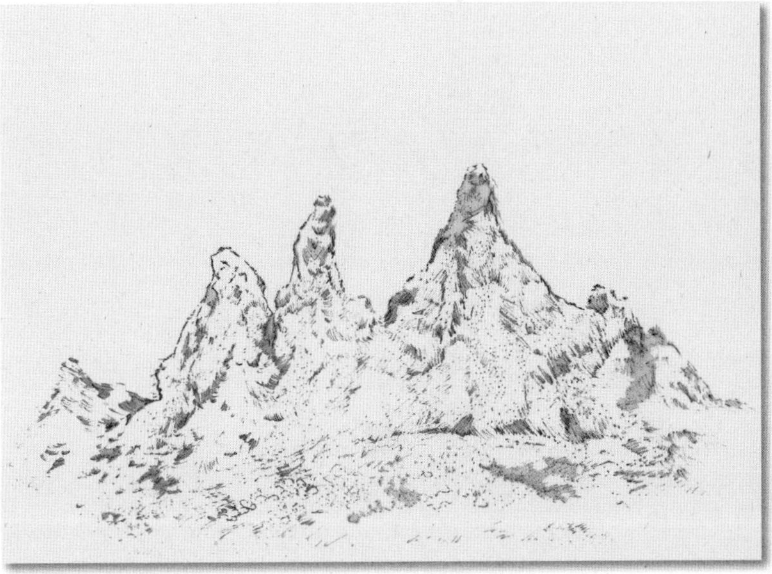

The stone has come to the end of her pilgrimage and is hungry. Please offer her three balls of rice, ಅರಿಶಿನ, ಕುಂಕುಮ, *and one plain.*

THE PROFESSOR
I am a priest and a scientist. I can measure you but I cannot nourish you.

THE SNAKE HILL
When you wear your coat you forget that your wife was here offering milk to heal your wounds from scorpion bites.

She took her last breath while hanging clothes.

SCENARIO 3
THE CLASSROOM AND THE SCORPION

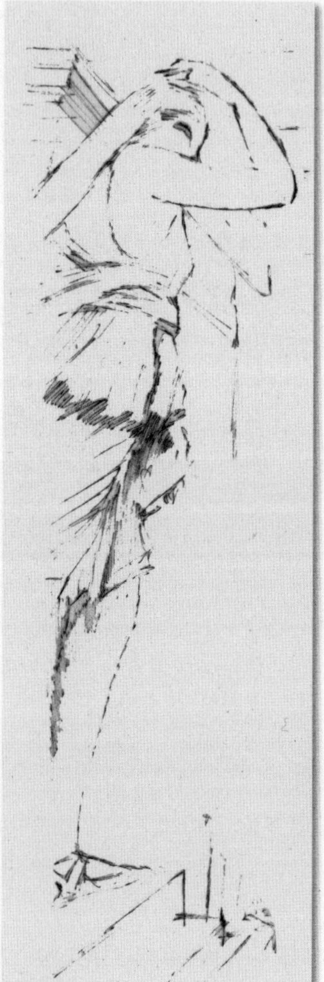

I, the black scorpion, carry stories across generations of broken spirits. Do you, the marble statue in the hallway of the university remember me?

THE CLASSROOM
the disguised companion walks in with the black scorpion on her left shoulder, sinking slowly underneath her skin.

There is nowhere else to go than under your smooth skin that silence your wounds from healing. I am your secret/sacred space.

THE CLASSROOM
the disguised companion invites us to get closer.

It feels
insecure?
nervous in the chest?
humble throat?
raging guts?
tired tongue?

I am not alone here

THE CLASSROOM
Disguised companion, who are you? Your black scorpion has awakened the other scorpions.

I am the disguised companion. Have you thought about her, the scorpion?
Has the scorpion slept next to you last night?

or did it take you to your secred space?

Was he on your palm or on your foot today?

They say he is either عابر سبيل (Passer-by) or *vijand* (Enemy)...

But have you thought of her as a guide to the path you endeavour or your voice to the silence you endure?

REFERENCES

Kolar Aparna, Beatrice Catanzaro, "You Are But You Are Not", *Approdi. Musei delle migrazioni in Europa,* ed. by Anna Chiara Cimoli (Milan: CLUEB, 2018).

Kolar Aparna, Saba Hamzah, forthcoming, "Languaging as Refusal", *Fennia, International Journal of Geography*.

Beatrice Catanzaro, "As If", *Routledge Companion to Art in the Public Realm*, ed. by Cameron Cartiere, Leon Tan (New York: Routledge, 2021).

Saba Hamzah, "Stranded: Stories from the Abysmal Sea, Feminist Intersectional Politics of Death", MA Thesis (Utrecht University, 2020).

Saba Hamzah, "Burn in Silence" (2023).

Saba Hamzah, Saba Hamzah, "Soliloquy to Floating Doom" (2021).

Saba Hamzah, "Structural and Epistemic violence in Historical Landscapes of Yemen", *Europeanisation as Violence: Souths and Easts as Method,* ed. by Kolar Aparna, Daria Krivonos, Elisa Pascucci (Manchester University Press, forthcoming).

bell hooks, "Choosing the margin as a space of radical openness", *Framework: The Journal of Cinema and Media*, n. 36 (1989).

Silence: The Currency of Power, ed. by Maria-Luisa Achino-Loeb (New York: Berghahn Books, 2006).

Linda Armano, Annamma Joy, "Encoding Values and Practices in Ethical Jewellery Purchasing: A Case History of Italian Ethical Luxury Consumption", *Sustainable Luxury and Jewellery*, ed. by Miguel Àngel Gardetti, Ivan Coste-Manière (Singapore: Springer 2021).

Linda Armano, "Quanto etica è l'eticità? Interpretazioni culturali lungo la filiera del diamante canadese", Anuac, n.11, (2022).

Lindsay A Bell, "Soft skills, hard rocks: Making diamonds ethical in Canada's Northwest Territories", *Journal of Global and Historical Anthropology*, n. 79, (2017).

Ann Kingsolver, "Representation as an Extractive Economy: Silencing and Multiple Marginalities", *Reflecting on Silence and Anthropology. Emergent Conversation* series, *PoLAR: Political and Legal Anthropology Review Online* (2015).

Jennifer J. Kish-Gephart , James R. Detert, Linda Klebe Treviño, Amy C. Edmondson, "Silenced by fear: The nature, sources, and consequences of fear at work", *Research in Organizational Behavior,* n. 29, (2009).

Rober Weller, "Salvaging silence: exile, death, and the anthropology of the unknown", *Anthropology of this Century,* n. 19, (2007).

Eviatar Zerubavel, "The Elephant in the Room: Silence and Denial in Everyday Life", (Oxford: Oxford Scholarship, 2006).

ACKNOWLEDGEMENTS

The Centre of Excellence in Law, Identity, and the European Narratives (grant numbers 312431 and 336678) at the Academy of Finland have supported Kolar Aparna's participation in this research. All drawings are by Beatrice Catanzaro, 2023.

↘ Kolar Aparna

is a postdoctoral researcher at the University of Helsinki, Faculty of Arts, Academy of Finland Centre of Excellence in Law, Identity and European Narratives (Eurostorie). In the last decade, she has been teaching on themes related to postcolonial Europe. Her work is focused on building situated knowledge as part of epistemic struggles around citizenship, exile, and borders. Aparna co-edited *Method as Border: Tuning in to the Cacophony of Academic Backstages of Migration, Mobility and Border Studies* (Social Inclusion, 2020), co-authored *Europe is no longer Europe: Montaging Borderlands of Help for a radical politics of place* (Nordic Journal of Migration, 2020), *Asylum University: Re-situating Knowledge-Exchanges Along Cross-Border Positionalities* (Pluto Press, 2018), among others. She is currently co-editing a volume with Daria Krivonos and Elisa Pascucci on *Europeanisation as Violence* (Manchester University Press).

↘ Linda Armano

is an anthropologist. She was awarded a Marie Curie Fellowship hosted at the University of Venice and the University of British Columbia. Armano's research interests include indigenous epistemologies, ethical issues in the mining industry, and global supply chains. Some recent publications are "The Acculturation Process of New Products through Known Products. Interpreting Ethical Certification of Diamonds through the Lens of Organic Food Produced in Italy" (Luxury: History, Culture, Consumption, 2023); "How ethical is ethicality? Cultural interpretation along the Canadian diamond supply chain" (Anuac, 2022); *Conceptions of Territories. Indigenous Land Management and Multinational Property in the Northwest Territories of Canada* (Tab Edizioni, 2022).

↘ Beatrice Catanzaro

is an artist, researcher and lecturer. She teaches at the NABA Art Academy, Milan, and the Accademia Unidee at Cittadellarte—Fondazione Pistoletto, Biella, Italy. She gained her PhD at Oxford Brookes University with the Social Sculpture Research Unit. Catanzaro's practice-based research questions the matrix of hegemonic social structures and imaginaries through dialogical processes grounded in long-term engagements and interdisciplinary collaborations. She co-founded the Woman Centre and Social Enterprise *Bait al Karama* in the Old City of Nablus, Palestine. Her work has been exhibited in museums and international venues such as MART Museum, Rovereto; Fundação Gulbenkian, Lisbon; Espai d'Art Contemporani (EACC), Castellón; and Rome Quadriennale, Rome. She lives and works in Milan.

↘ Saba Hamzah

is a feminist poet-scholar, writer, and educator, who navigates the intersection of knowledge production, memory, and social justice, with a decolonization approach. Her main devices are line and light, and the moments in between. Hamzah works as a research associate at the Tropenmuseum in Amsterdam and is a fellow scholar at Vassar College in New York. From fall 2023, she will participate in the IWP (International Writing Program) at Iowa University. Her commitment to educational innovation is reflected in her work with alternative pedagogies and artistic practices, where she seeks to stimulate critical thinking and challenge conventional norms, thereby shaping transformative learning experiences. Hamzah is a founder of the Yemeni Women Archive, a space for emerging knowledges from women's experiences and histories in Yemen and the diaspora.

A GLOSSARY FOR SOCIETALLY ENGAGED ART

↘ Barbara Holub
IN CONVERSATION WITH Grant Kester

In order to explore the role of dialogue in the constitution of collaborative art practices Barbara Holub invited Grant Kester to work together to create a glossary of terms associated with a dialogical conception of the aesthetic. Each assembled a set of keywords that were then combined to form the following glossary. In some cases, both provided definitions for the same concepts; in others they didn't, depending on their respective interests. The glossary can be read "between the lines," in the interstices and tensions between their respective orientations, as artist/practitioner and art historian/critic.[1]

1 See: Grant Kester, *The Sovereign Self: Aesthetic Autonomy from the Enlightenment to the Avant-Garde* and *Beyond the Sovereign Self: Aesthetic Autonomy from the Avant-Garde to Socially Engaged Art* (Durham, NC: Duke University Press, 2023).

AESTHETICS The concept of the aesthetic is inextricably linked with the somatic knowledge produced through our bodies. Like autonomy, it is characterized by a fundamental ambivalence. On the one hand, aesthetic experience provides a means of accessing the underlying mechanisms of human subjectivity, necessary for the implantation of Enlightenment ideals in a recalcitrant public consciousness. On the other hand, the aesthetic challenges the instrumentalizing modernist drive which treats the public as a cognitive resource to be programmed and controlled by the ideologies of the state. In its more utopic guise, aesthetics can help us challenge the hierarchies of mind over body, theory over practice, and intellect over emotion. Our goal must be, however, not a simple inversion of this ethical/epistemological binary, in which the body and affect are assigned preeminent value over reason. Rather, we must understand that all knowledge is produced at the interstices of mind and body, and self and other, each drawing the other out of its isolation. In conventional aesthetic experience, this dialogical tension is surrendered and the "thorn of alterity" necessary for sustaining it is reduced to a mere projection of the authoring self. In this manner, the aesthetic ends by enshrining the autonomous self, rather than by calling it into question. How might we reconsider the aesthetic in collective art practices in a manner that preserves this tension, rather than collapsing it into semblance? GRANT KESTER

An ongoing reproach of socially engaged art and art which engages with urban issues/in the urban realm/in urban public space is that this art does not consider aesthetics in a relevant way. This reproach needs to be challenged, since it is extremely relevant and important that artistic practices engaging in societal and urban issues conceive specific aesthetics according to their contexts, for creating a "situation" (see Situationists) with a specific visibility. We need to reconsider these practices both as relevant for the art discourse, for reconsidering the role of art in society—and also in terms of their artistic "autonomy." BARBARA HOLUB

AGREEMENT/ DISAGREEMENT Agreement and disagreement entered the rhetoric of engaged art in conjunction with the binary pairing of consensus and dissensus. In conventional art criticism, they are presented as two opposing principles. Agreement is the coercive force imposed by projects that operate through "collective" social forms, which are especially prevalent in practices developed beyond the institutional art world. By contrast, disagreement or dissensus are unique to art world-based practices which seek to destabilize dominant political narratives through various forms of cognitive assault staged in galleries and museums. This opposition is predicated on a principle of simultaneity in which the decisive character of the aesthetic encounter unfolds in a single moment of revelatory self-transformation, after which the viewer's consciousness is irrevocably transformed. Here, the capacity for provoking a form of critical insight is the singular province of the artist, while the viewer remains a passive receptacle of the artist's transformative intentionality. Engaged art practices understand aesthetic experience as durational and temporally extensive, moving through periods of both criticality and consensus; disagreement and agreement. They ask, moreover, whether we can imagine an aesthetic paradigm in which that these subjective modalities are not permanently assigned to fixed individuals (the artist vs. the viewer), but rather, are mobile and transient. In this view, insight is not carried into particular sites of resistance by a single, privileged agent, but rather, is generated through the act of resistance itself. GK

Art needs to allow for disagreement. Art is one of the last realms of society with the capacity to openly advocate for disagreement, for contradictions, for not fitting, and for questioning norms. Artists take on risk and need to be strong enough to stand up for disagreement. BH

ATMOSPHERE The atmosphere for creating a situation and a space of collaboration and dialogue is crucial for a productive process and fruitful project. This requires an awareness of what hospitality means, of setting grounds for welcoming an exchange beyond pragmatics, of allowing for non-linear arguments, for deviation, for pleasure, joy, and contradiction—beyond the pre-set expectations of all parties involved (commissioning party, city administration, artists, curators, etc.), as an open-ended process. BH

AUTONOMY Autonomy refers to our capacity to be self-governing (to create our own "norms"). In European philosophy, the concept of autonomy emerges in conjunction with bourgeois paradigms of possessive individualism, as the middle class sought to contest absolutist political domination in the seventeenth century. Autonomy carries two related meanings: autonomy as independence "from" an external force, and autonomy as the ability to exercise a transformative power "over" the external world. It thus possesses both a potential for liberation and a capacity for instrumentalization. This ambivalence is paralleled at the epistemological level, in the tension between the "critical distance" opened up as thought frees itself from domination, and the forms of knowledge that are mobilized as the sovereign self exercises its mastery over others. Norms are, by definition, shared social constructs. How, then, can we negotiate the tension between individual selves who seek to impose their own values onto others, and the dependence of any complex social system on beliefs which are consensually shared, rather than unilaterally imposed? How can we think autonomy differently? GK

Due to the long lasting debate, if socially-engaged art dealing with specific social, cultural, and political contexts can have its own autonomy, it is even more important that this autonomy be claimed—only then art can act and use its potential to contribute from a different perspective. BH

CHANGE

Change implies the alteration of a given (social) organism. In the context of the political, we can speak of a volitional change, intended to diminish forms of oppression and enhance the freedom and equality of a given society. Change occurs at varying scales and speeds. The definition of change is linked with, and dependent on, a specific ontological model of the social system within which change occurs. Is this system entirely uniform? Is it defined by points of fracture or incompletion? How does it re-constitute itself in response to efforts to transform it? Do some forms of change matter more than others? Many strains of the Marxist tradition rest on the ontological essentialism of "capitalism" as a fixed system of domination, allowing for only two possible modes of intervention: reform, which serves simply to validate the underlying integrity of a system based on fundamental inequality, and revolution, which requires the absolute overturning of that equally monolithic system. Is there another way for us to conceptualize change which is able to transcend this binary opposition? And if so, what use do we make of the ambivalent legacy of revolutionary change associated with the Communist tradition in the twentieth century? GK

The current universal quest for "change" has resulted in an obliteration of its (socially engaged) meaning.

Economic capital interests mingle with critical voices and radical engagements so that the original quest to help build a more just society has been jeopardized. Yet artists and urban practitioners continue to produce/keep insisting on producing (often times collaborative) situations for change and developing these strategies. Insisting, pursuing, against all obstacles. With an utmost investment of energy and dedication to the belief that art is one of the last reserves in society able to contradict the dominant and governing neoliberal rules and power systems; for propagating visions in spite of all obstacles. That is the potential and real power of art. BH

ENGAGEMENT The word "engage" is derived from the Old French *engagier*; meaning to pledge or to bind. A pledge suggests a commitment to something beyond the bounds of the self. In the context of artistic practice, it implies a sense of reciprocal obligation to the broader social world. This stands in contrast to a conventional aesthetic paradigm, predicated on the belief that art's significance doesn't derive from its practical effect on the world, but from the fact that art as such has no outwardly directed purpose at all. This notion is carried forward in the avant-garde tradition in a principle of radical non-utility that we encounter in figures such as Adorno, for whom the work of art must remain "hermetically closed off and blind" to the surrounding world; a world defined by corruption and impurity. In place of this degraded view of the social, engaged art practices understand the realm of the social as a space of both domination and potential resistance. The social refers, as well, to the resources of solidarity and collective action that might be mobilized to challenge this domination, and to the role that artistic production might play in advancing this resistance. How does engagement call upon us to reconsider the binary schema of inside and outside, purity and impurity, criticality and complicity, art world and the broader social world, that patterns conventional aesthetic paradigms? GK

The artist engages to an extent that assumes utmost responsibility—that is usually the prerequisite for creating a meaningful project. But that needs the engagement of all of the other parties involved on an equal level. The artist only gives up at the last moment—if and when he/she has to realize that the resources necessary are not available/provided accordingly. BH

EXCITEMENT Excitement is crucial for engaging in societal/ urban issues. Excitement about what can be achieved is a driving force for engaging (see ENGAGEMENT)—for carrying on and insisting beyond felt and experienced limits (see LIMITS). The artist wants to raise and pass on that excitement to the other people involved. BH

L IM ITS Limits of do-ability must be considered carefully along with the process—even though the artist sets out his/her engagement based on the conviction that there are no limits. The artist has to challenge limits. Otherwise, the artist cannot work in a meaningful way. But the artist also has to be able to recognize, whether at a certain moment the conditions required for a successful project are not provided anymore according to necessities. Then the artist has to stand up, defending his/her integrity and the integrity of the project. BH

LISTENING The artist—as well as the participants—must be open to listening. The condition of listening can be taken as a starting point for the artist's work. This implies acting as a "non-expert," coming in openly, listening to others instead of imposing knowledge or (unrequested)

advice—providing a situation of a non-hierarchical dialogue. Sometimes the participants must be informally "trained" to engage in listening. BH

MACRO-UTOPIA transparadiso[2] has developed and employed macro-utopia as artistic-urbanistic strategy for "Direct Urbanism": Macro-utopia operates by employing an anticipatory fiction which allows for the emergence of the latent, hidden visions that we usually ignore due to self-censorship. The conflicting interests of the various groups involved are used to develop a design practice geared to conflicts, whose first mission is to produce a psycho-cartography of divergent ideals and role models."[3] BH

MOTIVATION Motivation is the driving force for engaging, for transgressing the borders of the seemingly doable—be it in the professional working context, in the political realm, or in the personal context. The artist can amplify this (potentially latent) energy by creating specific situations to engage, since the motivation of an artist engaging in societal issues is closely connected to and driven by the desire to change (see CHANGE) conditions—and

2 transparadiso was founded by Barbara Holub and Paul Rajakovics in 1999 as a trans-disciplinary practice for addressing current urban issues from a critical perspective. transparadiso has been developing artistic-urbanistic strategies and tools for promoting "direct urbanism" as a socially engaged, process-oriented method of urban planning, counteracting the dichotomy of "bottom up" and "top down" urban planning (see: transparadiso, *Direct Urbanism,* Wien: Verlag für Moderne Kunst, 2013) refers to "direct action" by Emma Goldman and discusses strategies of engagement between "direct" and "silent," as in *Silent Activism* (see: Barbara Holub. *Silent Activism*, Berlin: De Gruyter, 2022).

3 "Macro-utopia" was first presented here: transparadiso: Barbara Holub, Paul Rajakovics, Bernd Vlay, "On Direct Urbanism and the Art of Parallel Strategies", *open* (Rotterdam: NAi Publishers, 2007); then revised in: Barbara Holub, Christine Hohenbüchler (eds.) *Planning Unplanned* (Wien: Verlag für Moderne Kunst, 2015).

to propagate visions and macro-utopias (see MACRO-UTOPIAS). In these contexts the artist acts beyond personal interests—except for the interest of contributing his/ her artistic experience and making that visible. BH

NEGATION Negation emerges in Hegel's philosophy as the motive force of human progress, dedicated to exposing the limitations of posited thought and driving it to a higher level of synthesis. Here positivity and negation are separate moments in the temporal unfolding of the dialectic. Marx will criticize Hegel for "prematurely" ending the movement of negation when he contended that world historical development had culminated in the modern Prussian state. Instead, it was essential to preserve negation as a form of absolute critique, necessary for forcing the capitalist system into the final, utopic synthesis of full communism. This principle is carried forward in the Leninist contention that any form of partial societal progress serves merely to justify ongoing capitalist domination. Instead, political thought must dedicate itself to the single-minded destruction of the capitalist system. This principle migrated into avant-gardist discourse in the belief that art can forestall its inevitable co-option only by abjuring any affirmative gestures of cultural production (thereby aligning art, symbolically, with vanguard political action). As a result of this dynamic, traditional paradigms of revolutionary praxis have been unable to provide a compelling account of the utopian future on behalf of which contemporary struggle might be waged. Can we envision a new concept of revolutionary transformation; one that allows the critical negation of existing reality to co-exist with the creative generation of new social forms? GK

OPENNESS

Referring to the final question raised by Grant Kester concerning "negation": Openness is needed—for exploring and insisting on the "unwanted"! BH

PASSION

Passion is closely connected to excitement (see EXCITEMENT): Passion is ultimately required for a durational engagement, for overcoming obstacles, transgressing the first excitement of artistic engagement. BH

REFLECTION

The artist has to reflect the process on an ongoing parallel level (and beyond completion of the project). This must not be confounded with "evaluation." On the contrary, reflection by the artist facilitates their ability to creatively control changing conditions throughout the process and for developing strategies and tools to redirect the project if necessary. What I argue for in *Silent Activism* is that reflection by the participants involved should happen on a personal level—counteracting the quest for evaluation, since the impact of the art project/intervention will resonate on a personal level on a longer term. BH

PREFIGURATION

The concept of prefiguration originates in the theological search for signs of Christ's eventual arrival in pages of the Old Testament. It appears in Latin in the fourteenth century as a "figuring beforehand," but "figurare" can refer not simply to similitude but also to "forming," "shaping" and "building." In the contemporary moment, it speaks to a human need to engage in speculative experimentation with new modes of social organization that challenge the alienation and hierarchy of contemporary life. The history of European aesthetic theory, from Schiller to Marcuse, can be seen in this light as the extrapolation, at the symbolic level, of alternative modes of being, and new ways of knowing the world and each other, that transcend the crude materialism of contemporary life. In social movement theory, prefiguration plays a central role as a vector for the experimental, and frankly utopian, exploration of new forms of collective creation and decision making. In this view, it is only by working through, in an experiential manner, the tensions and potentials of human sociality, that we can comprehend the new society that our political struggles hope to produce. It is this prefigurative evocation that provides the constituents of change with a sense of their own agency and creativity. How, then, do we reconcile the "vertical" hierarchies of conventional vanguard politics (necessary for the tactical engagement with dominant forms of power) with the "horizontal" processes of consensual will formation and creativity necessary to orient praxis towards its eventual goal? GK

RESISTANCE Resistance implies a form of externalized oppression, against which one will exert a liberating counter force. This gesture is not simply kinetic, but also epistemologically generative. The act of resistance produces new forms of cognitive and somatic insight. The knowledge of the body (how it "feels" to act back on a coercive force) is joined with the mental knowledge created by gauging the pragmatic effects of specific resistant gestures. Resistance implies a form of coherent selfhood necessary for marshalling the resources needed to resist. It also implies the modes of intersubjective openness and solidarity necessary to constitute a collective agency sufficient to overcome an oppressive force that is more powerful than any individual. At the same time, all resistance begins, and is sustained, at the level of the individual consciousness. How and why do we choose to resist? And what is the relationship between a mode of resistance that is registered at the level of the individual consciousness and body, and those forms of social organization that allow the transformed consciousness to be projected into the world in a transformative manner? GK

Resistance to what is demanded, if necessary. Understanding at which point and how to resist. Which means can we as artists employ in a specific situation? Strategically understanding and differentiating accordingly, whether we want to continue with the project or at which point the demands of the commissioning party jeopardize the integrity of our project. BH

SILENCE In certain moments it is important to be silent. Silence is closely connected to listening (see LISTENING) and to speaking (see SPEAKING). To understand silence as a productive artistic means—as interruption, creating a break for contradicting and counteracting the omnipresent request for "being loud," for communicating, for advertising one's achievements. Silence is experienced as disturbing, as irritation. Reconsider silence as quality instead of a lack of ability. A choreographic strategy. Leaving space for the participants, to expose them to the experience; to endure silence. Silence must not be confounded with keeping quiet, even though both are active artistic strategies. It is important to realize the moment, in strenuous discussions, when it is conducive to keep quiet. BH

SPEAKING In certain moments it is important to speak, to get engaged. It is important when it feels uncomfortable, when one needs to expose or to critique; to be strong, in these moments; to be aware of the moments when we need to speak up, to contradict, to claim a position. BH

SATISFACTION Creating awareness of what satisfies us as artists—in comparison to other fields of society. What do we need in order to feel that moment? For feeling that moment. How much do we need to invest? What is the equilibrium between engagement and self-exploitation—more and more, transgressing personal borders? How can we advocate for an adequate recognition for our contribution to society? Artists are predominantly underpaid and acting on a self-exploitative level (in spite of the request for "fair pay"). The increasing divide between socially engaged art practices and the art market, which operates more and more only as investment calls for reconsidering the role of art for society. David Graeber researched intensively on the topic of the discontent and dissatisfaction of employees due to meaningless work tasks in corporate companies.[4] Here, we should step in as artists and claim that our expertise be recognized on an equal level with other dominant fields of expertise, for repositioning the relevance of social, human, and humanistic values—for contradicting a global system based merely on economic profits. BH

UNKNOWING Closely connected to unlearning. Assuming a position of not knowing, as a disposition for communication on an equal level. BH

4 See: David Graeber, *The Utopia of Rules: On Technology, Stupidity, and the Secret Joys of Bureaucracy* (New York: Melville House, 2015).

↘ Barbara Holub

is a Vienna-based artist, emerged from her architectural studies at Stuttgart University of Technology to develop a societally engaged artistic practice centered around "Silent Activism." In 1999, she co-founded transparadiso with Paul Rajakovics, an interdisciplinary platform intertwining art, architecture, and urban intervention. Serving as the president of Secession, Vienna, from 2006 to 2007, Holub has lectured globally at esteemed institutions such as the University of Illinois School of Art and Design, Chicago, Vienna University of Technology and the University of Applied Arts Vienna. Notably, she received the Austrian National Art Award in 2018. Holub's recent works include the monograph *Silent Activism* (De Gruyter, 2022), along with projects like *WE PARAPOM!* (Chemnitz 2021-2023, 2025), and, with transparadiso, *NORMAL* (Graz Culture Year 2020-2021), *Times of Dilemma* (Valletta 18, Malta), and participation in the Vienna Biennale (MAK Vienna, 2021).

↘ Grant Kester

is a professor of Art History in the Visual Arts department at the University of California at San Diego and the founding editor of "FIELD: A Journal of Socially Engaged Art Criticism." His research focuses on the history and theory of socially engaged art. Kester's publications include *The Sovereign Self: Aesthetic Autonomy from the Enlightenment to the Avant-Garde* (Duke University Press, 2023) and *Beyond the Sovereign Self: Aesthetic Autonomy from the Avant-Garde to Socially Engaged Art* (Duke University Press, 2023).

PLACES AS MULTIPLICITIES

NOTES OF AN ACCOMPLICE

LISA MAZZA

A place is more than just a strip of land. A place is not a fixed, clearly-defined unit. Rather, it's a varied space which can be perceived and experienced in multiple ways. It can never be described in just one way, because it has a different meaning—or even multiple meanings—for everyone, though some knowledge and experience is shared. By trying to conceive a place not as a fixed point but rather as a relation between various elements, new perspectives open, and a network appears. Art encourages us to recognize and trace this network of relations. Social anthropologist Tim Ingold[1] writes of the importance of creating relationships between elements, be they human, organisms, or other things. Intra-relation, as he calls it, erases the distinction between things and their relations; things "become" their relations.

A cultural institution acts in a specific geographic, political, social, demographic, environmental, topographic, botanical, zoological, and more-than-human context which isn't

1 Tim Ingold, *Being Alive: Essays on Movement, Knowledge and Description* (Oxon: Routledge, 2011).

↘ Lisa Mazza

is co-director of BAU, an institute for contemporary art and ecology, founded together with Simone Mair and Filipa Ramos in 2015. From 2014-2020, she co-directed Lungomare with Angelika Burtscher, Roberto Gigliotti, and Daniele Lupo. In her multiple roles as curator, cultural producer, mediator, and editor at BAU she facilitates artistic production that experiments with forms of gathering in which the landscape, the human and the more-than-human are important sources of knowledge. Among the artists Mazza collaborated with are Inland, Cooking Sections, Futurefarmers and Katrin Hornek. In 2021, she was the associate editor of the anthology *More-than-Human* (published by Het Nieuwe Institut).

rigidly fixed, which reflects not a unit but a multiplicity, and is in turn thought of as such in connection with other multiplicities.

Lungomare in Bolzano is the embodiment of multiplicity. United in a desire to imagine the sea in the Alps, to dream of the non-existent, as a co-thinker and accomplice of Lungomare, I was able to share in this utopia for a limited amount of time. Inviting artists and their associated practices into a context opens up a negotiation of multiplicity. Building bridges outwards from local issues and placing these issues in a larger, more global, transdisciplinary exchange is so exciting. The interplay between the hyper-specific nature of a place, interwoven with other geographies, disciplines, and perspectives allows us to bring the unthought to the surface, to be daring, and to actively experience multiplicity. It's only through this expanded perspective that the questions and challenges of our time—climate crisis, migration, increasing social inequalities—can be confronted discursively, artistically, and with tangible actions.

Context-specific praxis can only be activated more deeply if the context is not just the object of research but also part of it, if we aren't simply researching something but researching "with" something, if relationships are established.

This becomes possible if research has a public dimension, if asking questions is linked closely to actively listening, and artistic work isn't heard as a monologue but rather as a dialogue involving many voices which many people can contribute to in different ways. If the places the projects are displayed are included as an active element rather than just a container, and if artistic work opens up public dialogue and creates communities—even temporary ones—then culture can be viewed as a space with far broader horizons.

Just as these imperatives have shaped Lungomare's work for two decades, as a cultural producer I have a sociopolitical responsibility to bring together and develop further practices of thought and practices of making, never ceasing to redirect our gazes to places they wouldn't reach alone.

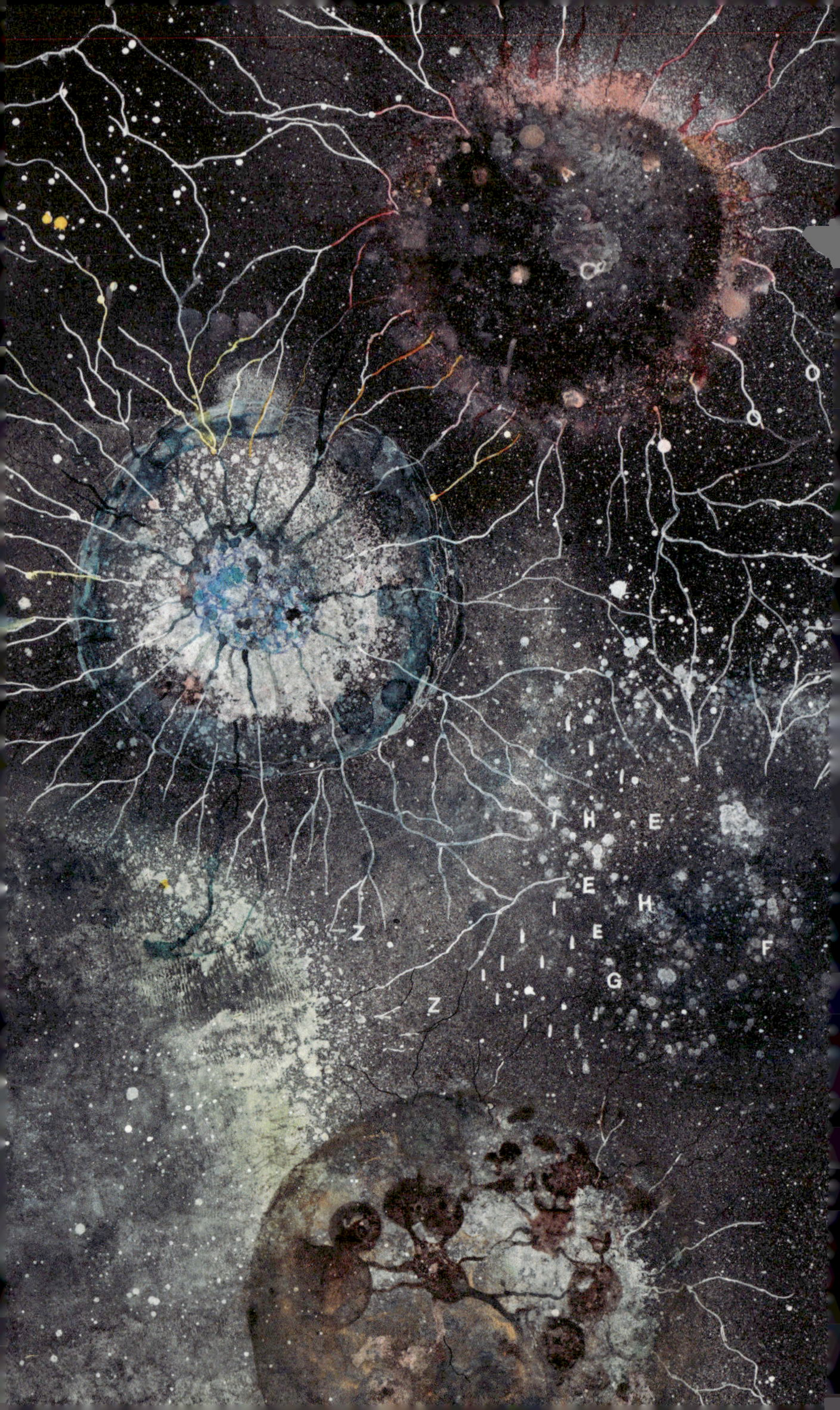

CHAPTER 2

THE PUBLIC SPACE AS A FIELD OF ACTION

DIALOGUES

↘ orizzontale
IN CONVERSATION WITH Jan Liesegang, Marinella Senatore, Francesco Careri, Lisa Carignani, Amélie Aranguren

↘ Erika Mayr AND Meike Schalk
IN CONVERSATION WITH Constantin Petcou AND Doina Petrescu

↘ Valeria Graziano
IN CONVERSATION WITH Tihana Pupovac

↘ Anna Colin
IN CONVERSATION WITH Thierry Boutonnier

NOTES OF AN ACCOMPLICE

↘ Roberto Gigliotti

DREAM ON!

ROMAN CONVERSATIONS

(ON THE STREET. OR AT A BAR)

↘orizzontale
IN CONVERSATION WITH Jan Liesegang, Marinella Senatore, Francesco Careri, Lisa Carignani, Amélie Aranguren

Loose conversations to imagine a participatory, healthy, wandering Rome. This Rome exists. It's a city seeking to resist the overdevelopment, hyper-productivity, and isolation the economic, social, and urban systems tend to push us towards. This Rome fails and, from its failure, creates sublime images. The conversation is all about Rome, as we try to recover its wondrous, friendly, generous, welcoming side. This story uses Rome as an example of a context to get back to thinking about the basis of our active, solid, gentle, close, and respectful practices in the cities we'll live in in the future and the cities we're building right now. We'd have loved to be with our characters sitting in a square, chatting in a bar, or wandering the edges of the city, but we didn't always manage to.

CHARACTERS
(in order of appearance)

JAN LIESEGANG
raumlaborberlin
in the role of narration architect

FRANCESCO CARERI
professor at Roma Tre University
in the role of wandering poet

LISA CARIGNANI
researcher
in the role of activist for the Pratone di Torre Spaccata

AMÉLIE ARANGUREN
Campo Adentro
in the role of rural creator

MARINELLA SENATORE
artist *in the role of* trailblazer

NASRIN MOHITI ASLI
orizzontale
in the role of the questioner

JUAN LÓPEZ CANO
orizzontale
in the role of the questioner

1 ONLINE MEETING. INDOOR. EVENING. TWO COMPUTERS. CONVERSATION RECORDED.

Jan dials in from the hallway of a hostel in Denmark. He's traveling with his students from Bergen Architecture School and taking a break. Nasrin and Juan are in a studio in Rome. Their environments are dimly lit.

NASRIN: We're writing a script straddling reality and fiction about cities as a sphere of action. You published something about the same thing, right? *Acting in public*?

JAN: Too old!

NASRIN: Doesn't matter, let's talk about it. If you could be any character, who would you be and what would you do?

JAN: Tough one. There are a lot of us at raumlaborberlin, and we've got different ways of being and doing. Me, I'm an architect and I'm interested in the stories behind projects. I'm interested in how impactful a narrative can be. There are still question marks over connections between people, spaces, narratives, and possibilities. And now, aware as we are of the climate emergency, everything's up for discussion more than ever before. Right now, doing things might be worse than not doing anything at all.

NASRIN: At orizzontale, we have a similar approach. We raise questions. Sometimes we feel like we're in a paradox—by trying to solve one problem, we create others.

JAN: Right, rather than giving answers we're raising more questions. However, I think living in the present means we also need to build an imaginary frame of reference. As architects, we have a vision, which means trying to give answers.

JUAN: "Acting in public:" What part of this declaration still stands today, and how has your practice developed towards other imaginaries?

JAN: We still live by that motto. The question is how to create more solid structures? Activism is needed, but now we also try to build relationships with institutions based on trust. We work within the system and try to negotiate with it, not just as space creators but as providers of alternative spaces at accessible prices, to create structures to give people long-term prospects. It's all about developing models.

JUAN: You were young when you wrote that book. So were we when we created orizzontale. This happened in two cities: Berlin, and Rome. Both of us wanted to respond to a lack of institutional care for things held in common good. But the Berlin you started in feels so different from today's Berlin.

JAN: Yeah, Berlin now is a conventional city. The exciting thing about Berlin was the wall, the gaps that created, the conflict between the two political systems and how they reintegrated. Now it's a city led by market logic. There are still gaps in the system, but finding spaces of freedom has become a real skill. There are a lot of social practices trying to turn spaces into common goods. Overall, though, they only manage that one percent of the time. Architecturally and territorially, there's a fight for space—natural space, space for people, space to build on, space to live on. I think we should start looking more toward the suburbs.

JUAN: There's a good book about suburban areas, *Remoria* by Valerio Mattioli.

NASRIN: When we work on Rome and the tension between the center and the suburbs, we view empty spaces as alternative resources, like the Lago Bullicante. Apart from physical empty spaces, suburbs are built with specific structures, including social ones. They're generally residential areas without any cultural activity going on. Life in some parts of Rome is a nightmare: gridlock, dirty air, cement, asphalt. The right to live in a city includes the right to do it healthily. How do we want to be in a city? What future do we want to build? Let's dream on!

JAN: That brings a lot of things to mind. One of those things is that Rome thinks of itself as a center—like the center of the Catholic world. That kind of narrative excludes the suburbs.

There's something else Rome and Berlin have in common too: Now, the interesting part isn't the center—the center has become too nice, comfortable. We can take our practices to the more precarious areas and create a new city there, though we'll feel marginalized to start with.

JUAN: Back to Berlin, how has your work changed the city?

JAN: I think the idea of cooperative city development has reached the higher levels of debate. A lot of planning goals are ones we could have written ourselves: common good, participatory processes, social city, neighborhoods, all that. Some of us are active in the debates going on in the city. We're trying not to turn into politicians, but to be political.

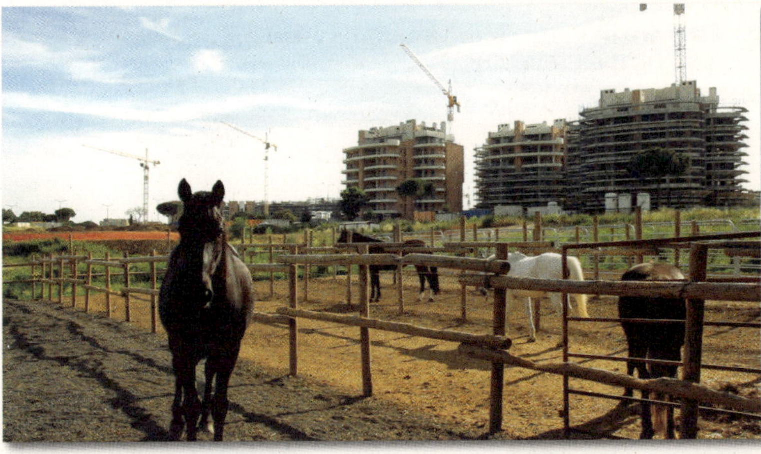

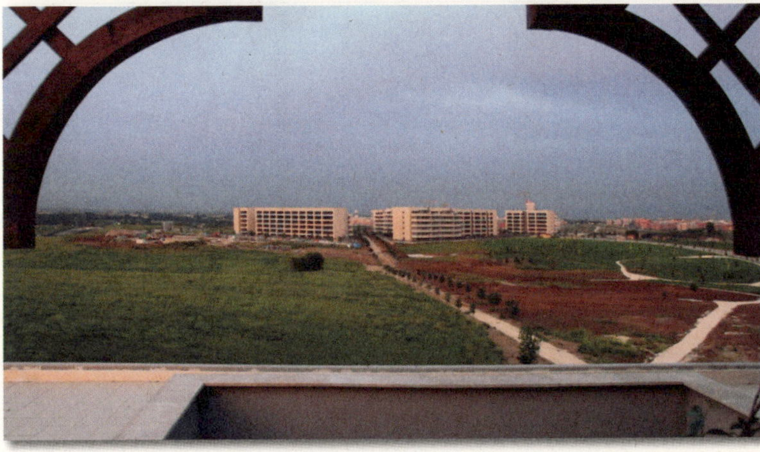

Frauke Gerstenberg, Jan Liesegang, *Libertà Vigilata*, 2011, 2 channels video, frames. Courtesy of the artist.

2 NIGHTFALL STILL AT THE COMPUTER. EVERYONE TRYING TO SIT COMFORTABLY.

We keep talking about politics and imaginary cities, and about the South and how important it is that Northern Europe doesn't become dominant. We laugh. Let's drink to that.

3 ROME. SWEET BUNCH BAR, VIA CASILINA 283. OUTSIDE. EVENING.

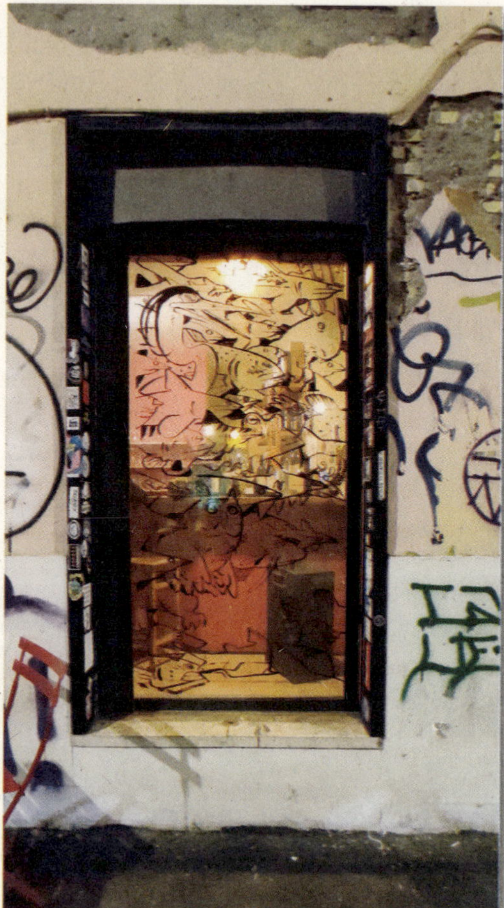

Detail of the Sweet Bunch window and bar during orizzontale's conversation with Francesco Careri, 2023, photo by orizzontale.

Juan, Nasrin, and Francesco wait for the bar to open. The street is lit by electric lights and passing cars. Pier arrives and lifts the shutters. We go in and Pier makes us three spritzes while we sit down. We pick up where we left off with Jan, talking about the South, empty spaces, and suburbs. Suddenly, silence falls. Gypsy Woman *by Crystal Waters starts playing loudly, and everyone laughs. Conversation continues while the stereo continues to play.*

NASRIN: Let's talk about empty urban spaces and cultural or academic gaps, you know all about those.

FRANCESCO: Unfortunately, the university is full of them!

[Everyone laughs.]

NASRIN: Inhabiting voids, setting off a process, putting forward exceptions to meet shared desires and needs. Yesterday Jan and I wrapped up our conversation talking about a Rome that can't be recreated from the center, only from the margins, the suburbs.

JUAN: How would you describe yourself?

FRANCESCO: The fun answer is that I'm a wandering poet. I often say that when out walking. If you say you're an urban planner, people think you want to take away their house. If you say you're an artist or an architect, people assume you have power. Poets don't have power: your life can't be disrupted.
The looks on people's faces! they always break out smiling. Beyond that though, I'm an architect, activist, academic...

NASRIN: Tell us about the relationship between academia and poetry. Academia is where we're supposed to be able to solve everything, but when you do research...

FRANCESCO: That means you don't know the answer! The important thing in universities, I think, isn't the relationship you have with your peers but with the people who aren't on the same level as you. They play a role in the institution, too. Students, for example. I teach three different classes. Civic Arts, which I love, I started teaching in 2006 and it's named after Geddes' *Civics*. A course on Theories of Architecture, and another on Architectural and Urban Planning. My approach is that I don't teach anything, we're all there to learn together. It's a Socratic approach, really, where we discuss things, things come up, and feeling a little inadequate is crucial. What I'm interested in getting across is that architects aren't just people who sit behind a computer working on Autocad. Let's get that clear.

NASRIN AND JUAN: We try to get away from the computer whenever we can!

FRANCESCO: In the '80s and '90s, building something in the public realm meant experimenting with space. What can we make with our bodies, hands, our very presence? The act of being present outside sets off energies and relationships. So, the first step is to go outside, sit down, and be asked "who are you?".

NASRIN: This makes architecture a space inhabited by bodies. In the practice of artist Marinella Senatore, the active presence of a body in a space means architecture unfolds. Would architecture exist without time and without life?

FRANCESCO: While we're on the topic of time, the slogan of my Civic Arts course is "when you lose time you gain space."

JUAN: Great slogan!

FRANCESCO: In Civic Arts, there are only three rules. The first I've just mentioned, "when you lose time you gain space." The second is that private property is a taboo you can overcome. And the third, trickier, rule, is that "you can't go back the way you came." You need to use intercoms, climb walls, go in through the window, force the space to see what happens. Our walks are really varied. When I suggest this in Lima, Bogotá, and Buenos Aires, they tell me I'm crazy and will get killed. But if you're in a group you can demolish the fears that a space holds.

NASRIN: Creating something rare, a disorienting event.

JUAN: Disarming!

FRANCESCO: When Cain killed Abel and was condemned to constant wandering, God gave him a mark, a sign: hands open and raised, visible from far away. How do you walk in the desert if you have to cross other people's land? Unarmed, hands up. That's what being a poet is: Asking for hospitality, saying you're passing through, that you want to cross someone's land, asking for passage. What I teach, really, is the mark of Cain. Building relationships with others. There's no handbook for this—you can only do it through experience, through relating to others.

JUAN: Relating to others helps create future scenarios. What is your vision of the future?

FRANCESCO: For Stalker's Rome, the emptiness was the unknown. We wanted to go around discovering what was going on in the margins. We started to walk around the edges and through the crevices, learning everything about a new world we now understand as bursting with potential. That's what we talked about at the start, right? In the center there's too much control.

A couple of days ago I took my kids for a picnic in Trullo in Monte Cucco. Stunning natural environment. People living there want a park. But what makes a park a park? Benches? Trees? This city has so much heritage right now the way it is, not because of how it can be transformed. The future involves stumbling into a place and us, you, and many other realities being in that place. Let's build a wild space for sharing, with a project that's partly social to host people who need it. That's the idea!

4 OUTSIDE A BAR. SIDEWALK. NIGHT.

Conversation shifts to good working practices, traveling the globe. From L'Aquila of Vuoti di interesse, *we move on to Chile with* Ciudad Abierta, *to Valparaíso and Talca, to the Architecture School in Bergen to the Faculty of Roma Tre. We think about doing a documentary about this dialogue. Then Nasrin leaves. Margherita arrives. We chat. The evening comes to an end.*

5 ONLINE. ROME. INDOOR. DAY.

Monday morning. Marinella is at home. She just got back from Milan's Salone del Mobile. Nasrin and Juan are in their studio. Marinella tells them what she has coming up, and about the School of Narrative Dance *she's organizing.*

NASRIN: We've been talking the last few days about an alternative Rome called "Amor," about giving healthy spaces to people who need them—and other species too, actually—and learning from the local cultures linked to the land. To us you represent the sphere of action through collective performances, acting through emotion and communicating intent. How would you describe yourself?

MARINELLA: For a long time, I described myself as an activist, but I reached a point where I didn't want to use that label anymore. That was when I was working with Black Lives Matter and had an accident at a protest, my health was really put at risk. Around that time, I met an artist called Carlos Aponte who was a big influence. Now I call myself a trailblazer, forging new pathways—especially for women who want to do this kind of work. There was a long period when I called myself a process author, but my biggest talent might be that I have a huge amount of life energy and I can activate that energy in others, too.

JUAN: Through the *School of Narrative Dance*. Tell us more about that.

MARINELLA: I had to create the school. Before becoming an artist, I used to teach. I love teaching because that's how I learn things. It lets me put things in other people's hands so that they can do something with them, albeit maybe something boring. Then in 2012 I created Rosas, an opera involving over twenty thousand people. When that came to an end, I had to leave that community. That was so hard. So, I decided to build a container to bring together the different strands of research into movement. The "dance" in the *School of Narrative Dance* refers to a very ancestral movement, less to do with choreography. It's more of a movement that comes from communities, that only makes sense to and within that community. I wanted to come up with something that would, in the words of philosopher Jacques Rancière, emancipate people.

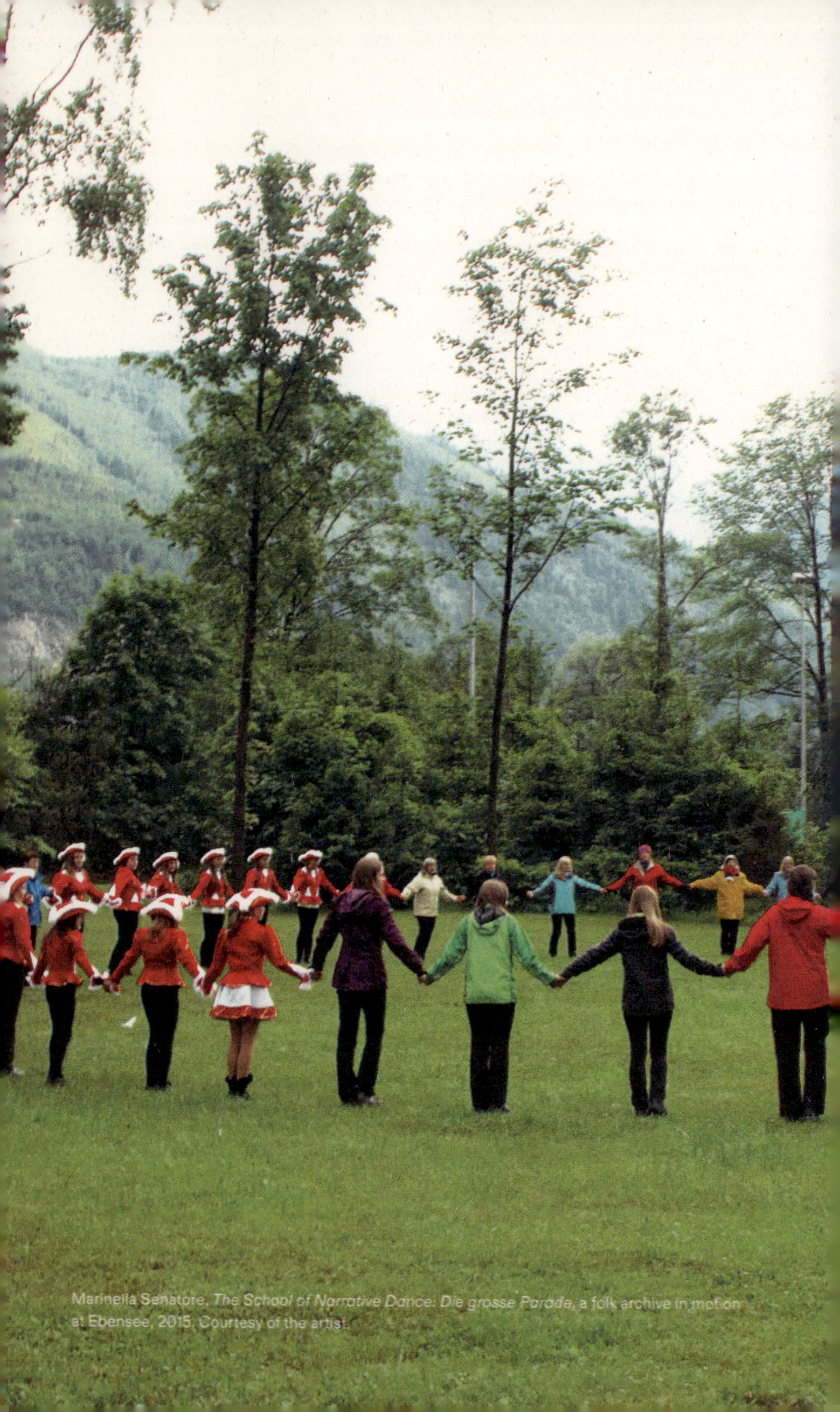

Marinella Senatore, *The School of Narrative Dance: Die grosse Parade*, a folk archive in motion at Ebensee, 2015. Courtesy of the artist.

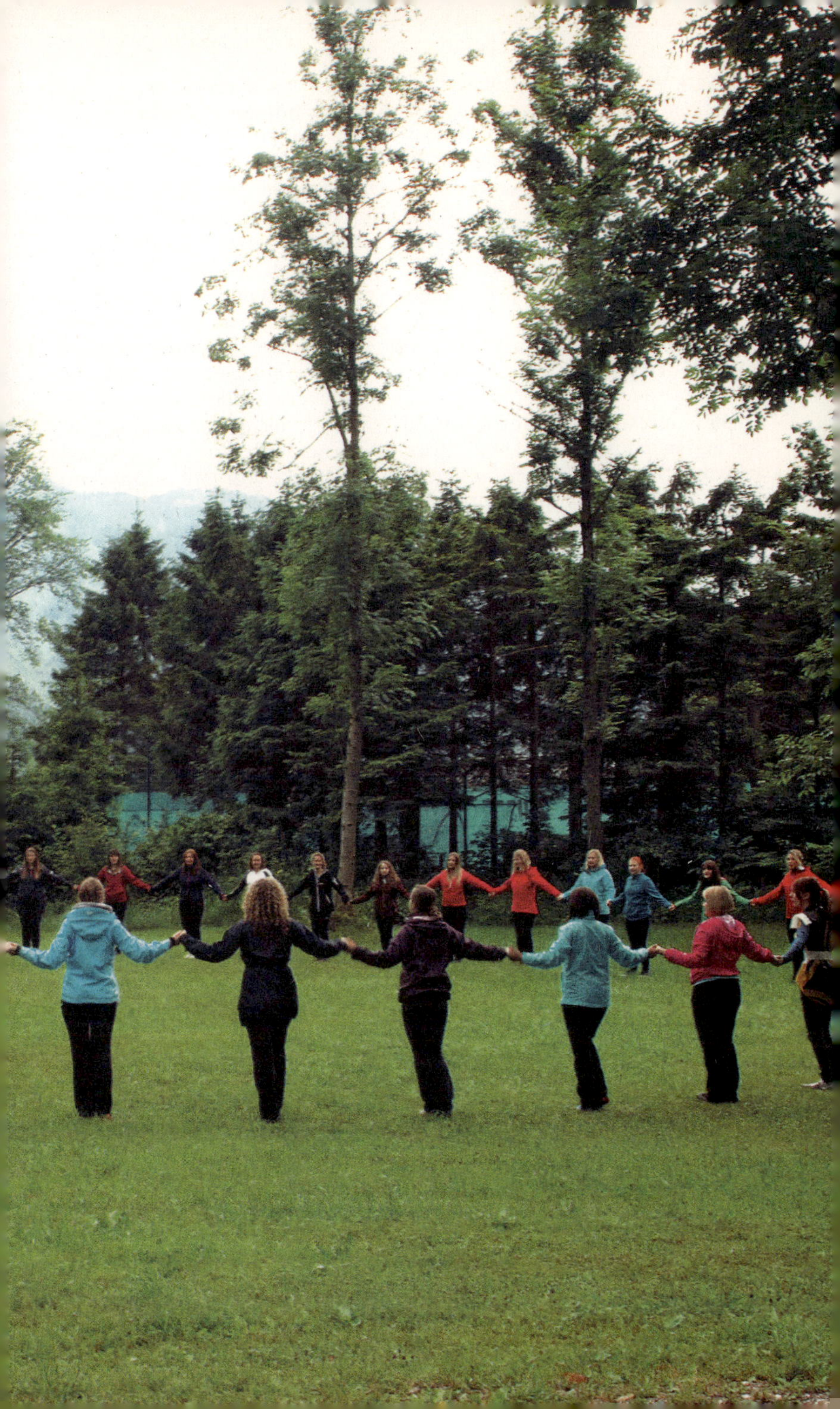

NASRIN: Thinking of the way the *School of Narrative Dance* works and of dance as ancestral movement representing the sense of community, how can we overcome tribal identities? Sometimes when we diversify by showing our own identities in society, we become increasingly fragmented. Overcoming social categories seems more and more difficult. How can we succeed without overpowering someone else?

MARINELLA: In our culture of performing and being productive at all costs—whoever that cost falls on—as well as being available, happy all the time, knowing what goals we've reached, there's no space for depression, the illness of the century. "Mental health" has become a dirty word. To me art is a way of finding your way around the world, one of the most ancient ways of doing so. I want my practice to break the wall between precarious and wealthy communities, because we know art is often created by wealthy, self-referential artists.

NASRIN: Can giving space to failure and changing what failure means be a way to level things out?

MARINELLA: We fail at everything we do, and every time we do we raise the bar exponentially. Failure is so normalized at the *School of Narrative Dance* that being able to change is relaxing. Performance teaches us and normalizes vulnerabilities like depression and loneliness. Inability has been key to the whole project. But how do we represent all of this and keep things dynamic? The overarching answer is the body—neutralizing spoken language and everything that comes out of our heads, using only the body instead.

NASRIN: It's amazing how much the body influences distances.

MARINELLA: All beliefs are subverted on the dancefloor. A different story unfolds, one of bodies talking, drawing near, not getting grossed out, getting grossed out when you don't want to or don't expect to. Then, maybe, something stops working. So, the choreography changes. Now my work uses spontaneous movements, using the body's own vocabulary. No two projects are alike. No two people are alike, after all, so why should my approach be? Participatory art, social art, community projects—all these mean taking risks.

JUAN: For us this practice is really meaningful, having an ongoing project and working with an idea developed in a space alongside the participants.

MARINELLA: My artistic joy comes from knowing I've launched processes which end up going off in directions I'd never have been able to guess. Like the yodeler who ended up singing with a group of trans majorettes. When he first met them, he saw those bearded majorettes as monsters.

JUAN: That's what makes it dynamic.

NASRIN: Tell us about your relationship with Rome.

MARINELLA: Well, it's my home, though I'm not here all that often. The biggest thing here was when we won the Premio MAXXI. At the awards ceremony, when the *School of Narrative Dance* was announced as the winner, participants gave such a loud roar, but some people from the arts scene just walked out. That's Rome. All kinds of people.

NASRIN: Right, that dichotomy is exactly what we're interested in learning about. That and the fact that suffering might not make us happy, but it can be the springboard for transformation, just like success and winning can.

MARINELLA: I think the thing that stops people being happy the most is that they don't feel a sense of belonging. The answer to that is community, the people you work with, the people you choose, the people in your neighborhood. Associations and social centers can be a family, a different kind of family. Communities not based on blood, class, or age. Rome is bursting with possibilities because it's a lot of different towns all at once, and there's a kind of simplicity in how things are here. We have to fight against the sluggishness of this city. It needs to be a much kinder place. Policies aren't working well at all. The solutions have to be totally different.

NASRIN: *School of Narrative Dance,* coming soon to Rome?

JUAN: A party?

MARINELLA: Invitations are important, inviting and being felt as though you're invited. Having a key ingredient that art needs: people. The people, the populace, and everything those words mean.

---

6 COMPUTER GOES OFF.
SUNNY OUTSIDE.

The conversation ends with the invitation to create a party. Thanks, Marinella!

---

7 PIGNETO SUBWAY STATION. OUTSIDE. DAY.

Meeting at Metro C, with Lisa and Amélie. We're going to walk and chat in the Pratone then have lunch together.

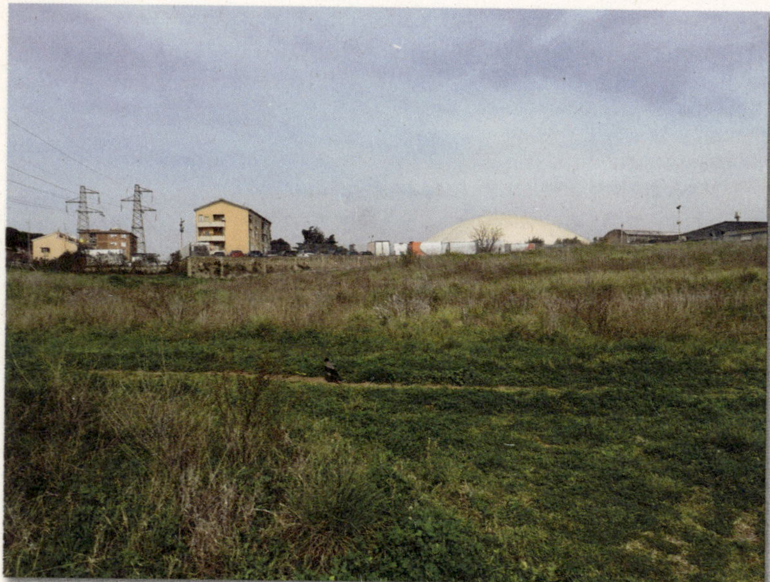

Pratone di Torre Spaccata (Rome), snapshot during the stroll by orizzontale with Amélie Aranguren and Lisa Carignani, 2023, photo by orizzontale.

8 METRO C. BENCH.
DIRECTION PANTANO.
INDOORS.

Amélie starts telling us about her research at the Academia de España while we wait for the subway.

AMÉLIE: I'm working on a map of social and agricultural events within the ring road around Rome, and its markets. I've started working with an activist group, women from Cervelletta who have a choir. They sing to protect the park.

9 PRATONE DI TORRE SPACCATA.
OUTSIDE.

When we get to the Pratone, conversation turns to Lisa. The sky is clouded over.

JUAN: The Pratone was both part of your university thesis and of the archeologist Camilla Silotti's. Now you're researching the relationship between architecture and anti-speciesism. Do you think your interest sparked off a citizens' response? What kind of struggle has broken out?

LISA: The citizens were already using the Pratone when the PNNR funds from the European Commission financed an expansion of Cinecittà studios last year. We decided to create a group called the Comitato Pratone di Torre Spaccata, to stop it being paved over and more ground being taken up. After all, land is precious, and it's not a renewable resource. We spent the first year raising awareness among the citizens with a lot of projects held in the Pratone. Then in October we launched a kind of public debate about turning the area from building land into public green space.

JUAN: Amélie, your experiences have some things in common. Tell us about your practice?

AMÉLIE: I'm part of Campo Adentro, an association founded on the idea of conceiving rural environments as spaces of contemporary creation based on three lines of action: artistic, teaching-learning, and agro-ecological production. We have a flock of two hundred sheep from which we get wool and cheese. It's in Asturias now, but spent a lot of time at the Casa de Campo in Madrid. Here we did some workshops on sound, movement, shearing, milking, and worked with local schools showing kids where wool, cheese, and milk come from. In Asturias we're restoring a village and we've just finished building a dairy. The village is an art and agro-ecology pilot project. We're also raising goats in the Picos di Europa, led by shepherd and YouTuber Nel Cañedo.

JUAN: At orizzontale we often wonder how to tackle rural issues in an urban context.

AMÉLIE: Right now, at the Centro de acercamiento a lo rural in Madrid we know that without support from the city and concentrated consumption the countryside could turn into a macro-farm.

JUAN: Here in Rome the city and countryside are highly interdependent. Lisa, tell us your thoughts.

LISA: Rome has a lot of green spaces, both wild and agricultural. Pratone is one of them. As a group we're trying to show how rich our biodiversity is, the animals and plants living there, how people use the space informally. I think defending the Pratone is important not just to make sure it's designated a public park that can be reorganized or redesigned, but so people can begin recognizing its intrinsic value, regardless of how humans use it.

---

10 WIND BLOWING. STRONGLY.

We take a break and talk about Rome and the dynamic building of new central areas over the last twenty years.

AMÉLIE: I'm interested in so many parts of Rome orizzontale introduced me to. Like the story of Cobragor, a movement born of the March 1977 protests which handed land to unemployed people for them to work on. Today it's an agricultural cooperative.

JUAN: Shepherding and other rural paradigms are part of Rome's soul.

AMÉLIE: I wrote to the city government to get a copy of the regulations. I know you have to pay for pastures because the grass is really high-quality. I still don't know what the rules around actually grazing animals are though, where you can do it, health measures, fees, and stuff. But Rome is certainly unique in Europe, because a full thirty-five percent of its land is agricultural, and also because of the many herds raised here, unknown to one another. I want to put them in touch—if they come together, they can open new dialogues.

JUAN: What other experiences are you bringing to Rome from Spain? Your Escuela de líderes pastores is fascinating.

AMÉLIE: The Escuela is a network of subjects trying to protect shepherding, especially nomadic shepherding. The *ganaderas* also have a movement – female shepherds who look after and care for their animals cooperatively, in a less violent way.

JUAN: Lisa, what joint initiatives and solidarity networks are you familiar with in Rome?

LISA: The Lago Bullicante Ex-Snia has been a focal point for over twenty-five years of struggle, made up of powerful victories and just as many defeats. District committees like the one in Certosa, with a community energy project. Associations like the non-profit A Sud ONLUS that provides legal counsel on environmental issues. Loads of these existing bodies put forward ideas of the city that are different from the official narrative.

---

11 IN PRATONE. THE WALK IS FINISHED AND THE GROUP IS HEADING FOR LUNCH.

Conversation moves onto the psychosocial benefits of citizenship. They talk about the need for green belts to protect from future heatwaves and issues with how livable cities will be in twenty years. The Pratone and Campo Adentro, and the other solidarity project mentioned, are contemporary struggles for the future and for future generations. Amélie watches the butterflies and points out that them being here shows that the Pratone is healthy. The group then disappears into the distance.

---

12 AT THE STUDIO DOOR. ROME. INDOOR. MORNING SUNNY. THE AIR IS FRESH. THE STREET IS EMPTY. A DOG BARKS. BIRDS CHIRP.

The Rome orizzontale imagines happens every day in the forums mentioned in the conversations we've had: communities, rural life, interdisciplinarities, interspeciesism, activism, new types of collaboration, learning and teachings, spatial practices based on solidarity. These are the pieces we put together to build our daily puzzle. These are attitudes that anyone can put to use for our citizens, even in different places remote from one another. This script is imperfect, but it allows us to take the time to host the people we spoke with. This is a breath of fresh air to re-energize ourselves. Now we head back outside, to act in the public space, creating our "Amor."

Amélie Aranguren

is a member of Inland, an art collective and a collaborative agency dedicated to agricultural, social, and cultural production. Inland confronts various problems of a system that is collapsing at its environmental, cultural, and financial levels by formulating critical tools and applying them through experimental practice. It builds on the premise that the rural area offers a physical and cultural space for the generation of diverse ways of life that differ from the hegemonic model. Inland runs the Centre for Approaching the Rural in Madrid, a space that hosts a Documentation Centre, a canteen, and a Self-Publishing Workshop. It has been shown in the Istanbul Biennale, Museum of Modern Art Medellín, Matadero, Centre Pompidou, Serpentine Gallery and many other places.

Francesco Careri

is an associate professor at the Department of Architecture of Roma Tre University, where he directs the Master of Environmental Humanities. In 1995, he co-founded the urban art laboratory Stalker. With Stalker, he develops the method of collective walking in the "actual territories," the indeterminate or void spaces of the city, which have long been disregarded or considered a problem in traditional architectural practice. His main publications are *Walkscapes. Walking as an aesthetic practice* (Gustavo Gili, 2002) and *Pasear, detenerse* (Gustavo Gili, 2016). With Lorenzo Romito, he published *Nomadismo Architettura Ospitalità. Esperienze e azioni dal camminare al CIRCO* (Bordeaux Edizioni, 2020). Since 2017 he is a scientific responsible with Prof. Fabrizio Finucci of the research group Laboratorio Circo and together with Prof Giovanni Caudo of the Laboratorio di Città Corviale.

Lisa Carignani

is an architect and a PhD candidate in Architecture: innovation and heritage at the University of Roma Tre, where she collaborates in a course of the Theory of Architecture. Her research focuses on the relationship between space and animals, to understand how the relevance towards their spontaneous and vital features could lead to deconstructing traditional tools of architecture. Today, she is an activist for Pratone di Torre Spaccata, a big wild area in Rome that is at risk of disappearing. She is also involved in self-building, photography, silkscreen printing, bookbinding, and different crafts and manual methods of doing and communicating.

Jan Liesegang

is a professor at Bergen School of Architecture and a founding member of raumlaborberlin, an interdisciplinary architectural practice that works on urban design, architecture, experimental building, art and research with a strong focus on the activation of public spaces in process-based, participatory projects. In his work and teaching, Jan is especially interested in exploring the limits of the narrative dimensions in architecture and strengthening the identity of urban spaces. Jan's latest projects include the recently opened public park, sauna, and river pool in Gothenburg, Sweden; a summer school and public activation project in an abandoned brick factory in Pristina, Kosovo; and the ongoing project for an inclusive artist house and academy in Cologne, Germany. He co-published several books: *House of Time / living in the now* (Triënnale Brugge, 2019); *Cantiere Barca* (2016); and *Building the City Together* (2015).

orizzontale

is an architects' collective based in Rome whose work crosses the fields of architecture, urbanism, public art and DIY practice. Since 2010, orizzontale has been promoting projects of common relational spaces, giving form to both dismissed and unseen images of the city. The collective has developed projects in Italy, Spain, Germany, Austria, Greece, Ukraine, and Portugal. *8 ½*, their mobile theatre designed in 2014, was awarded the prize Young Architects Program by MAXXI Museum and MoMA PS1. In 2018, orizzontale was awarded the Young Talent of Italian Architecture 2018 for the best Italian under 35 practice and in 2023 was invited to the 18th Venice Architecture Biennale in the Arsenale and the Italian Pavilion. The team is composed of Jacopo Ammendola, Giuseppe Grant, Juan López Cano, Margherita Manfra, Nasrin Mohiti Asli, Roberto Pantaleoni, and Stefano Ragazzo.

Marinella Senatore

is an artist trained in music, fine arts, and film. Her practice is characterized by public participation, initiating a dialogue between history, culture, and social structures. Rethinking the role of the artist as author and the public as a recipient, Senatore's work merges forms of protest, learning theater, oral histories, vernacular forms, protest dance and music, public ceremonies, civil rituals, and mass events, reflecting on the political nature of collective formations and their impact on the social history of places and communities. Her work has been exhibited widely throughout Italy and abroad, including Manifesta, Centre Pompidou, MAXXI Museum, Palais de Tokyo, Venice Biennale, and much more.

RESTORING LAND AS PLANETARY COMMUNITY PRACTICES

↘ Erika Mayr AND Meike Schalk
IN CONVERSATION WITH Constantin Petcou AND Doina Petrescu

In 2010 Lungomare invited us to initiate an intercultural urban gardening project in cooperation with the association Donna Nissà in Bolzano for *Summer Drafts*.[1] In our project *Cultural Landscapes*, we considered urban gardening as a way of caring for nature and for communities at the same time.[2] As visiting artists—a gardener and beekeeper, and an urban researcher—our practices have been engaging in gardening and beekeeping in art contexts, and in the developing of new roles for and relations between practitioners, different communities and institutions in art projects that question and intervene in the making of urban public spaces.

2010 *Summer Drafts* focused on questions of migration. With Donne Nissà, we developed a garden on a fallow site of the city district of Don Bosco in Bolzano which was known for its "semirurale" houses that had been built in the course of Mussolini's resettlement policies, which brought Italians from Southern provinces as workers to new factories in the German-speaking South Tyrol. The two story detached houses with gardens offered the newly arrived a home at the edge of the city and the possibility to survive on growing their own food. The popular houses were torn down during the 1970s, except for two, to give way to a denser city development.

Together with Donne Nissà, we wanted to connect to the history of migration and gardening of the site while enabling a dialogue on and with urban nature to highlight its biodiversity. Plants, bees, and other species carry an old knowledge about strategies of survival. We argue that connecting to this old knowledge can sensitize our thinking, and

1 2010 *Summer Drafts* was curated by Valeria Graziano and Paolo Plotegher. *Summer Drafts* started in 2008. It has brought together practitioners from various fields who engage in questions of community, participation, relationality, and dialogues, among other themes. Guests were invited for a residency in Bolzano and given the opportunity to develop a project with the support and in conversation with a local civil society organization. Read more on the platform's homepage, https://summerdraftsarchive.wordpress.com/summer-drafts-2010/, accessed 18 June 2023.

2 See our garden blog Kulturlandschaften, https://kulturlandschaften.blogspot.com. The Semirurali Garden in Bolzano became the first intercultural garden in Italy.

influences not only our view of the world but moreover our daily actions. By this, gardening as a cultural production revitalizes knowledge on the sites' history and connects it to current debates on migration as well as to environmental and civic practices. Since 2010, the garden has grown and become part of a local community, and an anchor point for social and ecological activities.

To reflect upon the garden and gardening as a mediator further, we spoke with the founders of atelier d'architecture autogérée—AAA, Doina Petrescu and Constantin Petcou, about planetary gardening, resilience, and *TERRRA*, their most recently started project in Romania involving a piece of rural land, owned by a cooperative with the focus on restoring the land and establishing a school for planetary gardeners following the thinking of the French landscape architect Gilles Clément.[3]

ERIKA MAYR & MEIKE SCHALK What does the concept of planetary garden and planetary gardeners mean to you?

CONSTANTIN PETCOU Gilles Clément's concept is in a way very simple. It refers somehow to the closure a garden needs in order to allow us to organize, observe, and understand how nature works. Because a garden originally means "a limited, closed space," for him the planet itself must be understood as a garden in order to be preserved and continue to remain an area for living. For me the concept of care is very important in this. Because having a garden is not only to use and exploit a natural system, it is to take care of it. Our impact on the planet is so strong that nature is not strong enough to continue to function any longer. A planetary garden is a space to be used with care and a long-term vision in order to ensure the future.

DOINA PETRESCU In addition to the concept of the planetary garden, it is the idea of planetary gardeners, the people that are supporting and maintaining the planetary garden.

3 Gilles Clément, *"The Planetary Garden" and Other Writings* (Pennsylvania: Pennsylvania Press, 2015).

Because the people who are usually specialized in doing the work in a "garden" do not necessarily have the skills that are required for a planetary garden. We are in need of people who have other skills that have more to do with ecological repair and who have another understanding of nature, not only on a local level but also on a global one. Therefore, Gilles Clément set up a school for planetary gardeners. There are already a few branches in different places in France. We propose to set up a branch in Romania, in Brezoi. We discussed with him the profile such a school might have based on the fact that there is a local knowledge, a peasant knowledge that we can find in the region which has this ecological dimension already. This is reflected in the ways of laboring the soil and maintaining the forest. Therefore, there is the idea that the peasants will be the teachers in the school. The trainees will be youngsters, students in landscape design, agriculture, and all other people that are developing a special interest in engaging with nature but missing out this dimension. So, this school would be both supporting the tradition that is getting lost just now (with the last generation dying) and the new generation that will perpetuate this knowledge.

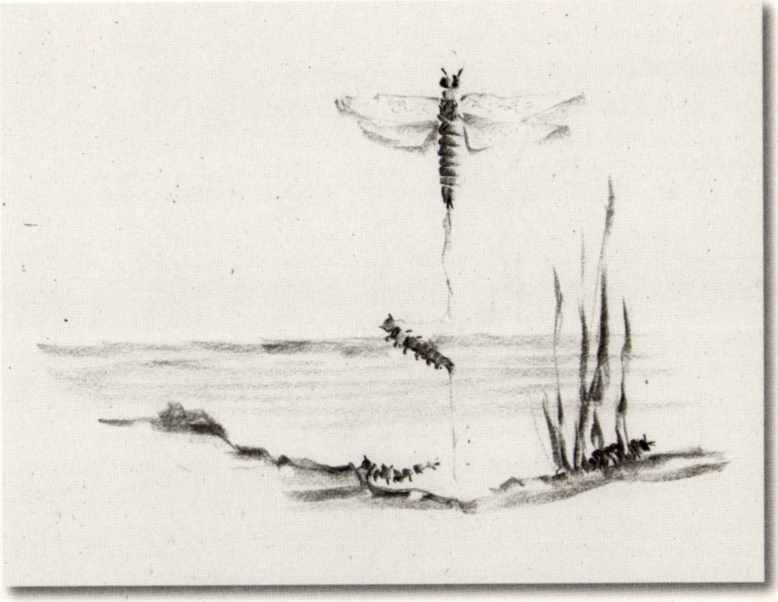

Gilles Clément, *Jardin Vertical*, drawing, year unknown. Courtesy of the artist.

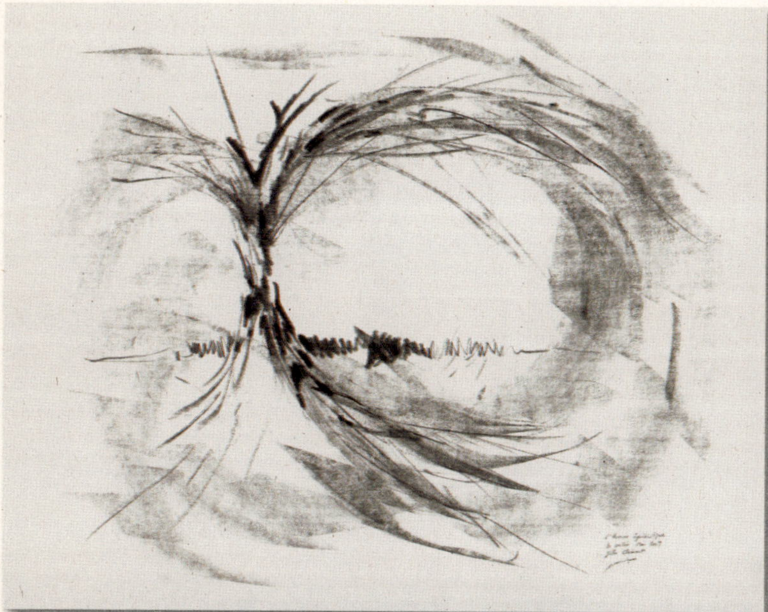

Gilles Clément, *L'arbre, symbole du recyclage permanent*, drawing presented at the lecture "Jardins, paysage et génie naturel", 2011, Collège de France, Paris, https://books.openedition.org/cdf/510, accessed 18 August 2023. Courtesy of the artist.

ERIKA MAYR & MEIKE SCHALK In your works you have been employing the notion of resilience, since more than twenty years, very specifically and far beyond narrower technoscientific understandings. How do you enact resilience and—to speak in your terms—*R-Urban* practices?

DP We set up our *R-Urban* strategy and hubs where the R comes from Resilience and from many other ecological R-s and also from "Rural," because we wanted to act in these suburbs where people (who originally came from rural backgrounds) have lost their connections to land. There is a population which now, a few decades after having moved into the suburbs has a very high rate of unemployment, has economic and social problems. For us resilience means dealing with this condition but also addressing the challenges of the future, there where the people live. The right to resilience is not only for the ones who are aware of climate change, but also for those that do not have the means to be aware, for those that are not ecologically literate but who are the first to be affected by the effects of climate change. So, these eco-civic hubs that are run by the residents themselves, would be a resource for the neighborhood, a place to learn, to practice and to start transforming daily life in order to adapt to the future, to learn how to practice. But one of the conditions is to do it collectively. For this reason, the operational concept of resilience in this case is rather the idea of co-resilience. "Co-" means collective but it can also mean commons and commoning. It might also mean an extended community in which nature and the non-human aspect are also included, being understood as a partner, as a "member" of the community.

For example, in the case of Colombes, a commune in the northwestern suburbs of Paris,[4] when one of the *R-Urban* hubs was demolished, the gardened land and the life which started on it were almost more affected than the community

4 The *R-Urban* Hub in Colombes was one of the first urban labs that AAA set up to test their strategy of urban resilience. Read more here: https://www.urbantactics.org/projects/rurban/rurban.html, accessed 18 June 2023.

itself. It was a very aggressive situation. Soon after starting to use this farming hub in Colombes, a new mayor of the city was elected, it was a right-wing woman, her partner was a developer, she reclaimed the farming site back for real-estate "development." So, we were forced to leave the site. We decided to relocate the hub because we knew from the beginning that it will have a temporary condition and we have consequently built it to be able to be dismantled and reinstalled in a similar way. We did find a new location in a neighboring city, at a walking distance from the initial location, so that the users were able to continue to use the hub. But we also looked back at what remained in the initial site after the relocation. In Colombes, we worked on improving the quality of the soil for a number of years, depolluting and adding compost. At the end we obtained a very good soil that was able to sustain the life of plants and insects. All this life was destroyed, because the mayor just poured tarmac on all of it!

So yes, we can speak of co-resilience also in situations of resistance to political factors. I think the idea of "gardening" is somehow a metaphor for co-resilience—and we have to always remember that we do live in a world which is a capitalist world, which is used by extracting and exploiting it aggressively on all levels. So we need to include this into all dimensions that we take into account when we talk about resilience.

CP Resilience is not only the capacity to bounce back from a stress situation but also to do it together. Working on this we hope to explore a collective way which forges a new social mentality.

In the twentieth century the population was dominated by Modernism, Economic Growth, and Consumption. And in the actual situation our society must invent a new collective imaginary about how to restore, at the same time with restoring the soil, the nature, how to restore ourselves, and the society, because we are more and more in a crisis, a big scale crisis which concerns the climate, democracy, and wars. It is very important to be able to restore at the same time the capacity to deal with democracy, with ecology, and with justice, and this is very difficult because in this crisis situation, there are not many tools or institutions, and not enough institutional capacity to encourage and support such radical change, the society seems very fragile at the moment from this point of view.

E M&M S How can we understand possibilities for urban and rural commoning on public and private land? And, how can we protect new types of contemporary commons with and without contracts?

DP In urban areas we have adopted a process and protocol. We start with a temporary contract for public land use, an annual lease, that would be renewed periodically with the city. However, more recently for one of the *R-Urban* sites that we were occupying in this way in the city of Bagneux in North France, we have established a contract, through which we have passed on to the City the custody of the two hubs that were built on the site belonging to the city with the condition (marked in a Charter signed by the City) that they will remain forever "common goods," and as such be protected as commons, by the city itself. There is as such a legal (and political) guarantee that they will always be used for commoning activities.

CP Enclosures happen all the time with the commons, with public space, with all these spaces that are not protected by law but are dependent on political will, the risk is that common use is interrupted by a political change, as it was the case in Colombes. Commons are fragile, this is why, as Doina said before, we signed this Charter with the municipality in Bagneux, afterwards, in order to keep the use of the space in the future with these commons-rules, in all political situations. But it is just a protective measure, we just tried it hoping that it will work.

In Brezoi, *TERRRA* has been currently established on private land, partially owned by a cooperative of around twenty-five researchers and activists from six different countries. In the future it will be in full cooperative use, but open to the public and the municipality to occasionally use it. The idea is to create an open *TERRRA* commons and start to build a network with it.[5]

5 https://www.c4r.info/en/actions/brezoi

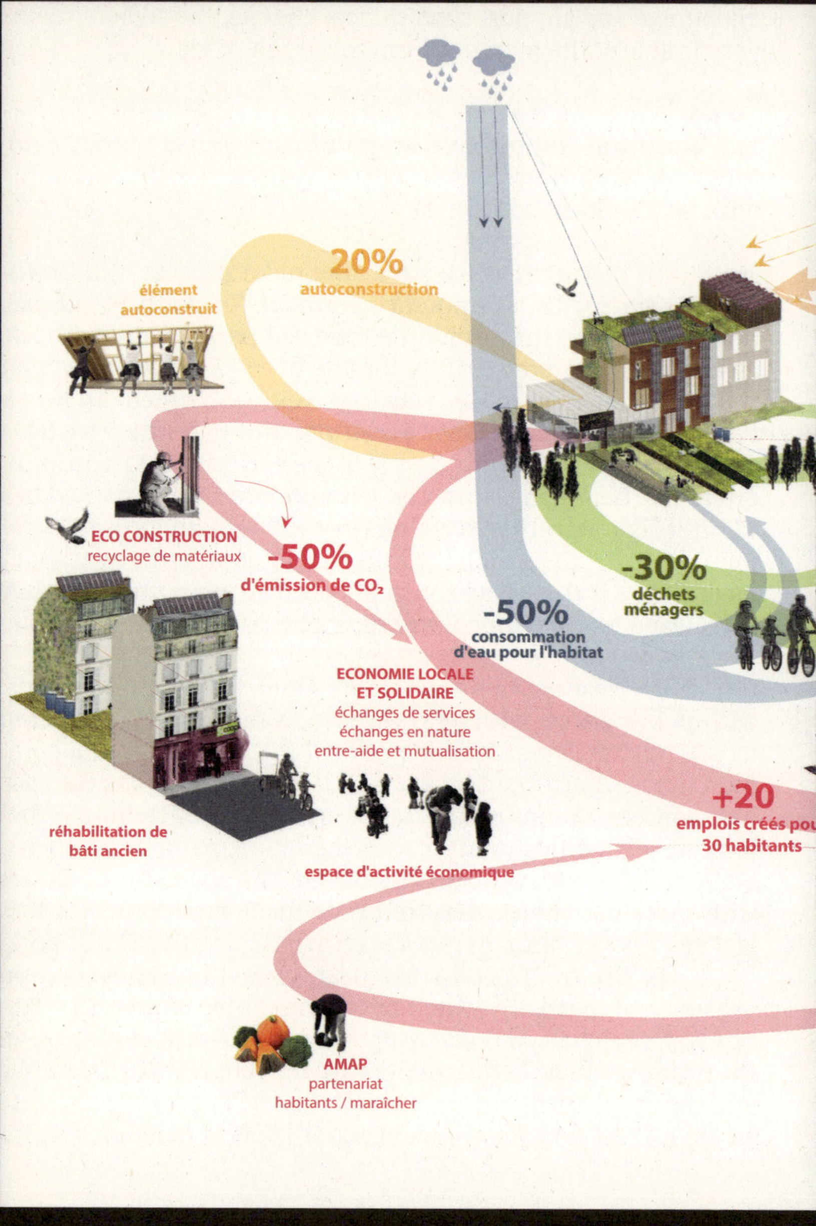

AAA, *Circuits courts résilients à différentes échelles territoriales*, Resilience diagram for *R-Urban* including a Recycling and Eco-construction Unit, an Ecological Cooperative Housing Unit, and a Civic Agriculture Unit.

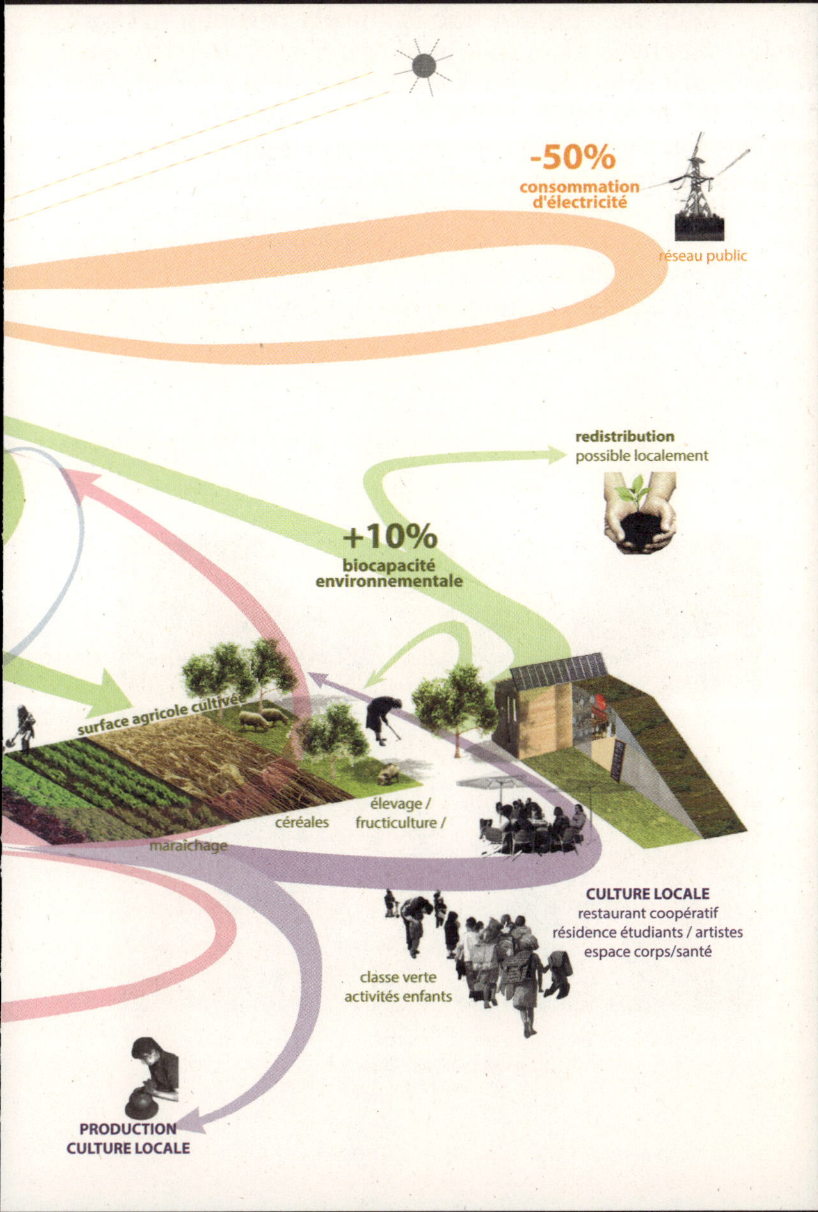

-50%
consommation d'électricité
réseau public
redistribution
possible localement
+10%
biocapacité environnementale
surface agricole cultivée
élevage /
fructiculture /
céréales
maraichage
CULTURE LOCALE
restaurant coopératif
résidence étudiants / artistes
espace corps/santé
classe verte
activités enfants
PRODUCTION
CULTURE LOCALE

D P Well, the *TERRRA* hub is already part of a network, the *R-Urban* network of civic hubs that have started to spread across Europe. But also setting up this hub in Romania, was a trial and error exercise, it was an occasion to prototype a new thing: there we will test how commons could sometimes emerge on private land. We need to claim for commoning not only public land but private land as well. For us this is also an attempt to explore the multiple possibilities that a civic hub can take on in different contexts, directly depending on the conditions and opportunities of the context.

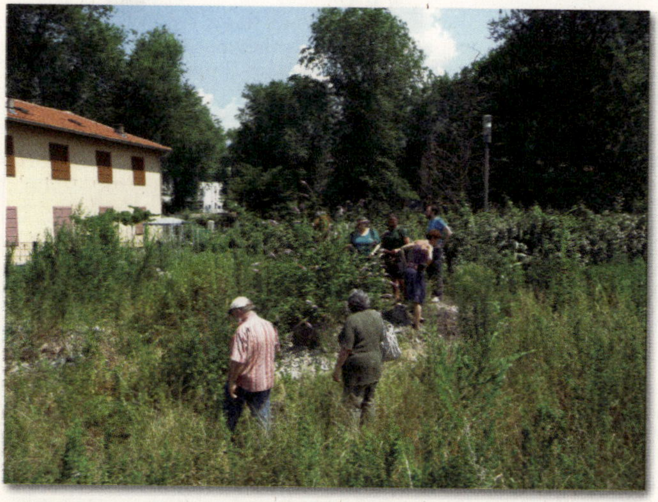

Erika Mayr, Meike Schalk, *Summer Drafts*, Urban Gardening Workshop, Bolzano, 2010, photo by Meike Schalk.

When we met the future gardeners of the Semirurali Garden 2010 in Bolzano during our workshop to lay the foundation of this garden, we learned that the reasons to start common gardening are as diverse as the people who have a passion for it. Gardening not only enables us to grow and harvest our own fruits and vegetables, but it also brings individuals together to share knowledge, tools, the work, their products, and enjoyment, as well as the responsibility for the soil, matter and materials, and the production processes they entertain.

In parallel to the workshop, we formulated a list of basic suggestions for the making and maintaining of urban gardens as a strategy for their survival which, considering the weak legal situation of urban gardens and the rising pressure of real estate development we have experienced during the recent years, we find it more relevant and urgent than ever today. We propose its points here once more as a guide for introducing planetary gardening as community practices. They can be summarized as follows:

> Prepare for common meals and vision workshops to enable the making of a common space.
>
> Read the site, value, and incorporate found elements on the plot for connecting the garden's ecological past and future.
>
> Collect knowledge about gardens and gardening, concerning their legal status, layouts, and geo-technical data by exploring existing examples and talking to other gardeners.
>
> Document different gardening practices in a garden diary or blog which can work like a manual or guidebook for the garden. In a blog or open diary, you can keep a record of intentions, practices, and developments. Others can learn from this example. Good public relations are important for maintaining the garden, for requiring funds, donations, and support. Establish friendly relationships to your neighbors for exchange and support.
>
> Through giving and taking seeds, plants, flowers, berries, vegetables, fruits, tools, advice, help, and information the urban garden will blossom.

For revealing knowledge of the garden—its species and economic networks—printed information can be displayed which communicates history and stories of the garden to newcomers and visitors.

Use the garden in as many ways possible to make it publicly accessible. Talking about the garden will anchor it as an important public place in the neighborhood and for the city, extend its lifespan, and consequently protect it from eviction.

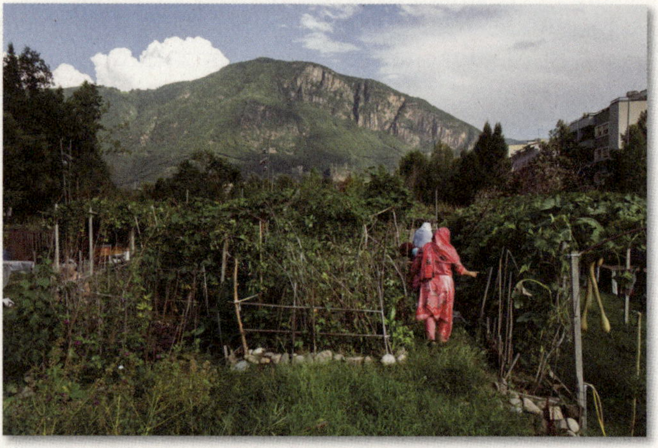
Semirurali Garden, Bolzano, 2023, photo by Kseniia Obukhova.

Beside collective practices of everyday life, regular educational activities and special events such as seasonal garden parties, performances, and common food experiences will publicize and inscribe the garden into the social and ecological life of the city.

↘ Erika Mayr

is a trained landscape gardener, horticulturist, and urban beekeeper. Her work and research are focused on aspects of urban beekeeping, as she acknowledges the potential of informal urban nature sites for the world of bees and for human inhabitants. In 2007, she started her own beekeeping enterprise *Stadtbienenhonig* for small-scale productions of urban honey. In 2011, Mayr co-founded *Stadthonigfest*, where she organised a yearly honey market in Berlin-Kreuzberg until 2018. Mayr shared her expertise in the book *Die Stadtbienen* (2012), which inspired many people to start with bees. In 2015, she was invited to become a "Bee-Ambassador" at the German Pavilion *Be(e) active* at the EXPO in Milan. Mayr relocated to Rome in 2020, where she transforms the green areas at the Accademia Tedesca Roma Villa Massimo towards a more bee-friendly and sustainable garden.

↘ Doina Petrescu

is a professor of Architecture and Design Activism at the University of Sheffield, UK. Her research focuses on issues of co-design and civic participation, gendered practices, political ecology, co-production, and resilience in relation with architectural and urban design. Petrescu conducted several research projects and is the author of numerous publications including *Urban Commons Handbook* (2022); *Architecture and Resilience* (2018); *Learn to Act* (2017); *The Social (Re) Production of Architecture* (2016); *Agency: Working with Uncertain Architectures* (2009); *Altering Practices: Feminist Politics and Poetics of Space* (2007); *Architecture and Participation* (2005).

↘ Constantin Petcou

is an architect and semiotician. Since 1996 he has been teaching in various schools and universities, including ENSA Malaquais, the University of Paris 8, Harvard and MIT Massachusetts. With Doina Petrescu, he co-founded atelier d'architecture autogérée (AAA)—an architectural practice that received awards in France, the USA, Romania, Belgium, and Japan. Petcou coordinated several research projects together with AAA and initiated the *Rhyzom network* and *R-Urban*, a strategy for urban resilience in European cities. He contributed to numerous publications and coedited *Urban/ACT: a manual for alternative practice* (2007) and *Trans-Local-Act: Cultural Practices Within and Across* (2010).

↘ Meike Schalk

is an architect and associate professor in Urban Design and Urban Theory at the KTH School of Architecture in Stockholm, Sweden. Her transdisciplinary research on architecture and urban issues combines critical inquiry into discourses of social justice in planning with practice-oriented research methods and equality, diversity, and inclusion policies and practices in architectural education. Schalk's recent projects and publications include *Between Technologies of Power and Notions of Solidarity* (with H.S. Kajita, J. Mack, and S. Riesto, Lars Müller, 2022); *Species of Theses and Other Pieces* (with T. Lange et al., transcript, 2022); *Feminist Futures of Spatial Practice* (with T. Kristiansson and R. Maze, AADR, 2017).

REFRACTIONS, BORDERLINES, AND UNBUREAUCRATIC POLITICS

↘ Valeria Graziano
IN CONVERSATION WITH Tihana Pupovac

VALERIA GRAZIANO I would like to start this dialogue by evoking an element of resonance with my first encounter with Lungomare and its community of practice, which in 2008 took the shape of a residency scheme that brought together a number of artists, theorists and activists to work with local migrant and antiracist organizations. Much of their work, at the time, grappled with the socio-political impact of the "Balkan route," the path followed by undocumented migrants attempting to reach central Europe. Since moving to the Balkan region, I became more aware of the recurrence of the idea of this part of the world's position as a territory "in the periphery" and "on the border." This trope of being situated in a "peripheral" space has been ascribed both to Lungomare in Bolzano and to the whole Western Balkan region covered by the work of Kooperativa, hence it might be fruitful to refute. What does it mean to define something as peripheral? Is peripheral close to "provincial" or "borderline?" Being borderline, in the sense of at risk of becoming dangerous, but also as simply close to borders, is also a slippage of signification that interests me. A second but related point has to do with both Lungomare and Kooperativa as entities that (re)produce cultural spaces in contexts traversed by minority politics. How can minority politics be progressive in the contemporary moment? Are minority cultural politics able to—maybe paradoxically—offer paths that lead us away from the scarcity-based approaches within identity politics?

TIHANA PUPOVAC Kooperativa was founded after decades-long exchanges, friendships and ties in spite of the state propagated violence, in spite of the newly established borders and in spite of the high predominance of identity politics and conservatism in our post-socialist spaces. In a way Kooperativa, as a community, poses the question about borders, who we consider neighbours, how are cultural ties built and developed, what internationalism means etc. Kooperativa also presents an endeavour to preserve what little is left of culture as a public space/good in our respected countries by sustaining not just a critical position but an openness to experimentation and collective endeavours.

VG In a recent collaboration with Kooperativa, I was invited to contribute to a summer school in Ohrid, North Macedonia, with the beautiful title *Liquid Frameworks, Solid Institutions*. The programme focused on participatory governance; the democratisation of cultural public infrastructure via a discussion of the different imports of notions such as public goods and commons; and practices of civic-public partnerships. I think that these three organizational measures are among the most vivid areas of experimentation and transformation of not only contemporary cultural organizations (rejecting the pressure to become more entrepreneurial or service-like), but also crucially the public sector, understood as the governance of collective needs. It is worth reflecting on how both in Italy and in the Balkan region, for more than a decade now, we have seen a flare of processes where cultural workers spearheaded activist mobilizations. Some of these militant scenes, in turn, also gave rise to political parties, especially focused on a municipal scale of intervention and struggle. I'm thinking here of recent processes in Naples, Rome and Milan for example, such as the efforts to institute a foundation of the commons, basic income campaigns, civic-public partnerships in the name of common goods. Meanwhile in Ljubljana cultural workers have been at the forefront of weekly protests that opposed the far-right regime of Janez Janša; and in Zagreb, they contributed to the formation of the Right to the City movements that led to the municipalist party Možemo in Croatia (and later to similar initiatives in Belgrade). This refraction between cultural sector and social movements (with incursions in representative politics) is a distinctive element that I think is connoting the forms of public agency we have known and contributed to in recent years, would you agree?

TP Yes indeed, although I would add that there is a paradox in how art and culture reproduce the public sphere as such, because the critical and political stances it can put forward still depend upon institutional and third sector funding and resources. This civil society position it often finds itself in carries with it this ambivalent condition. This poses limitations on what you can do, how you can transform yourself as an organization and how you can access or even (re)produce the public sphere. In this sense, art and culture do not share the same trajectory as other organizations that take care of the political, be it a party or a union for instance. If I can be critical, I think in a way we sometimes get stuck in mimicking what a political organization should be. Yet, art and culture deal with politics and policy, which are both very distinctive aspects underpinning any notion of the public sphere as a space of action. Recently, Anton Jager in "Everything is Hyperpolitical"[1] proposed that after 1989, with the neoliberal turn, in order for the hyper-individualized subject to emerge in the political arena, public institutions had to be dismantled, which also affected arts and culture, pushing many artists and cultural workers into the civil society sphere. In the European periphery, arts and culture, having taken on the role of the critical public voice, survived also thanks to foreign intervention and development funds. So what we have today is a scenario in which artists and cultural workers are behind some extremely urgent social and political campaigns. If we understand the public sphere in terms of democracy and democratization, in the context of Yugoslavia, it was precisely and ironically at the dawn of parliamentary democracy that arts and culture took over the role of what funders like to call "the watchdogs" of democratic processes. So, when thinking of the art and cultural sector, this is a sector that is infused and embedded in social movements, yet it is a distinct social formation with its own limitations. Being in the public sphere is not simply a matter of dialoguing, and opening space for dialogue, a lot of it revolves around organizing, rethinking processes of decision making, and confronting those in power.

1 https://thepointmag.com/politics/everything-is-hyperpolitical/, accessed 23 June 2023.

VG When you speak about addressing the paradoxical mode of existence and social reproduction of the cultural sector, I feel the need to unpack further what is nested inside a problem that has been spoken about in terms of NGO-ification of the sector as a specific impotence in acting in the public sphere. I see two orders of problems here. On the one hand, there is the ever-present question of "institutionalization"—aka, a gradual entropic movement that traverses most group endeavours and systems. It can manifest as a slowing down, a lack of energies, as a routinization of practices and bureaucratization. So, one question is how do we avoid skeletonization, if this can be avoided at all, what are the modes that can replenish a practice that wants to engage with the public?

On the other hand, NGO-ification describes a specific way of understanding dialogical practices in a depoliticized way, in a default manner. This became really apparent to me during the last few years of doing research and organizing in the field of care struggles. The recentring of care across activist and cultural interventions is of course a welcome and much needed shift. But after the last years of pandemic and crisis, I think more and more folks are wondering what scenarios will open up next, in a context where self-organized care initiatives or practices sustained within the cultural sector (often in the guise of "art projects") keep filling in gaps and cracks left open by a zombified public sector and a predatory market with overt monopolistic tendencies. So, reclaiming the political demands of such stepping in, reclaiming a way of practice that, unlike NGOs dominant lingos, is a partisan intervention in the public sphere. It is not about complementing the failings of the state or private run services, but about carving out a space from which demands can be made upon public resources. If we understand politics to be the process of decision making about what a society should do with its surplus, as it was the operative definition underpinning workers self-organization in Yugoslavia, for instance, then we have a clear picture of what vectors to follow as we witness the current vicissitudes of art and culture. NGO-ification and the efforts to avoid it in the sector should be understood in a context of violence, the slow, mundane violence of funding strategies and bureaucratic procedures. We cannot assume this as an internal fault of the sector.

TP Indeed. The distinction between politics and policy in more classical terms can also be formulated as a distinction between the State and civil society. This coordinate is historically lost in many ways, what was once considered civil society in the sense of mass organizations (parties, unions etc.) no longer exists. The historical significance of mass organizations has been lost in the present. Today, what we call civil society is either highly professionalized para-political organizations and think tanks or at best groups of enthusiasts who are willing to take over the burden of social reproduction that the State was so happy to hand over (for instance various aspects of care, space for minorities and marginalized groups as well as arts and culture). What I'm interested in is to try to articulate how art and culture as civil society falls within this paradox of differentiation between politics and policy.

VG In this sense, the modalities of action of the art and culture sector are very different from the ones available to militancy, understood as a voluntary political activity that does not rely on the monetization of its values in order to reproduce itself.

TP Militancy and activism used to rely on unions and other organized forms of solidarity. This infrastructure is no longer available, unions, much like cultural and artistic organizations, have long ago become para-institutions of sorts which are now faced with the daily concern of their own reproduction. The transformative potential of organizations also depends on the fine balance between available resources, surrounding social relations and militancy.

VALERIA GRAZIANO

We have inherited a myth that narrates the birth of the modern cultural sector as intertwined with the foundation of the republican nation state. I'm sure you have encountered some versions of this story. You might have been taught, for instance, about how during the French Revolution, the rioters repossessed the art collection of the King in the name of all citizens, and opened the Louvre as a public museum. A similar story traces the foundation of national theatres as a pivotal moment of democratic emancipation of the public sphere as we inherited it. Yet, what is often neglected in this class-less and Eurocentric accounts is the parallel story in which most working class and anti-colonial organizations during the same period, whenever given the chance, have also been reclaiming arts and culture for their members, in ways that were internationalist, class-based and political partisan since inception. What is relevant in this minor tracing is that the contours of the public sphere that emerge via this alternative genealogy of the sector is an idea of the time spent on art and culture that is not about participation in citizenship, it is not about personal refinement, it is not about a statement of polity. Rather, the possibility of art and culture to emerge as an organized sector is tied to a refusal of the labor time. It is freed time, rather than free time, so to speak. Reclaiming a space for culture for the sake of leisure is an extremely radical gesture in this perspective. Of course, within working class movements there were a lot of anxieties and tensions around this. For instance, many party and union cadres would push for the creation of an pedagogical approach to the culture offer of their organizations. They wished for the workers to educate themselves in their time off, to become more versed in revolutionary political theory. This tension between "betterment—through—education" and more straightforward activities of "enjoyment" runs through most working-class cultural organizations that I have been studying from the turn of the last century, such as workingmen's clubs, people's houses, recreational centers, theatre groups and choirs, etc. There is an unresolved conflict between the didactic impetus and the recreational one within the Left itself.

TP I'm reminded of Kazimir Malevich's provocative essay "Laziness as the Truth of Mankind," where paradoxically laziness, rather than labor, holds the promise to more productivity and communism. In Yugoslavia, this was wonderfully parodied in the work of Mladen Stilinović who took inspiration from Malevich's text for his own musing on the role of the artists. There is a famous self-portrait, in which Stilinović is photographed in bed, arms resting theatrically above his head, eyes shut. On top of it, it is written "artist at work." This work plays, on the one hand, with the trope of rethinking the dynamics between leisure and work but also production and creativity. But on the other hand, it also plays with the capitalist idea of the reproduction of the artist as a kind of *bon viviant*, a highly individualized, nineteenth century romantic type, who just survives out of his pure genius and addictions. While of course anyone who has ever practised arts or become invested in creative labor knows that it is a relentless commitment that requires not just the means to sustain creativity (and we can be critical of this notion), but crucially, it requires spaces of collectivity. No labor happens alone.

VG In the face of this hyper-individualization, paradoxically, the reliance on networks, platforms and scenes for the valorisation of one's practice is heightened. In this respect, the public sphere is no longer simply a space of appearance and circulation of culture, but, from the perspective of the hyper-individualized art and cultural worker, it is also a site of hustling, coinciding with the possibility of getting the next gig, the next project. Accumulation of reputational capital to balance the precarity of the sector is a problem we need to consider in terms of how it can erode the health and potency of the art and cultural sector (let's think, for instance, of all the "the chaos, hostility, racism and censorship that have engulfed"[2] the 15th edition of Documenta curated by the Ruanagrupa collective), especially in a context in which an increasing amount of labor time ends up being spent on fighting the centrifugal tendencies of these homophilic structures.

VG Art and culture, amidst the collapse of the welfare state and the oppressive forms of life promulgated by austerity and financialization, can maybe offer a space where to recompose notions of deep democracy, not representative forms based on majority consensus, but as a radical commitment to plurality, rooted in the idea that encouraging and preserving diversity is the very basis of a demos. A fun question to ask of the sector might thus be: "How could we organize taking care of the public, of doing politics, at a scale, in a way that does not feel like labor, and even worse, as bureaucratic labor?" What formats of unbureaucratic politics can we invent? This notion that serious politics takes place in formal meetings which, as Barbara Ehrenreich put it, had to be experienced "in a sitting position, requiring no form of participation other than an occasional speech, and conducted according to strict rules of procedure"[3] emerges within European modernity. It was an incredibly violent narrowing-down of what it means to take part in forms of public sphere—at the expenses of other forms of togetherness such as collective dancing or trance states, for instance, which were disdained as the practices of colonized people. What is passed over in this approach to democracy as deliberation are all those instances of struggle where carnivals would lead to riots, and many other spaces where one could have very serious conversations without this as the organizing principle. How can we do politics in a way that is not an endless bureaucratic meeting?

2 "We are angry, we are sad, we are tired, we are united," letter from Lumbung community, https://lumbung.space/pen/pen.lumbung.space/we-are-angry-we-are-sad-we-are-tired-we-are-united/, accessed 19 April 2023.

3 Barbara Ehrenreich, *Dancing in the Streets: A History of Collective Joy* (London: Granta Books, 2008).

TP It might be interesting to reflect on how what you just brought up in terms of the potential of pre-modern forms of public discourse might resonate with the hypothesis that we are witnessing a return to feudal forms of accumulation and of governance. Let's think for instance of the scrambling of public and private spaces, the return of personally-revered leaders, the spread of millenarist theories. How we get on the other side of this remains a difficult question to consider. For me, the carnivalesque that you mentioned for instance, also reminds me of the 1990s. We had that quality in the alter-globalization movements, in queer parades, for instance. But even those moments on the streets came out of organized spontaneity. While we should be aware of the shortcomings of modern institutionalized forms of collectivity, we should also be cautious not to fetishize spontaneity. I would also answer your question of "Do we believe that there is agency that can be specific to the cultural sector as it performs its administrative functions?" with a yes. It would be naive to expect it to reproduce itself as an avant-garde, but this does not need to mean that it cannot produce its own forms of radical effectiveness.

↘Valeria Graziano

is a visiting lecturer at the Institute for Applied Theatre Studies, Justus Liebig University Giessen, Germany, and associate researcher at the Centre for Advanced Studies, University of Rijeka, Croatia. Her work focuses on cultural practices and modes of organizing that foster the refusal of work, a redistribution of social reproduction, and the possibility of political pleasure. Recent work includes "Repair Matters," a special issue of *ephemera. theory & politics in organization* (2019); *Pirate Care Syllabus* (2019-2021); and *Figure It Out, Comrade!*, an ongoing inquiry on forms of plebeian illegalism (2023-present).

↘Tihana Pupovac

is the coordinator of Kooperativa—Regional Platform for Culture based in Zagreb, Croatia. For more than ten years, she has been active in the local and regional independent cultural scene. From 2012-2016 she coordinated the regional network Inappropriate Monuments, while from 2019-2021 she was the coordinator of the MaMa cultural centre. Pupovac is one of the initiators and editors of the *MaMa on Demand* podcast. She deals with Rousseau, Rousseauism in post-Marxist theory, as well as the theory and critique of post-socialism as a doctoral student at the Institute of Philosophy, ZRC SAZU, Ljubljana. Her interest, furthermore, includes feminist and psychoanalytic theory.

ACTING WITH TREES

↘ Anna Colin
IN CONVERSATION WITH Thierry Boutonnier

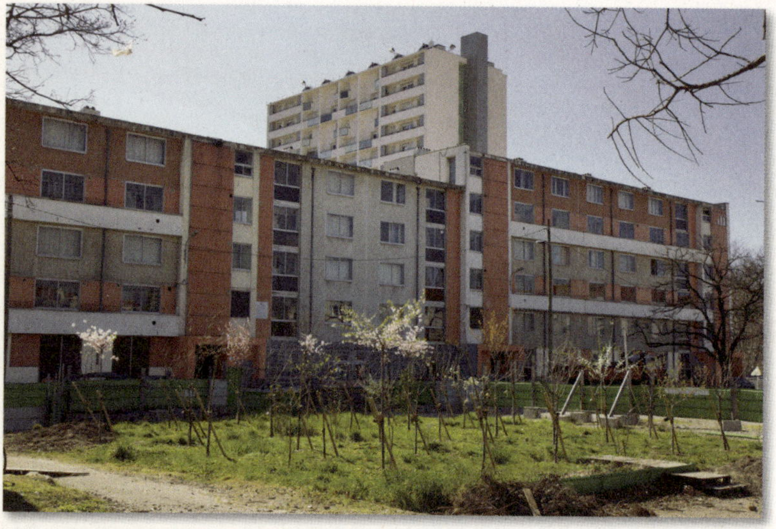

View of the nurserie for *Prenez racines!*, Lyon, 2012, photo by Thierry Boutonnier.

ANNA COLIN Let's start this conversation with how we met. It was at the Valence School of Art and Design (ESAD), in France, at the end of January 2023, where you were working and where I was giving a talk about the relation, both fruitful and fraught, between curating and horticulture in the context of *Weather Report*, a research project initiated by the art historian Johanna Renard and the filmmaker Florence Lazard. While I'm very new to this field, you have been working with arboriculture in your art practice for the past fifteen years or so, in particular in the urban realm through the creation of long-term collective planting projects, where you position trees as "co-habitants."

On the way back to Lyon, you introduced me to the book *La Troisième Voie du Vivant* (*The Third Way of the Living*) by the biologist Olivier Hamant.[1] Hamant sees in the characteristics and behaviors of biological systems models to rethink, for example, socio-economics and organizations in a time of resilience and necessary de-growth. He describes the components of living organisms as "imperfect," "sober," "under-optimal," and "counter-performing," yet able to remember for multiple generations. The idea of robustness, in contrast to performance, which Hamant puts forward in his book, is one you wanted to discuss in this dialogue. How do you understand that term? How does it connect to your arboricultural art practice? Or perhaps put in a more roundabout way, how can a situated understanding of trees and plants inform a public art practice?

THIERRY BOUTONNIER I understand robustness as an expression of our relationship with radical otherness, to paraphrase the botanist and biologist Francis Hallé. This is a simple way of describing what I have observed through the art of arboriculture. The robustness of living things emerges from variability, heterogeneity, slowness, delays, errors, randomness, redundancies, and inconsistencies. Robustness is the path to viability. As Olivier Hamant puts it: "One could thus

1 Olivier Hamant, *La Troisième Voie du Vivant* (Paris: Odile Jacob, 2022).

define sub-optimality as the ability to evolve over time by using internal weaknesses, not as problems to be circumvented, but as a springboard for adaptability."[2]

I've been working with trees for a long time. I tend to say that I don't sculpt dead wood, but that the form follows the living wood with people. In this way, social plasticity takes form in urban tree nurseries. It gives rise to a diplomacy of the tree. Arboricultural art means harnessing the power of plants, extending the capacity to act, stimulating communities and overcoming injunctions—first and foremost, the injunction to achieve results. These complex practices remind us of our ignorance and urge us to be humble. So we have no choice but to maintain our curiosity and care for the Earth's living creatures.

Arboricultural art gives form in the sense of the tree. In other words, the visible aspect is the fruit of complex interactions in which authority is shared with what helps us breathe. "We" act with trees. Arboriculture is the cultivation of trees. Most of the trees that make up our forests, hedgerows, and orchards are the result of thousands of years of experimentation and selection. Arboriculture brings together knowledge and practices handed down by different tree-dwelling species, including hominids, which predate sapiens by more than seven million years. Living in trees, eating their fruit, growing their seeds, selecting leaves for one's medicine cabinet, making arches for one's bed—these are fundamental attempts by beings to live and survive in their environment. Inhabiting trees, being welcomed, inviting oneself, whatever the shape of our tables, the height of our frames... we continue this art of commensality. Thus, arboricultural art inspires many other art forms: from architecture to gastronomy, from circus to literature; its apparent, cryptic or filigree ramifications are infinite. My aim is to share these virtues with members of the public through practice. Is transmitting through the practice of a gesture a form of care?

2 Ibid.

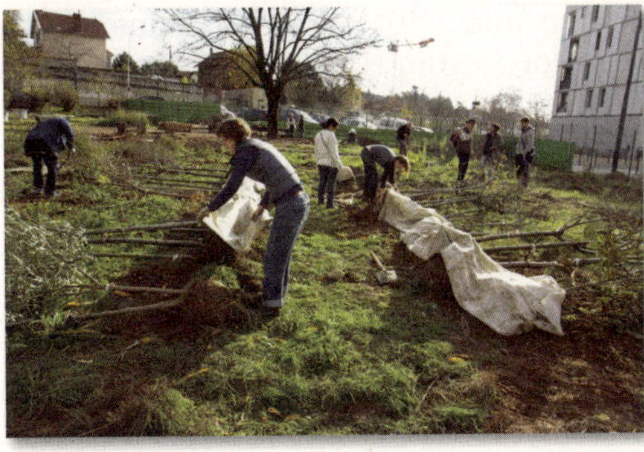

Transplantation preparation for *Prenez racines!*, Lyon, 2014, photo by Thierry Boutonnier.

AC I would say it is safe to agree that virtuous transmission is care. Since you are raising the topic, among other things I have (like many cultural producers today) been grappling with in my work are precisely the ideas of care, legacy, and maintenance, which have been used and misused for some time now and are all too often misaligned with the everyday practices of cultural producers and art institutions, both mainstream and alternative. These ideas have a very different reality whether you are working on a garden, an allotment or a micro-forest, or are developing a public, participatory art project, looking after an art collection (or a *herbarium*!), or sowing the seeds of a collective, an organization, an institution. Whether or not we agree with these terms, their implications and their misuses, in these diverse contexts, care, legacy, and maintenance all connect to the broader notion of time. As the sociologist of time Barbara Adam puts it: "a vast range of time-spans 'coexist' simultaneously" in the so-called natural environment, extending "from the imperceptibly fast to the unimaginably slow, covering processes that last from nanoseconds to millenia."[3]. I think that, ultimately, if I have turned to gardening, it is not only to change my relationship to time (and the relentless clock and calendar time associated

3 Barbara Adam, *Timewatch: The Social Analysis of Time* (Cambridge: Polity Press, 1995).

with working in and with art institutions), but also to be forced to let go of assumptions, to lose control, and to learn the much-needed art of patience and waiting. Is time robust?

T B If we talk about "commodity time," about cutting costs, maximizing profits, about the quest for efficiency to optimize every moment... then our time is limited and we are missing out on life. If we are talking about soft watches and dendro-chronology, then the arrow of time is spinning. Relationships with radical otherness are infinite, and these life trajectories open up mixed durations, inviting us to a robust co-presence. Time measured by the rhythm of our needle-beats is an inversion of the experience of the living and the thickness of the present. Donna Haraway and Kim Hendrickx teach us to think about active pasts and possible futures in a thick present. So the time of our atomic clocks and our ways of connecting to these injunctions of efficiency is not as robust as that of connecting to the unexpected. It's a question of weaving ourselves into feedback loops to make space and

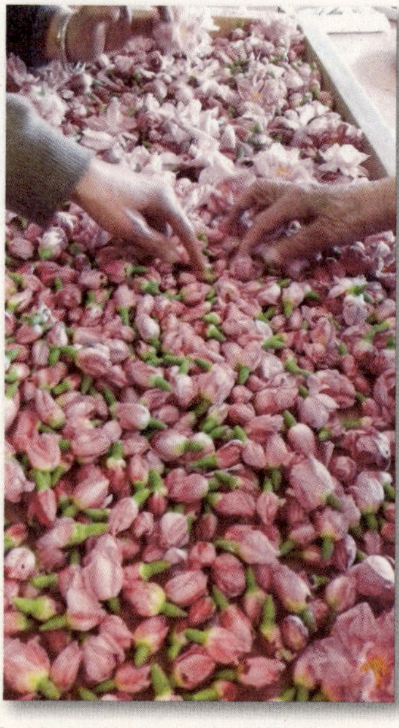

Harvest of roses for *Eau de rose*, Vaulx-en-Velin, 2022, photo by Jacqueline El Ouarraki.

time more complex. A living soil expresses well the thickness of the present and its deployment in space. Working with trees invites us to mingle with this thickness through touch and proprioception. They help us translate, pass on or invent names for these invisible beings who animate us through their proximity. It is as if the breath of our words became entangled in these bushy encounters. Through collective works such as *Prenez racines!*, *Eau de rose*, *Appel d'air*... we sense how relationships involve us and induce forms that are not really what we expected... Perhaps this is the stewardship of these tree-like presences: inducing the collective. An unspeakable difference between an "in-tension" of the plant towards light and the shaded "intention" of humans.

AC One of the specificities of the projects that you have just named is that they are mostly started collectively from the ground up (although they might at times be the result of a commission initiated by urban planners), and that they do not bear connections to art institutions. If art institutions—and by this I mean, possibly a bit simplistically, non-agile structures that might involve brick and mortar, a collection, having to bring a large number of people through the doors and be omnipresent on social media and the press to justify funding—are to take part in the debate and action around Earth care and the climate emergency, which they are clearly keen to do, then what part can and should they play, if any? Do we need ecocentric curatorial and production agencies? Or are we better off relying on grassroots, local, interdisciplinary initiatives and networks to best support the type of practices, thinking and action that you have been describing? Can art institutions join in the exercise of co-presence?

TB I'll start with *Prenez racines!*, an urban tree nursery that was initiated in 2009 in a district, said to be peripheral, of the Lyon conurbation. Together with the Maison des Jeunes et de la Culture Laënnec Mermoz (a youth cultural center) and its artistic director Géraldine Lopez, we proposed to local residents, who were experiencing urban renovation works for the last seven years, to choose trees and plant them, first temporarily and then definitely, in their neighborhood.

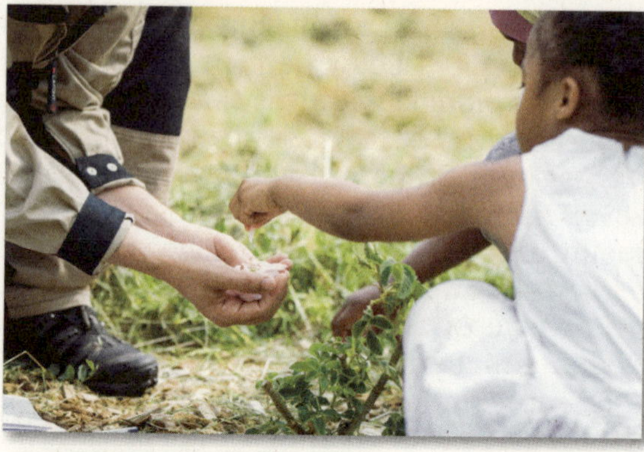

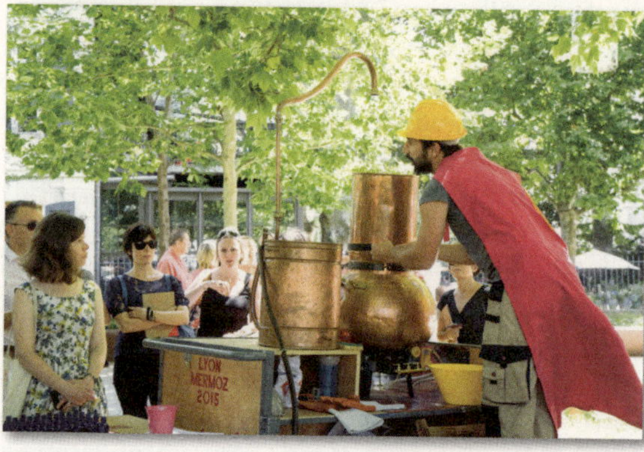

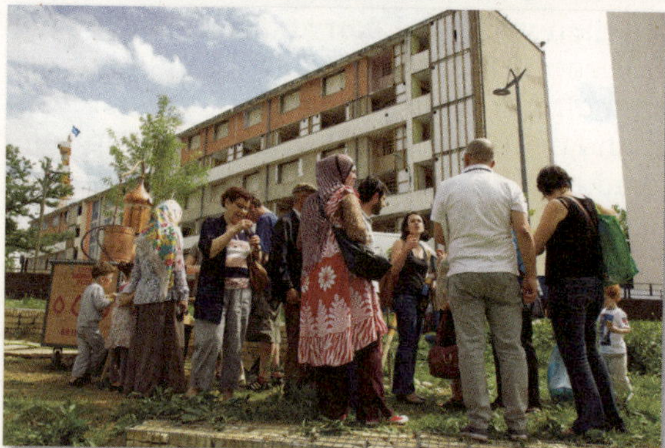

Roses picking for *Eau de rose*, Vaulx-en-Velin, Rose distillation for *Eau de rose*, Lyon Gerland, 2018, photos by Blandine Soulage-Rocca. Rose distillation for *Eau de rose*, Lyon Mermoz, 2015, photo by Thierry Boutonnier.

Thanks to the diplomacy of these trees, we have smoothed over the angles of real estate, introducing a sympathetic relationship with the earth. In this way, we collectively conceived and planted an orchard at the foot of a 750 m^2 edifice. From 2009 to 2015, these trees and the local inhabitants developed connections and to this day I am still in contact with them; in 2023, I was invited to join in for the festival *Vivant!* around artworks conceived by young adults in the district.

Since then, similar arboricultural workshops have flourished, as is the case of *Appel d'air*[4] in Nanterre, in the framework of commission emanating from the Société du Grand Paris (which looks after the infrastructural interlinking of Paris with its surrounding suburbs), to populate the forecourts of train stations with trees under the care of local residents. We chose to work with a particular tree, *Paulownia tomentosa*, and have been getting to know its vigor, robustness and the capacity of its roots in the face of pollution, water stress... Often, with the inhabitants who become co-authors of these forms of life, we surround ourselves with scientists to guide our observations. This was the case of *Eau de Rose (Rose Water)*, where we collated fragrant and flavorful hydrolats from rose bushes planted in different districts. With LBVpam, the Laboratory of Vegetal Biotechnologies Applied to Aromatic and Medicinal plants in Saint-Étienne, we worked with chromatography to observe different olfactory signatures in the soil of Mermoz, Vaulx-en-Velin, Givors, Gerland, Rillieux-la-Pape... So, whether it is through air or soil quality, rose perfumes or crop trees, the participants get acquainted with a singular common.

To go back to your question about the role of institutions, these can have different missions, such as acquiring art objects and conserving them, or maintaining eco-labels such as national parks to look after cultural ecosystems of reference. In the face of ecological and technological disruptions, which are plunging into the great acceleration of the

4 Thierry Boutonnier, *Appel d'air*, since 2017, https://projetcoal.org/en/actions/projects/appel-dair/, accessed 5 May 2023.

Anthropocene (or Plutocene) and its tragedies, whose disasters are so staggering that we lack the words to describe them, the "institutions" (which know how to make themselves heard by the most powerful) need to organize discussions with all sections of the population in the place where they are located. We need to question the propaganda at work, which consists of fabricating (social and ecological) denial. Institutions must not contribute to the appropriation and erasure of the works of humanity or the destruction of complex relationships with the living. Whatsmore, the cultural industries that contribute to chauvinistic, virilist, negationist, racist and ecocidal visions, such as the digital, film, sports or foodporn (= junk food) industries, should no longer receive any support from public institutions.

Finally, as you have intuited, I think that relations in an act of neighborhood—where artists act the most in the place where they are with the greatest diversity of alterity for indeterminate durations—transform these same neighbors in their relations to the millieux. These collective bricolages give us a capacity to make do and perhaps transform our relationships with our surroundings in a more lasting way. By trying to suspend time, aren't institutions actually accelerating it? Aren't they also helping to derealize the world? And is neighborliness possible in a world of massicification of asymmetrical interactions?

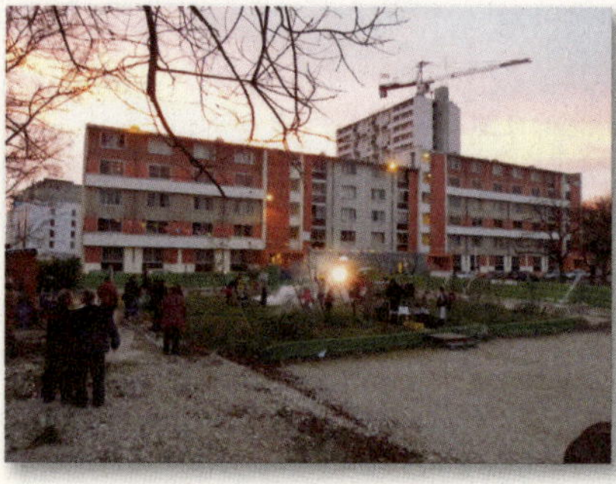

Tree party for *Prenez racines!*, Lyon Mermoz, 2012, photo by François-Régis Vallax.

↘Thierry Boutonnier

is an arboricultural artist who sets up urban tree nurseries together with citizens to transform our relationship with ecosystems. Boutonnier works with neighbourhoods, local councils, and trees. He also works with COAL, Coalition for Cultural Ecology, a European organisation founded in 2008. Backed by the power of plants, the collective projects he has developed include *Et in Arcadia ego* (Lausanne Jardin, 2009), *Prenez racines!* (Lyon, since 2009), *Appel d'air* (Grand Paris, since 2016), *Eau de rose* (Lyon Biennial of Contemporary Art, since 2013), and *Biodynamiser le parking* (far° Nyon, since 2019). He has exhibited in France and internationally, and his articles have appeared in *Les carnets du paysage, Sociologies, and Observatoire des politiques culturelles*, among others.

↘Anna Colin

is a curator, educator, researcher, and gardener. Her practice and research are engaged with social practice, alternative forms of pedagogy and modes of instituting, and critical and participatory landscaping. Anna was a co-founder and director of Open School East, an independent art school and community space in London, then Margate (2013-20), whose experience she is recounting in a forthcoming book published by La Villa Arson, Nice (2023). Colin trains in horticulture and permaculture design, works as a lecturer on the MFA Curating at Goldsmiths, University of London, where she is collaborating with Ros Gray on the development of an Art Research Garden, and is co-curator, with Camille Richert, of *Chaleur humaine*, the second edition of the Dunkirk Art & Industry Triennale (2023-24).

CHERRIES IN BLOOM

NOTES OF AN ACCOMPLICE

ROBERTO GIGLIOTTI

Something unique happens in Bolzano every March. Part of the city transforms—specifically, the area in front of the main university building. It's very creatively named Piazza dell'Università, University Square, in a city where the street and square names have more meaning than mere reference to famous people or events, rooted instead in historical conflicts that have never been resolved. This unbuilt plot of land lies in front of a building which by its very nature should be an accessible place, where both knowledge and experiences are shared, and which has been turned into a meeting space. The building itself is closed, air-conditioned, and in the eyes of its administrators is dangerously close to being able to be used "inappropriately." It's under video surveillance and patrolled by security staff ready to step in in the case of any "disturbance." When the humanitarian crises in 2014 sparked a wave of migration to Europe, in this building all the sockets on the first floor were closed and locked to stop them being improperly used to charge mobile devices. In this building, even now, after 6 p.m., you're met by armed, uniformed guards tasked with maintaining peace and order. The building was designed in the early 2000s with

↘ Roberto Gigliotti
is an associate professor in Interior and Exhibit Design at the Faculty of Design and Art of the Free University of Bozen-Bolzano. He works on museography with a focus on the practices of exhibiting architecture. He is vice-president of the Kunstverein ar/ge kunst and has co-founded Lungomare in 2003 and co-curated several projects for the cultural association. His book *Overexposed Architecture 2000-2020. Twenty years of architecture exhibition* will be published by Spector Books in 2023. With Nina Bassoli he co-edited issue 123 of the journal *Turris Babel* titled *In the public space* (2021). Currently Gigliotti works on the research projects *Curating Bolzano fascist legacies. A sustainable approach to a city's dissonant heritage* and *Positioning and re-positioning narratives and images of destinations in contemporary trans-media tourism discourses* within the frame of the *Interconnected Nord-Est Innovation Ecosystem* project financed with PNRR funds.

the idea of it being a symbol representing where knowledge meets the fabric of the city, reflected in the shape of the building itself. It has four entrances (well, now for security reasons it has one entrance and three exits) allowing anyone to use the ground floor of the building, making it an extension of the urban space surrounding it. The square welcomes people throughout the year, especially students, staff, or professors as well as the students from the nearby middle school and regulars from the student bar with its outdoor seating or the nearby kebab stand (which is even open on Sundays, imagine that! When the town empties of many of its inhabitants, tempted away into the surrounding countryside, ready and willing to enjoy whatever free time they have, if they can afford it). The trees, planted according to a clear pattern, are surrounded by horseshoe-shaped benches letting people sit and rest in the square. Vehicles are allowed on the roads making up two sides of the square, isolating it slightly from the town it's part of. These streets are a kind of invisible barrier. Passers-by live their lives outside of the square proper, part of the rhythm of this provincial town. On the square, some gravitate towards the university building, while across the street others go about their business.

Prunus x yedoensis (Yoshino Cherry)

The trees on the square are *Yoshino* cherry trees, covering the surface in uniform rows, evenly spaced, in a grid pattern. They're silently present—practically invisible during the winter, their trunks mostly used to lock up the countless bikes that fill this square in Bolzano's compact historic center. As the seasons turn, something slow, almost invisible, yet inevitable happens. The shadows of the imposing buildings around the square aren't cast evenly over the surfaces. The light breaks into the rigid geometry the square was designed to have. Some areas get more sun, which is where people gather in the winter cold—those are the same places where the first buds appear on the cherry trees before starting to gently bloom. Then, over the course of a couple of weeks, this stone square, unchanging for most of the year, becomes the stage of a dynamic, vibrant event. It's all over in just a few days, but the phenomenon is as powerful as it is transient. When the blossoms peak, a vibrant white cloud of petals hangs just above the square. Locals flock to see it. I saw some of the first tourists stopping here to take photos, swarms of bees crossing the square, filling the air with their buzzing, students sitting on the ground to admire the blossoms, friends and families having *hanami* picnics bringing in new traditions from far-off lands… the square draws everyone to it. The invisible barrier is broken. Poetry, for a few moments, overrides the strange contradictions of this space.

Over the last twenty years I've often come across Lungomare's ambitious projects in which events like the one I've just described take center stage. This experience taught me not to ignore the power of situations right under everyone's noses which can be a powerful tool for transformation. I'm therefore struck by the political power of a transient event, like flowers blooming, which lasts only a few days and at the end of which the curious, the tourists, and the residents stop mixing with those who visit the institution day in, day out. The square, as a space, goes back to its drudgery and stops being a place where the city's many identities mix, returning instead to a space behind an invisible line separating people who go about their lives, indifferent to what those across the line are doing.

PARADOXES OF PLENTY #53

(LIVING SYSTEMS)

↘Marzia Migliora

The drawing *Paradoxes of Plenty #53 (Living Systems)*, by Marzia Migliora, was created for the book *AS IF – 16 Dialogues about Sheep, Black Holes, and Movement*. It is part of a bigger cycle of work by Marzia Migliora. The title refers to a chapter of a book by English journalist Tom Standage, *An Edible History of Humanity*, from 2009. In this book the author reconstructs a specific idea of modernity through the history of agriculture and its subjugation caused by the production of food as a consumer good—the introduction of monocultures, intensive production, pesticides, genetically modified organisms and everything else which has facilitated humanity's supposed control over the natural cycle of growth.

In her drawing, Marzia Migliora has constructed a larger world of interconnectedness, grouping cells and galaxies in movement, a macro- and microsystem, a living community and their relationships to one another. A system arising from varied perspectives in constant exchange, nourishing itself, mutually destroying itself and at the same time reconstructing itself. Fine veins become sensors that cautiously seek ways to find each other, to make contact—organisms blur and new temporary and provisional living worlds open up. It outlines the history of a shared world, a potential alphabet for a community comprising people, animals, plants, and spaces. The paradox becomes a possibility, an action and a right to question the meaning of freedom, civilization, environment, and democracy.

↘ Marzia Migliora

is an artist who uses diverse mediums including photography, video, sound, performance, installation, and drawing to explore memory as a tool for articulating the present and the role of labor occupation in social spheres. Her works engage viewers through the presence of the element of absence, inviting exclusive connections with the artworks and laying the ground for infinite interpretations. Exhibiting internationally, including at Fondazione Prada in Milan, Venice Biennale, Castello di Rivoli, Museo MAXXI in Rome, FACT Foundation in Liverpool, and Magasin CNAC in Grenoble, Migliora delves into the complexities of human participation in the social realm.

Marzia Migliora, *Paradoxes of Plenty #53 (Living Systems)*, 2023, drawing, mixed media on paper 70 × 100 cm. Courtesy of the artist and gallery Lia Rumma Milan/Naples.

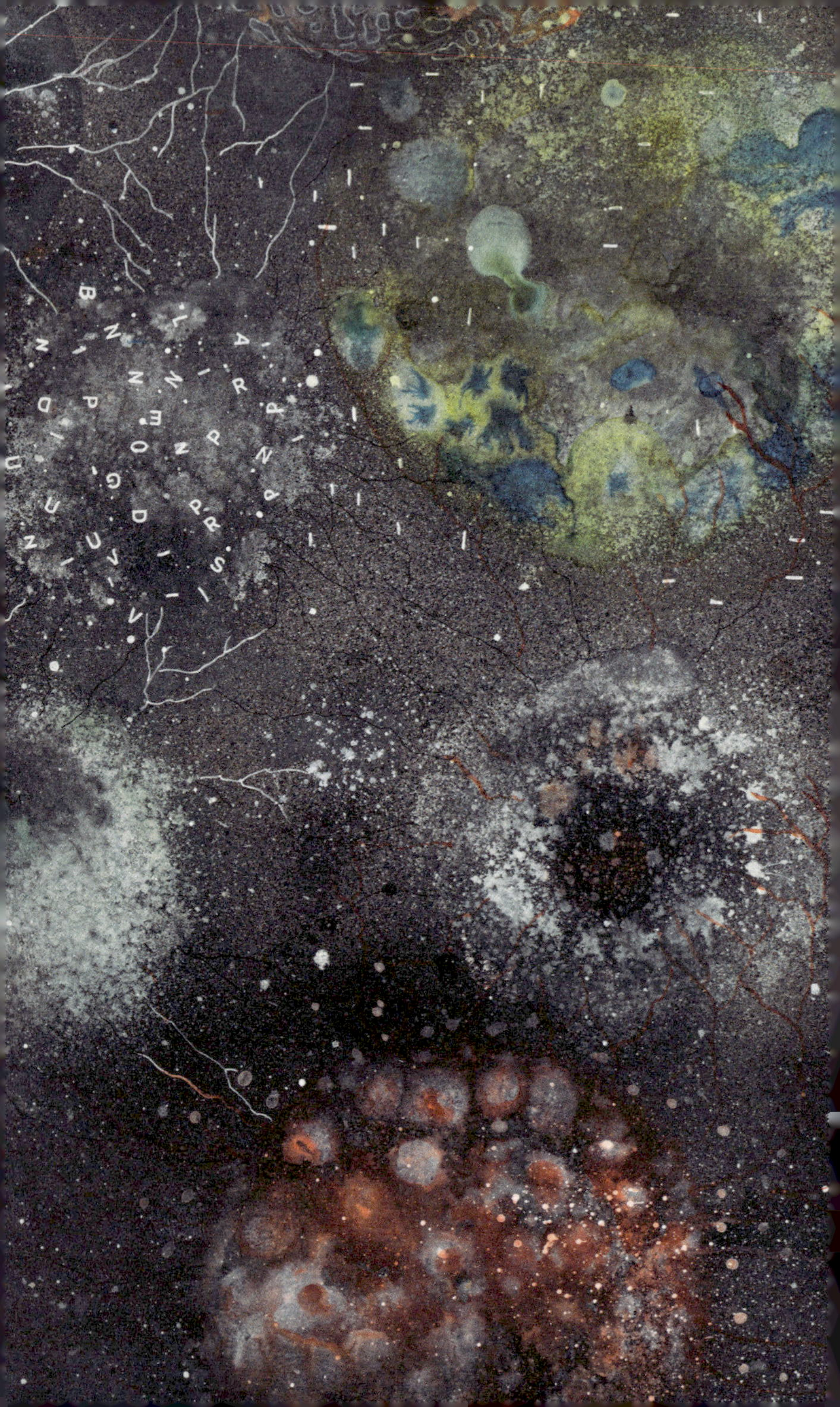

CHAPTER 3

SHARING KNOWLEDGE

DIALOGUES

↘ Rosalyn D'Mello
IN CONVERSATION WITH
Akansha Rastogi, Sharmistha Saha
AND Parissima Taheri-Maynard

↘ Luisa Lorenza Corna
IN CONVERSATION WITH Marina Vishmidt
AND Anthony Iles

↘ Pablo Calderón Salazar
IN CONVERSATION WITH Lorenzo Gerbi

↘ Cecilia Canziani
IN CONVERSATION WITH Federica Martini

NOTES OF AN ACCOMPLICE
↘ Frida Carazzato

NOTES ON MATERNAL DISCOURSE

↘ Rosalyn D'Mello IN CONVERSATION WITH
Akansha Rastogi, Sharmistha Saha
AND Parissima Taheri-Maynard

In her moving essay "Speaking in Tongues: A Letter to Third World Women Writers," Gloria Anzalduà cites from a lecture Luisah Teish gave to white feminists to illustrate how racial inequality affects the way Black women experience time.

> *If you are not caught in the maze that (we) are in, it's very difficult to explain to you the hours in the day we do not have. And the hours that we do not have are hours that are translated into survival skills and money. And when one of these hours is taken away it means an hour that we wouldn't have to lie back and stare at the ceiling or an hour that we don't have to talk to a friend,* she said.

These words speak to me as I wrestle, daily, with earning a livelihood as a freelancer and a mother of colour in South Tyrol. As an immigrant straddling the notional and geographical divides between first and third world, I am often made to feel like I am not entitled to time. While motherhood is a universally alienating experience, if you are queer and/or Black, Indigenous or a Person of Colour (BIPoC), your subjectivity ceases to matter, because you become systemically invisible. If you "appear," casual racism reminds you that your body and mind do not belong to their present context.

Under the aegis of trans-local exchanges of knowledge proposed by Lungomare for this book, I chose to seek out other mothers of colour who also feel oppressed by the unequal demand motherhood places on them. Motherhood involves constant improvisation, consistently accommodating unpredictable variables and transgressing working environments that disregard our humanity or hold us to unreasonable standards of productivity. How to sustain an intellectual career while inhabiting such a consciousness?

I asked three mothers of colour how motherhood intersected with their intellectual practices. Did they find themselves enriched by the new conditions of dependency that "held" them in tight relations with their children? How are they reclaiming space within their careers? How are they steering historical and political gaps? Lungomare proposed the question of "how to deal with the elephant in the room."

My contention is that motherhood is the elephant in every intellectual room, because maternal subjectivity has been historically marginalised under the guise of being non-universal, mundanely domestic and too intimately tied with flesh, blood and milk, too physiologically messy to allow for intellectual enterprise. These edited excerpts center the real-life accounts of mothers of colour who shared with me their experiences with building, nurturing and inhabiting intellectual environments against the grain; daringly taking up space within cultural domains historically reserved for cis-white men and women.

Parissima Taheri-Maynard,
Psychologist, Educator, Community Worker

How did you build *Wir sind auch Wien?*[1]

It began in 2018 with a Facebook page meant to share content related to mental health and its intersection with experiences of racism. I had no social media "influencer" history and did very little to promote the page. Still, many people quickly found and followed us. I kept doing this for a while with no real intention of creating a real-life meet-up until I saw a post by WE DEY—a community for BIPoC artists with a stunning community space in the 7th district in Vienna—asking for applications for workshops around the topic of self-care. I applied with the idea of doing a kitchen table talk for BIPoC people to speak about mental health. Twelve motivated people signed up and we had a lovely conversation with a clear intention: we needed more. I then set up the BIPoC Psychological Safer Space with regular meetings for a fixed group of BIPoC to speak about mental health. It ran for about three semesters alongside two other groups that started up, until the pandemic paused us. Unfortunately, WE DEY has stopped existing. In the meantime, I also became a mother, and am quite protective of our evenings, which is when the group used to meet, so

1 *Wir sind auch Wien* (We too are Vienna) is a platform for BIPoC (Black, Indigenous and People of Colour)-focused mental health.

it is on pause for now. However, many other things are now taking place for *Wir sind auch Wien*, as we have quite an Instagram following and are lucky to be invited to various settings. Since 2019, Farah Saad and I lead *Wir sind auch Wien* together. We now hold seminars, one-off workshops and "intra-visions" for organisations and individuals. We have since also expanded our team and now work closely with great BIPoC psychosocial practitioners and facilitators.

Did motherhood influence your practice as a psychologist?

I was on maternity leave for one year and did only a few workshops here and there, mainly online because of COVID-19. The next year, my partner took paternity leave. I returned to an approximately twenty-five hour work week. I am employed part-time as a psychologist at PROSA, a school for young refugees, and I freelance. This balance has been supportive in motherhood. Having one foot in employment has its benefits; maternity leave, care-days, sick-days, etc. Knowing your salary will end up in your account no matter if you are able to show up is a luxury. It is only with this security net that I was able to navigate postpartum the way that I did.

Has motherhood affected my practice? Absolutely yes, in every way! I believe the biggest skill I have learned is excellent time management. Not only do I have to think of my child before taking on any professional or personal endeavour, but also my partner. Especially when Rio was small, there were many job offers I couldn't accept. I felt like I was falling off the grid. Farah took on a lot more work so that *Wir sind auch Wien* could stay active. She still shows so much love and flexibility when my plans change short-notice because Rio is ill or something comes up. My mental tolerance for difficult topics is much lower than it was before motherhood. I often struggle with listening to stories of trauma, which is part of my job. So, I try to turn to supervision and have reduced one-to-one sessions massively for now.

My team is everything. Thinking things through together, organizing ourselves together, responding to things together has turned out to be the best way for me to work and is absolutely worth the often-lower payment, due to Farah and I splitting it. Offering safer spaces for BIPoC to come together has been wonderful too, as I also profit from the community care. That is the kind of work I love to do and with enough of that, it is possible for me to do the often more uncomfortable work with white people, which requires a certain type of armour to navigate.

I have felt that I am missing out on various intellectual and social events that take place in the evening, which is most of them, due to working hours of most people. I have also felt the pressure of not turning down work events because being a Black woman it feels too easy for institutions to replace me. That sense of responsibility has been quite stressful and makes me grateful to have such a great extended team of BIPoC practitioners and facilitators I can refer to when I do not have the resources. But mainly I have now met many other mothers of colour who have inspired me and shown me strengths that I did not know of before. Farah and I have so many plans for *Wir sind auch Wien*. It's important for me to take it slow. I don't want early motherhood to be focused on all the things I cannot do, so I need to not set myself up for that feeling by overbooking myself. So, we will continue to do the projects we are already working on and maybe sneak in a few extras here and there until Rio is a little bit bigger and I can organize my time differently. Staying patient is a challenge that motherhood is helping me work on.

Akansha Rastogi,
Senior Curator of Exhibitions and Programming,
Kiran Nadar Museum of Art (KNMA), Delhi

What is the curatorial vision behind *Very Small Feelings?*

The show comes directly from my journey towards motherhood. From mentally, emotionally and bodily preparing myself for this gift of life to being pregnant, delivering and caring for a new-born, all of it happened while pitching the exhibition to Dhaka Art Summit (DAS) and KNMA, conceptualising and realising it in its different aspects. I was technically on maternity leave while developing *Very Small Feelings*. But since it is a collaboration between KNMA and DAS, I was working from home throughout my pregnancy and postpartum, except for the one and a half month after delivery. Motherhood filled me with so much joy and in return I swirled the exhibition towards questions of rights of children as culture citizens, their relationship with contemporary art, arts and pedagogy, practices of artist educators and artists who collaborate with young learners, and artist-parents.

The exhibition brings together forty-two projects; a mix of new commissions, historical works, performances, books and artists' creative prompts turned into installations, personal and institutional archives activated from the lens of cultural practices related to childhood and children and transgenerational exchange. *Very Small Feelings* explores childhood as a transformative energy and a place that one can enter and exit at will, and where the origin of the self begins and flows into the dynamics between family, community, world and selfhood. We stage this exhibition through known and forgotten stories, tales, popular characters and cartoons that many generations relate to and imaginary figures that invited artists conjure. Participating artists tease, question and engage with the narratives deeply embedded in one's consciousness. This exhibition is so much about the power of the oral and auditory, its joys and everydayness, the performativity of telling and retelling stories we know and how they change with each transference from one ear to another.

I consciously decided to not take my then six-month-old baby with me to Dhaka during the install period. I knew my schedule would be crazy tight. I went eight days before the opening and we worked crazy hours handling multiple crises, shipment delays, artist crises, equipment issues etc. This long separation was, of course, the major event in the life of a newborn and my new life, too, as a mom. My co-curator Diana Campbell and the entire team at Samdani Art Foundation were very supportive and understanding. I would be crying or choking at least twice or thrice everyday while installing, after seeing his photo, or after a Whatsapp update. Colleagues around me gave me the time to calm down and return to work each time. I really needed this smooth normalisation of crying or expressing sadness, communicating my feelings of missing him as part of my work and being. With so many processes, hormonal changes postpartum, my emotional and mental landscape has been very fragile and having the space to openly express myself without judgement was so crucial.

How do you nurse your intellectual career?

Becoming a mom has only strengthened my will to make things work. I'm getting to my best ideas only now. I'm shaping the most beautiful and meaningful projects of my life. It is hard to divide time and energy but I'm depending and drawing on this large pool of collective energy to bring things to fruition. I fail most days. My son, who is learning to crawl and pull himself up, teaches me every day to fall a zillion times with such joyous smiles. Another thing that is helping me out is working on my calendar and to-do list. I don't have the luxury of time to waste.

I miss mom groups and artist-parent groups in the arts. There are so many artist-parents, yet it is such a no-go subject and an invisible aspect of creative practitioners' lives. I want to be able to talk about my baby to everyone, solicited or unsolicited without feeling awkward or judged. If anyone wants to engage with me, they have to recognise these other sides to me, that of being a mother and caring for a baby. I don't want to separate my work in the arts and culture from my life. Also, I can't take my baby with me to work as we don't have a creche in the museum. I really wish we had that and there was a way to support working moms in the arts, more so when we travel. Traveling and finding ways to support your own work in the arts is so difficult and expensive.

Sharmistha Saha,
University Professor, Postdoctoral Fellow, Theatre Practitioner

Where are you right now?

I am in New York on a Fulbright-Nehru Fellowship for Professional Excellence; a visiting scholar at Tisch School of Arts. I had a rough relationship to pregnancy. I also was sick through most of it. I contracted COVID-19 during my first trimester around March-April 2021, when the Pandemic was the worst in India. I wanted to escape all the nausea, food aversion, extreme weight loss, pain, leaking etc. I felt leaving India would help and so I applied for the fellowship even before my son was born. I already knew that I had received the fellowship by the time I gave birth on a midnight of December 2021 after five hours of labor followed by an emergency C-section. By then, though, I no longer wanted to escape from my child. Still, the pain, stress, and postpartum depression made me want to escape my situation. It's not easy to be a mother in a world where the "maternal" is so vulgarly dehumanised as the great self-sacrificing creature. I want to be able to talk about me without feeling guilty. The truth is my son is beautiful, still, I didn't want the reality that I was part of after birth. So, when we decided I was taking up the fellowship, initially I tried to bring my son with me. However, Fulbright does not pay enough for childcare and New York is very expensive. Given the circumstances, my partner's family assured me they would help take care of my son. I left for New York, having reduced my fellowship period from two semesters to one, since I couldn't stay away from my son for so long.

In New York, I am simultaneously working on two projects. One is my research, which is within the intersection of performance studies and post-colonial studies. I address questions of community identity, cultural performance and value *vis-à-vis* "intercultural theatre" through archival research, interviews etc. The other is my creative work. I am collaborating with playwright Tatiana Kouguell-Hoell to develop a performance on personal letters of war that I have collected over a decade. Gertrude Stein had once said that war is not an event marked between dates, but it has a before, between and after. We try to look at the personal letters in that light. Although I never planned it, Tatiana and I have ended up making a short film, *New York, Letters of War*, based on some of the material.

Do you feel supported by the world as a mother of colour and an intellectual?

I must admit everything I am doing now has been possible because of the rock-solid support from the women who work at my home in India and my mother-in-law. If there are women behind a man's success, I think there are once again women behind women's successes. I do think here, in the United States, they find it harder to see how a mother could leave an infant back home for the sake of her work. The "maternal," within the symbolic order, according to writer and psychoanalyst Julia Kristeva, is an unshakeable codified being. She must be a care-giver, else she isn't worthy of being a mother. Even the most liberal schools here find it hard to digest that caregiving is not only the mother's job. The socio-political-economic reality of the United States is largely reflective of that too. It is ingrained in society that mothers do not work their way to motherhood, but it is their ontological state of being.

I don't think in India that is the case. Because of the family structures we have in India and not to ignore the cheap labor of household help, a mothering woman can be more than the "maternal" there.

When I was in India it was challenging. I had not made any creative work in a while. Even for the courses I teach at IIT Bombay, I hardly got time to renew my readings. However, I have had wonderful colleagues and collaborators who were always understanding of my situation. Like I said, the women who work at my home have made my ambitions possible. I think in countries like India middle class women's dreams are built on the labor of the working-class household help. I am guilty and glad, especially given the lack of institutional or state support in raising children, like in some European countries such as Germany where I have lived for a very long time. Institutions such as nation states, which we have claimed to be the mother figure, are built at the cost of the mother's dreams!

Motherhood has significantly altered my working methodology. I am not able to "waste" time. All my work needs to make sense for me to make time for it. That is not very useful for creative work, which requires contemplation, failure, collaboration. Love takes over sometimes. I need to master this dance of love and labor.

↘ Rosalyn D'Mello

(she/her) is a feminist writer, art critic, columnist, essayist, editor and researcher currently based in the Italian Alps. She is the author of *A Handbook for My Lover*. D'Mello writes a weekly feminist column for *mid-day*, and a monthly memoir-based art column on contemporary art for STIR. She was a fellow at Künstlerhaus Büchsenhausen (2021-22), an Ocean Fellowship Mentor (2021), and the recipient of an India Foundation for the Arts research grant (2019-2022). Her writing has been internationally published and anthologised. She is represented by David Godwin Associates.

↘ Akansha Rastogi

is the senior curator of exhibitions and programming at the Kiran Nadar Museum of Art (KNMA), Delhi, India. Her research and writing focus on exhibition histories of modern and contemporary Indian art, institutional memory and histories of visual arts, museum studies and storytelling. Since 2019, she has been leading a multi-year program at KNMA under the framework of *Young Artists of Our Times*, for which she curated four exhibitions and thought forms, including *Very Small Feelings* co-curated with Diana Campbell (2023), *Right to laziness... No, strike that! Sidewalking with the man saying sorry* (2020), *Summer's Children* (2019), and *Smell Assembly* (2019). Rastogi served as an associate curator of the India Pavilion at the 58th Venice Biennale (2019).

↘ Sharmistha Saha

is an assistant professor of Performance Studies at the Department of Humanities and Social Sciences, Indian Institute of Technology Bombay, Mumbai and a theatre practitioner. As a Fulbright-Nehru Research Fellow, she works on the project *Community identity, cultural performance and value: politics of intercultural exchange between the "west" and postcolonial India* at the TISCH School of the Arts, New York University, USA. She is the author of *Theatre and National Identity in Colonial India: Formation of a community through cultural practice* (Springer/Aakar, 2017). She completed her PhD in Theaterwissenschaft from the Department of Philosophy and Humanities at the Freie Universität, Berlin and was a DFG postdoctoral fellow at Dahlem Research School, Berlin, Germany.

↘ Parissima Taheri-Maynard

(she/her) is a psychologist and university lecturer, and the founder of *Wir sind auch Wien*—a platform that specializes on the intersection of mental health and experiences of racism. With her team, she offers safer spaces for BIPoC (Black, Indigenous, and People of Color) to explore topics regarding self and community care, as well as training possibilities for mental health care practitioners. In 2020, Taheri-Maynard explored topics of mental health, positionality and accountability through the exhibition *SELF REFLECTION*, which was part of the Wienwoche festival.

HOW THINGS CONTINUE

↘ Luisa Lorenza Corna
IN CONVERSATION WITH Anthony Iles AND Marina Vishmidt

Preamble

From 2007 to 2015, we ran a film collective called Full Unemployment Cinema (FUC)[1] which organised screenings "about and against work" in London. The venues, mostly squats or self-organised spaces, didn't charge us for hosting the screenings, and allowed us, in turn, to keep our events free. Indeed, we put "our own labor" into the project, but at the time many of us were unemployed, or at least underemployed at the time of its initiation, and the political landscape around us felt slightly more tolerant, less ossified than it is today. We ran a blog where we announced the screenings, that became, over time, a digital archive of our activities. And we crafted small pamphlets gathering excerpts of texts that illuminated the shifting transformations of work.

The conversation that follows takes its lead from the demise of our collective in 2015. We started our conversation by drawing a map which helped us to recall the moment when everything started and all the other events that fed into our project. In the final drawing FUC is just a knot amongst many others adding up to a constellation of artistic and political endeavours where it is impossible to decipher any hierarchy or temporal order. Recalling our experience in a diagrammatic form was for us a way to deflect the emphasis on its exceptionality, and stress instead the links between our project and other initiatives happening around us. We hope that our memories and the accompanying considerations can offer to other people an occasion to reflect on the (ever changing) conditions for organising cultural initiatives that seek to resist commercialisation. This was our goal at the time, and still is ten years later, even though it is pursued under different guises.

1 Other members were John Cunningham, Caterina Sartori, Chris Jones, Jakob Jakobsen, Grace Schwindt, Kerstin Schroedinger.

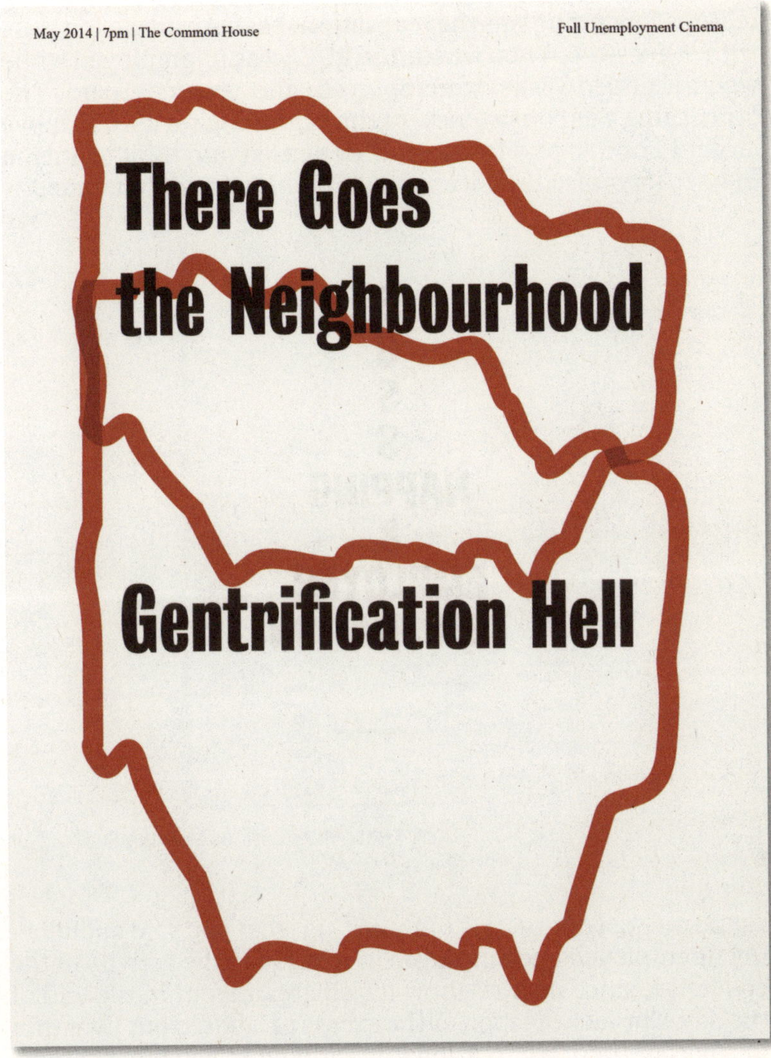

Full Unemployment Cinema, booklet cover for screening, Common House, London, 2014. Courtesy of the artist.

ANTHONY ILES We were saying we should talk about the beginning again, for the sake of the recording... one of the key reasons for ending was the realisation that we were all too busy with other stuff. When we started FUC I was unemployed while when it ended I was overemployed, and yet underpaid. The other thing was consistency. At the beginning we used to move around London and by the end we settled and built a cinema in a self-organised squat space at Colorama, and that ended.

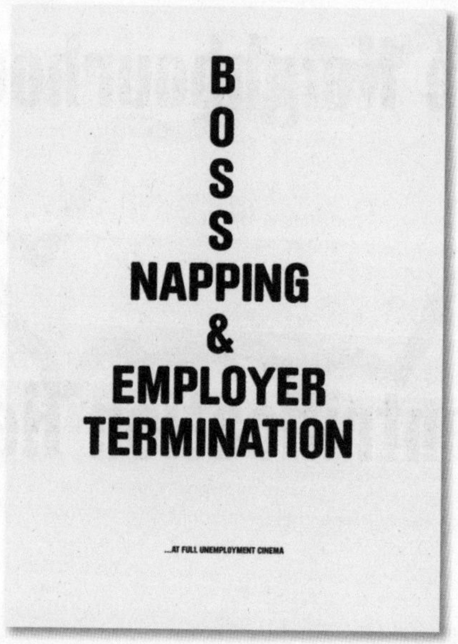

Full Unemployment Cinema, booklet cover for screening, Double Bill Cinema Club, London, 2013. Courtesy of the artist.

LUISA LORENZA CORNA It's interesting what you said about being unemployed and employed in relation to the activity of the collective, since it shows how it's all about labor in the end of the day. The lack of labor, or the excess of labor in our lives (not to say the—poor—conditions under which we labor), largely determined our availability to other experiences such as FUC, which was a collective of cinephiles interested in films on and against labor. I am pointing to a parallel between what we were living and what we were watching. Clearly we weren't looking for solace in the movies, but for an occasion of sharing an experience through the mediation of the filmic.

MARINA VISHMIDT Returning to the end of the collective, for me there was also a certain ambiguity about the group and the initiative. On the one hand, it didn't want to become institutionalised, but it seemed to have lost momentum.

LLC This initial exchange, and especially what Marina says about "losing *momentum*", brings to the fore two aspects pertaining to FUC as to many other self-organised initiatives. The first one is their ephemerality, the second one is the "public." To start with the first one, FUC emerged at a conjuncture when a series of favourable conditions intersected, but then, just as it came to life smoothly and organically it dissolved without much ado. Perhaps saying these types of initiatives are destined to dissolve is fatalistic, but we all knew it was a very fragile thing.

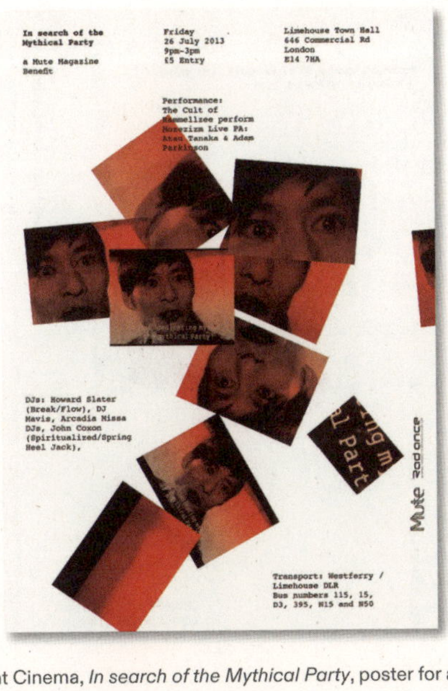

Full Unemployment Cinema, *In search of the Mythical Party*, poster for a fundraising event, Limehouse Town Hall, London, 2013. Courtesy of the artist.

AI Indeed, even though the fragility you invoke also has to be related to broader conditions. In recalling our history and demise, we should pay some attention to the economic context with its cyclical crises and financial bubbles, and the way it played out in London, a financial capital par excellence. We are talking about the long wave of the 2008 UK financial crisis here. It was clear that the bubble would be reignited and become a rule in 2011. By saying that I am suggesting that we should talk of ephemerality with a specific moment and location in mind. London, for example, is very specific in its accelerated ability to generate and destroy.

LLC I have forgotten to elaborate on the second point—the public. I made it clear "public" wasn't the right term since it presupposes a neat division between who produces and who consumes the spectacle whereas in FUC the two categories were often overlapped. There was a group of *aficionados* that suggested what to screen, helped with the logistics a bit, shared resources. This took a lot of pressure away from us, not only organizationally, but psychologically as in, we didn't have to

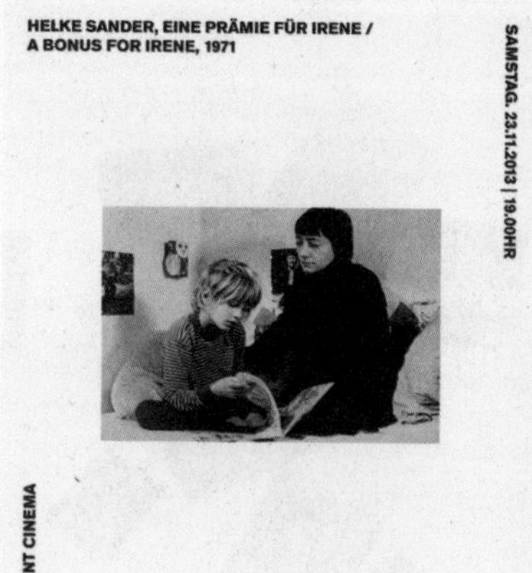

Full Unemployment Cinema, poster for screening, Lothringer 13 Halle, Munich, 2013. Courtesy of the artist.

please the audience with good programming, the outcome of each evening was beyond our control—and for the best!

How to survive in this world

LUISA LORENZA CORNA Talking about other film collectives, Marina, you were also part of Cinenova,[2] which to my knowledge is still alive... How could it survive the turbulent changes we are recalling? Didn't it become, unlike us, a registered film archive? And am I correct to say that one the strategies to survive as an art or film collective is to create an archive? As an alternative to institutionalising, or perhaps, as a more acceptable type of institutionalisation. But this indeed raises all sort of issues, since becoming an archive also means diverging energy from the present to the past, from responding to what's happening here and now to preserving what has already taken place. So, can we say that these types of transitions make organizations more inert?

MV Yes, but we resisted that as Cinenova. We are a distributor!

LLC True, but to be a distributor you need a catalogue, that is, an archive of movies ordered according to specific taxonomic criteria which you "own" as a distributor. And it is by virtue of "owning" a catalogue that you can access funding...

MV True, in fact, tangentially related to what we are talking about, another episode comes to mind. A Cinenova member at some point decided to do a PhD on Cinenova and got funding for doing it.

LLC Again, doesn't this account for the appropriation of the work of a collective? As in, you get individual funding to write about collective work. How does the organisation benefit from it? Or you think it is, instead, one of the few ways one must pay

2 Cinenova is a charity founded in the 1991 for preserving and distributing the work of feminist film and video makers.

back, retrospectively, the "labor of love" that has put into an organisation without substantial funding like Cinenova?

AI Now that you say that I remember someone did a PhD on Exploding Cinema and its mode of collaborative practice. And I also remember that at a conference at Goldsmiths, an academic referred to one of our first screenings, when we invited a few workerist militants such as former Ford worker Brian Ashton to discuss the film *Finally Got the News*. Both these two examples show academia's parasitical relationship to independent cultural initiatives, which often becomes little more than case studies extricated from the complexity of their contexts.

LC Sure, but as we mentioned before, access to academic money was also a way to deflect those fundings from the academic ivory tower and inject them into the wider world. It's not black and white. We should recall that there were departments abiding with this idea. Think of the business department of Queen Mary University run by Stefano Harney where Marina did her PhD. "Business" was a good cover-up for hosting and funding lefty people who were politically active elsewhere, knowing that that money would have sustained their work "outside" the academic space... I'm thinking for example of the archive of radical texts generation-online.org set up by Arianna Bove and Erik Empson, the Precarious Workers Brigade, or again The Nanopolitics Research Group, also founded by people studying at Queen Mary, which resulted in a book published by Minor Composition.

Teaching and learning

MV One of the most successful screenings we organiszed was perhaps *Scuola senza fine* (1983), a film directed by Adriana Monti in collaboration with female students from the "150 Hour" adult education course. The course was a pedagogical experiment implemented in Italy by a number of unions at the beginning of 1974 and allowed workers paid leave to attend 150 hours of secondary or university classes per year.

LLC This memory brings up another topic I wanted to discuss with you... teaching. Over the last ten years we were all involved in different pedagogical experiences in and out of academia and we experienced the ever-degrading conditions of teaching. The number of protocols in place, and the politics undergirding them, have undermined the very possibility of a generative exchange between staff and students.

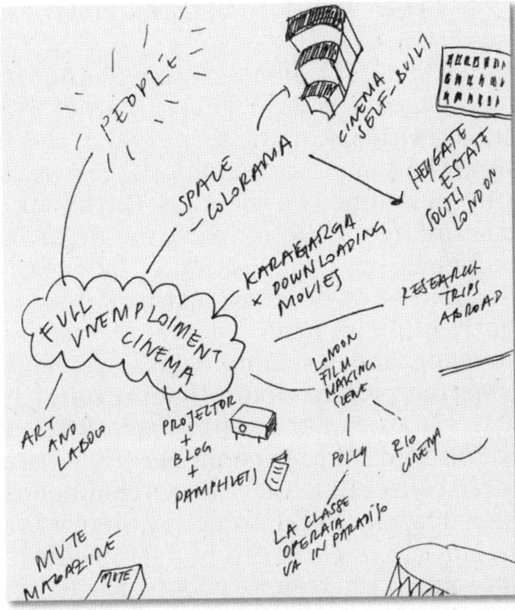

Luisa Lorenza Corna, mind map for *Full Unemployment Cinema*, fragment, 2023. Courtesy of the artist.

AI I agree and I think of all the educational events and workshops I have been part of, those outside the frame of university and art schools were way more interesting that the teaching I did within and for the university. This begs the question where "real" spaces for learning are in the current scenario.

LLC I feel that teaching has become "the manual" labor we have to do to be given time off for our "intellectual" research. It's all very sad, since teaching should be part and parcel of one own's research rather than its obverse. But it looks like academia succeeded in severing research from teaching, and this reflects in a division between members of staff who do research, and others that are employed as teachers. I take this as an example of how capitalism and its institutions constantly demean those labors entailing care and direct engagement with people—reproductive labor, so to speak.

Being close to art in the making

LLC Another aspect I wanted to discuss is our relationship to art and an artistic scene. When we started FUC we were in close contact with an artistic scene which was making art in response to the same preoccupations we were addressing through our programme of screenings. Questions of gentrification, the shrinking of public space, the financialization of culture, the increasing casualisation of labor were pressing issues at the core of our friends' artistic works, which were predominantly filmic in form. They were "making" movies, we were "showing" movies. Films were social bonds. And we were also, Marina perhaps more than anyone else, writing about our friends' art, but in a way that was different from traditional art criticism. Writing about our friends was a way to support shared causes that their movies channelled in a highly sophisticated formal way. I would say there was an alliance of practices. How do you define your relationship to art nowadays? What prompts you to write about an artist or a scene?

AI We should perhaps clarify what we mean by art in this context, as to me art is also a "way to frame" things, in order to get a bit of funding from the art world and take advantage of artistic platforms. This applied to FUC as well—we were a film collective with an interest in labor, but we sometimes presented ourselves as an art collective to be able to teach, for example, at the Royal Danish Academy of Art in Copenhagen.

LLC Yes, but I'd say that we didn't just relate to art in an opportunistic manner, art was for us also a horizon in some way.

MV Yes, but this takes us back to the point you raised which is about art and sociality. Making art and attending certain art events was part of our shared lives, while today we often encounter things in isolation. Certainly we are still in need of sociality and discussions around movies, but technological development has allowed us to gain access to filmic resources remotely, with little effort. And this had consequences which affected groups like Full Unemployment Cinema.

LLC I have another question bridging the history of FUC and our common interest in art, labor and autonomy. In particular, you, Marina, have been grappling with the question of autonomy in a number of written texts, the major one being the book you co-authored with Kerstin Stakemeier.[3] Anthony commissioned the publication and I reviewed it for *Parallax* journal. Only now I realise that that book brought the three of us together and was a catalyst of friendships and intellectual rumination. I like to think of books in this way, as pretext, so to speak, for generating social space where the affective intermingles with the intellectual. But to return to where I started, I wanted to bring to our attention the idea of "art abolition" which was already there in the background of your common book project and which Kerstin Stakemeier has revisited on occasion of the show she curated with Anselm Franke at the HKW (*Illiberal Arts*, 2023). There is not time here to address the show in all its complexity, but I wanted to use it just a pretext to talk about how we can "in practice" challenge the art world as the deputed place to make art, by contesting its problematic grounding. The *Illiberal Arts* show claims to do that, but I was a bit sceptical about its success, for I don't see how—quoting Anthony—you can contest the borders of art by curating another show. I would dare to say that FUC was more successful in this regard, or just more thoughtful. There was, on our part, an attempt to be in the art world without wanting to carve out a stable space for ourselves in that system, nor

3 Kerstin Stakemeier, Marina Vishmidt, *Reproducing Autonomy: Work, Money, Crisis and Contemporary Art* (Cornwall: Mute Books, 2016).

to establish a discourse, or make grand claims. We played on a certain invisibility in the broader scene, so to speak, while we tried to be visible, and known, to our regular audience of cinema goers.

AI Yes, we always keep the art world a little bit at a distance, in order not just to collapse into it. But this indeed requires a lot of careful thinking about the forms we create, the people we reach, the places we use. And it also requires freeing oneself from the luring idea of being successful in the art world...

Other places and forms for struggling

MV Perhaps there are other spaces, other fronts, not immediately linked to art and culture, into which we put our time and energy now. For example, I would like to know more about the work you do in your housing estates...

LLC Sure, this is a good follow up and works as counterpoint to the way we defined ourself before, as increasingly institutionalised and withdrawn from an underground cultural milieu. For if this is true to some extent, is also true that we are just active elsewhere. So, for example, Anthony and I are active in the residents' association of the estates where we live, Marina was joint secretary of the trade union branch at Goldsmiths, University of London. I have a feeling that a shift occurred five-six years ago. If before 2015 we were struggling to save spaces for culture, now we are struggling to save place for living and working under decent conditions, and we are much more belligerent than before. We are experiencing one of the most brutal neoliberalist epochs, and this obliges us to exist, so to speak, "in a survival mode," without time for idle and joyful culture militancy.

AI Marina, I would like to know from you how your role in the union changed your perspective on organised politics more generally?

MV I acted as joint secretary of the Goldsmiths University Union branch for a couple of years, which also coincided with the eruption of the COVID-19 pandemic. This meant living in a continuum of work, union militancy, and every-day duties to keep myself alive. So there wasn't really any space for the sociality and the fun that came hand in hand with FUC... But that moment was also an occasion to understand how a trade union really works. After a short while it became apparent that the dysfunctions of the union mirrors those of the academic institution. And this meant, paradoxically, that the more fight was happening, the more the horizon of change was so subsumed into the procedures of that institution. Indeed, cyclically, people coming from grassroots experience joined the organisation and raised the bar of the struggle, but adapting to the mode of operating of the union and abiding with national guidelines was unavoidable. Yet, despite all its limitations, contributing to the union was unavoidable...

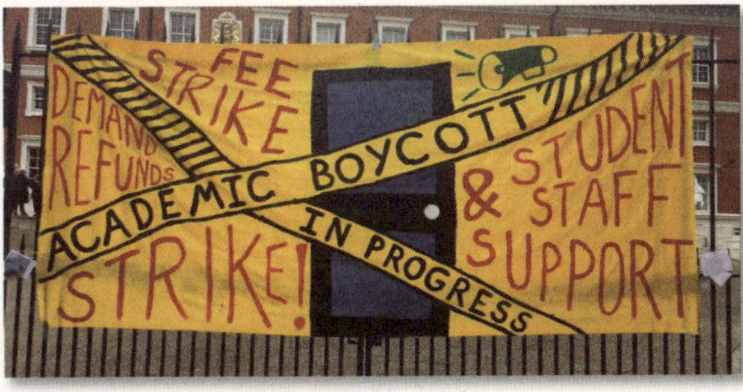

A protest banner outside the Goldsmiths University, London, 2023, photo by Luisa Lorenza Corna.

LLC What you say about the limitations of the union also applies to housing associations...

AI I agree. In the last two-three years, I tried to revive the "residents association" of my housing estate but while I was doing it, I was constantly confronted with the structural limits of this organisation. Resident's associations are conservative, and there's some truly awkward aspects to organising where you live, not with an elective community, but with people you just happen to be around. I have been trying to tune its members into contemporary struggles, but I never thought I could get rid of this form completely, in spite of its limits... Other friends I know who are housing activists tend to be completely inactive around their immediate living situation, almost as a matter of policy, we laugh about that, their situation and mine. I personally love it, but it is a massive struggle, at times really limiting and most people around me seem to think I have gone mad. Moreover, I frequently encounter intellectuals who are clearly alienated by or otherwise misunderstand my efforts to struggle with the people I live, often very poor people, the impression is that these others cannot relate to it as their struggle. I've no idea who they imagine they are struggling with or for, it seems many disempower themselves and others through petty circuits of self-distinction.

In place of an end

M V For me it was very exciting to show these films, many of which I've never seen, and then to have the possibility of discussing them, and conversely sad when it became sometimes more of a routine and that discussion didn't really happen. For me it was always about how we could both be very intentional but also very loose about how we did this, and perhaps over the years of the FUC those desires shifted in and out of balance. Which was also, as we've said, influenced by all the other things going on in our lives. And yet in some ways it still feels totally possible to start it up all over again.

↘ Luisa Lorenza Corna

is a lecturer at UWE Bristol and a visiting lecturer at the Master of Critical Theory at the University of Milan Bicocca. Her main concern is the relationship between politics, art, and architectural theory. Parallax, Historical Materialism, Radical Philosophy, Art Monthly, Texte Zur Kunst and Jacobin magazine are just some of the journals that have published her work. She is now completing, with Jamila Mascat, an anthology of Carla Lonzi's art historical and feminist writings for Seagull Books. Corna is currently working on her first monograph tentatively titled *Fugitive Lives*, which examines the theme of leaving the art world from the point of view of the critic.

↘ Anthony Iles

is the commissioning editor for the series *Documents of Contemporary Art* published by the Whitechapel Gallery and MIT Press and an associate lecturer at the University of Northampton. He was a founding member of Full Unemployment Cinema, a London-based collective that screened films about work and the struggles against it in independent, self-organised venues. Since 2005, Iles is a contributing editor with Mute / Metamute magazine. He co-authored several books, one of which with Josephine Berry, *No Room to Move: Art and the Regenerate City* (Mute Books, 2011), and one with Tom Roberts *All Knees and Elbows* (2012). Iles worked as a contributing editor to the anthologies *Anguish Language: Writing and Crisis* (Archive Books, 2015), and *Look at Hazards*, *Look at Losses* (Mute/Kuda, 2017), and contributed to *The Commonist Horizon* (Common Notions and Lost Property Press, 2022).

↘ Marina Vishmidt

is a writer and editor. She teaches at Goldsmiths, University of London. Her work appeared in *South Atlantic Quarterly*, *Artforum*, *Journal of Cultural Economy*, *Mousse*, and *Radical Philosophy*, among others, as well as in several edited volumes, including *Speculation for the Documents of Contemporary Art* series (Whitechapel, MIT 2023). She is the co-author of *Reproducing Autonomy* (with Kerstin Stakemeier, Mute, 2016), and the author of *Speculation as a Mode of Production: Forms of Value Subjectivity in Art and Capital* (Brill 2018, Haymarket 2019). Vishmidt is a member of the Marxism in Culture collective and is a board member of the New Perspectives on the Critical Theory of Society series (Bloomsbury Academic). In 2022, she was the Rudolph Arnheim Visiting Professor in Art History at the Humboldt University in Berlin and will take up a professorship in art theory at the University of Applied Arts in Vienna in the autumn of 2023.

ON SEPARATIONS

↘ Pablo Calderón Salazar
IN CONVERSATION WITH Lorenzo Gerbi

It is difficult to conceive of our world without the classifications that make up its different parts. Before you are born, most people will be asking your parents: "Is it a boy or a girl?" unknowingly highlighting some of the most fundamental divisions of modern society, those of sex and gender. If you were to contest this widely accepted framework, you would probably be accused of indoctrination or privileging "ideology" over "science." Being raised and educated in such compartmentalizing thinking, it is no wonder how easily we accept and normalize these separations in our everyday lives. Antonio García Gutiérrez refers to these separations as strategies in a "system of classification": "in today's world, the "classificatory" logic of ancient times continues to reproduce through conventional or tacit dichotomies, through oppositions that show only one side of the."[1] Arturo Escobar further discusses these "dualisms," stating that the problem is not the existence of the dichotomies "per se," but how these have been used to create hierarchies and separations.[2] This logic of disjunction is at the basis of the

1 Antonio García Gutiérrez, *En pedazos. El sentido de la desclassifcación* (ACCI: Asociación Cultural y Cientifica Iberoamericana, 2018).

2 Arturo Escobar, "Notes on the Ontology of Design", M. de la Cadena, M. Blaser (orgs.), *Sawyer Seminar, Indigenous Cosmopolitics: Dialogues about the Reconstitution of Worlds* (UCDavis, 2012).

metaphysics of reason,[3] which traces its origin to Greek philosophers Aristotle and Plato's three laws of thought, which were then further reaffirmed by philosophers like Descartes (*res cogitans versus res extensa*, mind versus body, etc.). Especially two of those three laws—the law of identity (A=A, each thing is identical with itself) and non-contradiction (A≠non-A, contradictory propositions cannot both be true in the same sense at the same time)—contributed to erasing an ambivalent (or polyvalent) approach to reality and reducing it to a bivalent one, a dichotomic and reductionist logic that structures reality in oppositions.

The present text is an extension, a written testimony, of a conversation we have been having throughout the last months, a conversation about separations. The separations we present are not exhaustive, nor do they have a particular hierarchy or structure of categorization; they are simply cutting lines we found on the path of our conversation and, by walking on/through/across them, we might have contributed to diffusing them to some extent. Some separations are clustered together—with no particular pattern or rationale—and further discussed; others are just listed at the end of the text. Like Nada in John Carpenter's *They Live*,[4] we decided to put on the glasses that would allow us to see these separations more clearly, and through this text we want to invite you, dear reader, to do the same.

3 Umberto Galimberti, *Il corpo* (Milan: Giangiacomo Feltrinelli Editore, 1987).

4 John Carpenter, *They Live* (Alive Films, 1988).

In *The Practice of Everyday Life*, Michel de Certeau refers to "strategies" as actions enacted by the powerful as a way to further consolidate their positions; in contrast, he suggests that "tactics" belong to the weak, as ruses attempting to challenge and subvert relations of power.[5] In proposing this framing, he created a dichotomy that separated the thinkers, who would reflect on the world from a distance (strategists), from the doers, who would engage with the world on a street-level (tacticians). This division—which can also be associated with one between theory and practice—is a cornerstone of the compartmentalized approach in modern thought, and it limits us to occupy either one of the two positions. However, Maria Lugonés suggested the role of the "streetwalker theorist," someone who would disrupt this dichotomy by being able to both "reflect on" and "engage with" the world; who can assume a strategic position and have an overview of the operating space, and also a tactical role to intervene directly in this same space.[6] This separation is also associated with certain spaces or contexts: academia is the space for theory (or research) and the "outside world" is the field for practice. Whereas in academia non-research-based practice is frowned upon, across different fields of practice academics are seen as pretentious people standing on their ivory towers. This dichotomy (which, in all fairness, is relatively less evident in the creative fields) is

5 Michel de Certeau, *The Practice of Everyday Life* (Berkeley, CA: University of California Press, 2011).

6 Maria Lugones, *Pilgrimages = Peregrinajes: Theorizing Coalition against Multiple Oppressions* (Lanham, MD: Rowman & Littlefield Publishers, Inc., 2003).

highlighted from both sides of the supposed division and reinforces the compartmentalized quality of modern thought. How can we allow for an overflow and more active articulation between the two sides of the—so-called—dichotomy? "Researching in the field" and "practicing in the academy" might be the first step to begin collapsing this separation which only benefits the powers that be.

MODERN – PRE-MODERN KNOWLEDGE / OBJECTIVE – SUBJECTIVE KNOWLEDGE / UNIVERSAL – LOCAL KNOWLEDGE / REDUCTIONISM – HOLISM / SIMPLIFICATION – COMPLEXITY

In the foreword to Morin's book *On Complexity,* Alfonso Montuori introduces a list of oppositions that compare modern knowledge—structured through the "scientific method"—to pre-modern knowledge:[7] objective knowledge of objects in the exterior world, rather than subjective knowledge of interior moods, opinions, experiences, and so on; quantification, and therefore "objective" data that could be measured as opposed to qualitative data that is "subjective" and cannot be measured; reductionism, or a focus on parts rather than wholes (holism); determinism—or finding laws of cause and effect that determine events as opposed to chance events that cannot be predicted by laws (contingency); certainty, rather than uncertainty; absolute, rather than "relative" knowledge; universal knowledge (applicable anywhere and everywhere) rather than particular, local knowledge (applicable only to certain specific settings); one right way of looking at a situation, rather than a multiplicity of perspectives, and the search for that one right way;

7 Edgar Morin, Robin Postel, *On Complexity* (Cresskill, Nueva Jersey-United States: Hampton Press, 2008).

either/or thinking, borrowed from Aristotle, which rejects any form of ambiguity or paradox.

From the Enlightenment on, pre-modern knowledge was labeled as primitive, because of its spiritual component and connection with religious ideology, in the battle for intellectual freedom against authoritarianism and superstition fought by science. "Seventeenth- and eighteenth-century science indeed was an instrument of liberation and enlightenment. It does not follow that science is bound to remain such an instrument. There is nothing inherent in science or in any other ideology that makes it essentially liberating. Ideologies can deteriorate and become stupid religions."[8]
This deterioration is evident in how scientific facts are taught at school from a very young age in a stultifying and acritical manner. Science is exempt from criticism, becoming "as oppressive as the ideologies it once had to fight."[9] It has found the truth in the scientific method and now follows it, losing its role as an instrument of change and liberation.

The last consideration is nevertheless not a conservative scepticism towards science—and the undeniable advances it brought to society—but instead is a critique of its attitude, which can imply the exclusion of other voices and the undermining of different ways of grasping the reality around us. How can we question the modern organization (and formation) of knowledge and its derived methodological truths and assumptions while opening up to pre-Enlightenment knowledge? Could the opposite variables from Montuori's list above, as well as the separations mentioned in this text, help us think about "dis-organizing knowledge" and

8 Paul Feyerabend and John Preston, *Knowledge, Science and Relativism* (Cambridge: Cambridge University Press, 2008).

9 Ibid.

apprehending the complexity of reality? This process of dis-organizing passes by dismantling the structures in which the current knowledge operates; through the selection of meaningful data, by separating, unifying, centralizing and arranging into hierarchies, all these operations are driven by logical principles of disjunction, reduction, and abstraction that guide our perception of the world, without us being conscious of them. According to Morin, these principles form the "paradigm of simplification," first theorized by Descartes by separating "the thinking subject and the thing being thought of." This simplification fragmented the complex fabric of reality by repressing disorder, ambiguity, and uncertainty, leading to the belief that the resulting ordered reality produced was reality itself.

FICTION – REALITY / TRUE – FALSE

In the published transcripts of his Berkeley Literature Classes, Argentinian writer Julio Cortázar recounts an anecdote of when, as a child, he lent a novel by Jules Verne to a friend; a few days later, his friend returned him the book and said: "I can't read it, it's pure fantasy."[10] Beyond the fact that he could not conceive of this as a reason "not" to read a book, Cortázar realized that his relation to fantasy—or fiction—was not the same as it is for many other people; "the fantastic for me wasn't what it was for other people; for me it was one aspect of reality, which under certain circumstances could manifest itself, but it wasn't some kind of outrage within an established reality."[11] Just think for a moment on the expression "the real world," so often

10 Julio Cortázar, Álvarez Carles Garriga, Katherine Silver, *Literature Class: Berkeley*, 1980 (New York: New Directions, 2017).

11 Ibid.

used and abused in learning spaces to refer to contexts of work, and assuming there is a fantasy—or fictional—world in contraposition. But beyond the (false) dichotomy, the great ditch dug between fiction and reality, what we find problematic is the way in which fiction is treated in a derogatory way, similar to Cortázar's childhood friend: why do we see it as something that has nothing to do with life? Why do we associate fiction with falsehood and reality with truth? Speculative design makes use of narratives that might be labeled as "fictional," but they might say as much—if not more—about our daily life as a wooden chair, a cold beer or an old tree—all of which are undeniably perceived as "real." This is because "fiction" is made of the same matter as "reality": conventions that are, at a certain moment and place, widely accepted by a large social group. From media to religion and from entertainment to literature, we are "storytellers" par excellence, and we should never underestimate the extent to which these stories we tell shape our world(s).

HUMANS – NATURE / ECONOMY – ECOLOGY / CULTURE – NATURE

Nature is a word that part of humanity invented to differentiate itself from an other, self-defining by opposition. As if humans were not part of nature, by naming it, we turn this other into an object, something we can use to our advantage. This way of looking at nature is embedded in our culture, it is a meme that originated together with the Western world. One of the first institutional definitions of nature is the one depicted in the Bible: nature as a garden, something we can harvest from, at our disposal to satisfy all our needs. It might seem a distant metaphor, but it is a solid foundation of the problematic capitalistic relationship we hold with the planet we inhabit. The same attitude is at the base of the separation between economy and ecology: our environmental household (*oikos* in Greek) has just been partially studied, understood and felt through ecology (*logos*, learning about), but most of all has been managed (*nemein*) through the economy (*oikonomia*), a cultural construct that imposed an artificial logic of value exchange in which humans are the main beneficiaries, regardless of all the non-human agents involved. What if ecology had informed an economy that looked at nature as a model, a closed system that grows, flourishes and decays, where flows of matter, lives, and energy feed each other and balance each other out simultaneously?

THINKING – FEELING /
OBSERVER – OBSERVED /
CIVILIZED – SAVAGE (BARBARIAN) /
HUMANS – NATURE

Orlando Fals-Borda was a Colombian sociologist working with indigenous, afro-Colombian, and peasant communities of the Caribbean coastal region in the 1960s. Confronted by the lack of appropriate frameworks in the social sciences to conduct research in such contexts, he developed Participatory Action-Research (PAR), a research approach with communities that had explicitly political and transformative intentions.[12] Representing a contraposition to the rationalistic tradition of modern science, he presented himself as a *sentipensante*, a neologism combining the words *sentimiento* (feeling) and *pensamiento* (thought). In collapsing this dichotomy, he was making a point for ways of conducting research that do not create hierarchies and separations between the rational and the emotional. This could be evidenced in one of his most famous publications, *Historia Doble de la Costa (Double History of the Coast)*, a book with a dual narrative, each of which is represented in

12 Orlando Fals Borda, "Investigating Reality in Order to Transform It: The Colombian Experience", *Dialectical Anthropology* 4, n. 1, (1979).

one side of the book's spreads; left pages had the "academic voice" representing rationality—even if carrying a certain level of sarcasm towards the scientific tradition—and the right pages were written in a more "personal voice," which represented the emotions and affects. But PAR had a much more profound political project, one which challenged yet another dichotomy imposed by research in the social sciences: that between "the observer"—the researcher, who would also be historically associated with rationality and seen as the "civilized"—and "the observed"—the communities being studied, who could be associated with the emotions and seen as savages. By including participants in different phases of the research process, they were giving agency to those who were not allowed to have a say on how knowledge was constructed or what counted as valid knowledge. Furthermore, the research process was explicitly transformative, which meant that it did not (only) aim at better understandings of the participants, their contexts and communities, but strove to transform their immediate realities for the better.[13] Lastly, working in a territory rich in rivers—with their subsequent basins and wetlands—of the Colombian Caribbean coastal region, Fals-Borda appropriated the image of the *hombre hicotea* (or "turtle man"), an anthropomorphic figure that collapsed the division between "humans" and "nature" and suggests new ecological relations.[14]

13 Ibid.

14 Douglas McRae, "El Hombre Hicotea y La Ecología de Los Paisajes Acuáticos En Resistencia En El San Jorge", *Tabula Rasa*, n. 23, (2015).

ST^U^DENT – TEACHER / IGNORANT – INTELLIGENT / LEARNING – TEACHING

In his book *The Ignorant Schoolmaster,* French philosopher Jacques Rancière defines the teacher as an explicator: she/he is introduced to the life of a child, who learned everything by his/her intelligence until that moment, including something very complex like the mother tongue.[15] Rancière's vision starts with the equalizing premise that all humans can understand what other humans did and understood. He defines explication as the myth of pedagogy, which divides intelligence into two: an inferior intelligence (the one of the young child) and a superior one, powered by reason and method, which allows the teacher to transmit her/his knowledge. The inferior intelligence is strongly activated by the will, the sense of urgency, but also by the constraints of the situation: in other words, one can learn by oneself when one is motivated (by need or obligations/limitations). The mastery of the teacher, according to Rancière, should consist in leaving his intelligence out of the picture in order to allow students' intelligence to grapple with that of the studied material.[16] From this consideration, Rancière derives his notion of the "emancipatory master," who has the capability of forcing students to use their (inferior) intelligence to deal directly with the material without his explication. Since, according to Rancière's vision, explanation is stultifying and not needed, he theorized the notion of the ignorant teacher as somebody who is teaching by asking questions about what he/she doesn't know.[17]

15 Jacques Rancière, *The Ignorant Schoolmaster: Five Lessons in Intellectual Emancipation* (Stanford, CA: Stanford University Press, 2007).

16 Ibid.

17 Ibid.

Paulo Freire, in his *Pedagogy of the Oppressed*, also plays with the separation between teacher and students. He offers a model of education where this equality between teacher and students finds its dimension in a pedagogical situation created around a shared issue/urgency.[18] The latter offers, as mentioned above, the needed intrinsic motivation to activate inferior intelligence. He defined this model as problem-posing education, opposite to the banking model of education. In the latter, there's no intention to make students aware and critical of the oppressor, so knowledge is transferred passively and passively received by the students-containers; the teacher creates the discipline, the students are disciplined by him/her. This kind of teacher can be identified as Rancière's stultifying master, the explicator. In problem-posing education, the educator is the student and the student is the educator: the educator is a sort of middleman, an ignorant schoolmaster, a kind of facilitator/organizer that shares the same interests as the students.

OTHER SEPARATIONS

OBSERVED – OBSERVER / COLOURED – WHITE / ACTION – REFLECTION / TIME – SPACE / US – THEM / I – WE / LIVING – NON-LIVING / RIGHT – WRONG / EXPERTS – NON-EXPERTS / TALKING – LISTENING / OPPRESSOR – OPPRESSED / DOING – BEING / KNOWING – ACTING / WEST – THE REST / NORTH – SOUTH / PRACTICE – RESEARCH / MAN – WOMAN / HUMAN – NON-HUMAN / SUBJECT – OBJECT / PART – WHOLE / SPECIFIC – GENERAL

18 Paulo Freire et al., *Pedagogy of the Oppressed* (New York: Bloomsbury Academic, 2020).

In discussing these separations, are we making the boundaries of each category more clear or more fussy? Are we drawing a line where before some people did not see one? Or are we erasing the dividing lines we find on our way? As Antonio García Gutierrez[19] says, any strategy of "declassification" will have to pass before by means of "classification;" so before blurring the lines, we have to make them as visible as possible. The paradox remains unsolved: we have still presented a series of separations, of perceived oppositions we encounter in our everyday lives, while calling for a less compartmentalized vision of knowledge and society. However, each set discussed in the text could also be seen as a "loose piece" of a larger picture; no, not "parts" of a "whole"—which is another dichotomy—but pieces that make sense in and of themselves, and that can be articulated between them in different ways. García Gutierrez describes these as "pieces" (*pedazos*)—a rough translation from the *tojolabal* (Mayan language spoken in Chiapas) *xet'an* —, which help us build knowledges (plural used deliberately) beyond dichotomies and separations[20] or, as Escobar would say, beyond the "hierarchical classification of differences" imposed by coloniality.[21]
Now, dear reader, we invite you to put on the glasses we used, so as to better see the separations: what do you see? What did we miss? Complete the list, reflect on and discuss them, so as to be able to break them into "pieces" and de-compartimentalize (y)our experience of everyday life.

19 Ibid., García Gutiérrez.

20 Ibid.

21 Ibid., Escobar.

↘ Pablo Calderón Salazar

is a designer, researcher and educator currently based in Brussels, originally from Colombia. Since 2021, he has been working as a postdoc researcher on articulating an interdisciplinary approach to situated creative practices at LUCA School of Arts in Belgium. His current research builds upon his practice during the last decade, where he has been exploring the potential roles of designers—and creative practitioners at large—in triggering, supporting, and enabling socio-ecological transitions. Calderón Salazar has published several academic papers and contributed to numerous non-academic publications. His most recent project, *L'Agence Saint-Gilloise*, represents an active creative practice dealing with designing social narratives in/and/for public space.

↘ Lorenzo Gerbi

is a designer, curator and educator based in Eindhoven, the Netherlands. He is the co-director of Baltan Laboratories, a cultural "indisciplinary" lab focusing on societal issues through a relational approach, creating spaces to rehearse living otherwise. In his practice, he proposes a rupture in the broad discourse around inter-, trans-, and multi-disciplinarity by adopting an "indisciplinary" approach that relies on temporarily removing disciplines to help develop a better collaboration attitude between them. He is a co-author of the publication *HumaniTies and Artificial Intelligence* (European Commission, 2022) and Editor-in-Chief of *Fictional Journal*. His project *Raise Your Voice* is part of the exhibition *Italy: A New Collective Landscape* at ADI Design Museum (Milan, 2023).

DEAR SISTER

↘Cecilia Canziani
IN CONVERSATION WITH Federica Martini

Rome, Italy, 12 May 2023

Dear Federica,

This spring it seemed like the sun was never going to come out, and instead we were reached by the news of a dramatic flood in Romagna, the report of the damages, photographs of rivers bursting their banks and towns drowning in mud. I was reminded of Marie Velardi's *Atlas de Terre-Mer*:[1] a book of watercolors whose subject is the disappearance of coastal regions across the globe. At first glance the paintings look abstract, or resemble Rorsarch blots, but they're actually accurate depictions of the impact that climate change will have. They are interspersed with the words of a letter telling an ancient tale of water being conquered by a mysterious people, ending with the decision to return the earth to the sea. I've been seduced by the idea of withdrawl as a form of resistance for some time now and am fascinated by the idea that unfolds in this piece of writing: stopping the struggle, allowing yourself to be overcome, losing your boundaries—none of this is yielding but instead is a way of inventing a new way of living alongside the world. After all, this is what we have been used to do in the cultural spaces we visited and founded. These are hybrid places, where different knowledge and disciplines can move around freely, knowing that a poetic response can help reinvent policies and politics. Places born of desire, curiosity, by doubt in action. Places where you and I first learned things that changed us, and changed the way we interact with the world and with other people.

1 Marie Velardi, Book 1 *Monographie* (2006–2019), Book 2 *Atlas de Terre-Mer*, with contributions by Isabelle Cambourakis, Hannah Entwisle Chapuisat, Emilie Hache, François Michaud, Valérie November, Karine Tissot, Sylvie Zavatta. Coédition L'APAGE.

When I invited you to write a dialogue on the topic of shared knowledge, you suggested exchanging letters instead. Symbolically, letters create space for intimate exchange between the "I" and the "You," allowing the narrative of one person to pass through the other, creating space for the other, while also providing an effective metaphor for the space we seek to shape as curators and researchers and which, I think, grows from a need that is, at its core, individual. To give a specific example, two years ago Ilaria Gianni and I founded IUNO, an independent research center. The first step was bringing together the threads of a conversation which had faded when we both stepped back from co-directing a contemporary art foundation a few years back. Our first action was to bring our books in and build a shared library intertwining her readings and mine, as a way of giving a solid form to our current interests. Opening up to one another meant being able to make space for the people who started to visit us at IUNO. Our program is led by our own inclinations but also informed by input and suggestions from visitors. The path isn't very linear but moves instead in the zigzags that nurture us as individuals and as a community.

A few years ago, in a scorching late August, on the occasion of a summer school[2] you organized, we walked in the streets of Rome, led by Marie, looking for plaques commemorating the many times the Tiber burst its banks, showing how high the water got. I'd never noticed them before, and it changed the way I look at the city: sometimes now I feel like I'm walking underwater. The experience of making art this way sensibly changes our perception of the world, which is an aspect that never stops fascinating me.

The summer school was our first opportunity to work together, mixing our students and fostering dialogue between different disciplines (an aspect that is typical of everything you do, by the way). *Becoming a River. Liquid Disasters and Speculative Stories* was the beautiful title that framed the

2 "Becoming a River. Liquid Disasters and Speculative Stories", Istituto Svizzero Roma (2019).

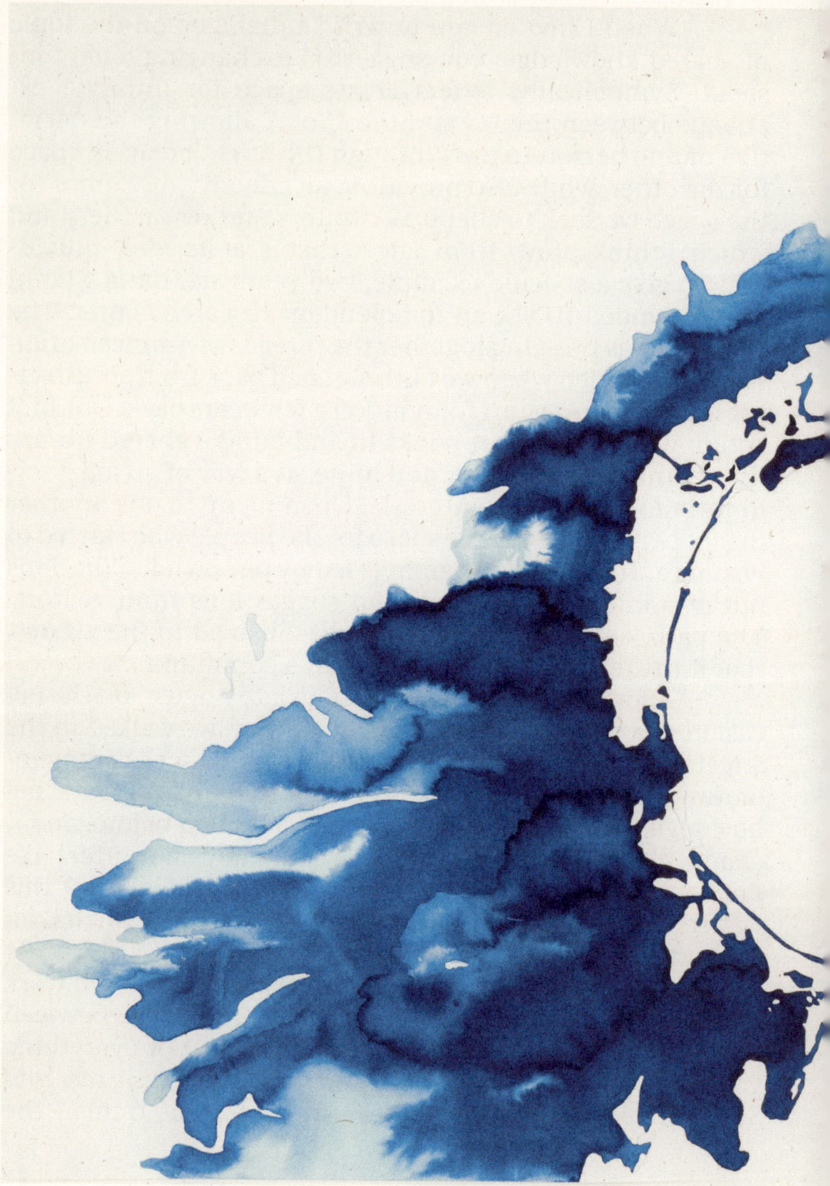

Marie Velardi, *Terre-Mer (Venezia)*, pencil and watercolor on paper, 75 × 109 cm, 2014, photo by Claude Cortinovis. Courtesy of the artist.

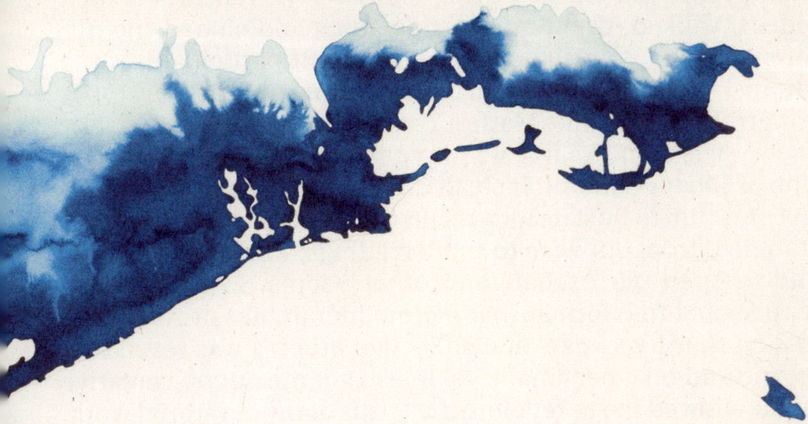

timely topic you chose. During that week we talked, watched videos, walked, drew, attended lectures and shared the different practices and knowledge that each participant in the group brought with them, in order to come up with new types of narratives. Just like Marie's *Terre-Mer* maps do.

The same year, I was invited to curate a solo exhibition of Chiara Camoni. Instead Chiara and I counterproposed the museum to host us for a recurring residency, a project that stemmed from our wish to share readings, words, and actions and to open our exchange to other people. Experimenting with such a free format that had no hierarchies or roles, and feeling that I was part of a collective process was revelatory for me and on a personal level it also got me out of a creative rut. It allowed me to redefine the terms of my curatorial work. I'm interested in thinking together, in co-creation, in being in the middle of things, without knowing quite where things are headed. Art historian and feminist Carla Lonzi uses the word resonance to describe how self-awareness is the end of a process you reach through being recognized by another individual. We perceive ourselves acoustically so to say, as an echo, within a relationship. The word resonance represents for me the possibility to rethink curating, and at the same time it introduces another argument for our discussion: the fact that feminism has been shaping our way of working, in a way we're both increasingly aware of, by bringing to the core of our approach listening, reciprocity, and the idea that life and the meaning of life continuously overlap, as Carla Lonzi wrote. At IUNO you can find exhibitions, workshops, and seminars, of course, but also a kitchen and a bedroom, which make space, and time, to stay for as long as you need to.

The *Terre-Mer* metaphor seems to me a good one for imagining a protocol (a word I am stealing from you) of curatorial practices based on knowledge exchange: things have to pass through us, bring us to crisis point, in order to change our perspective and our way of being both toward and within the world. You always said there are some kinds of investigations that are image-based, that have a sort of modesty, but are nonetheless precise. They are forms of investigation that sometimes struggle to find a home because neither galleries nor more politically-engaged spaces know how to manage them. Instead,

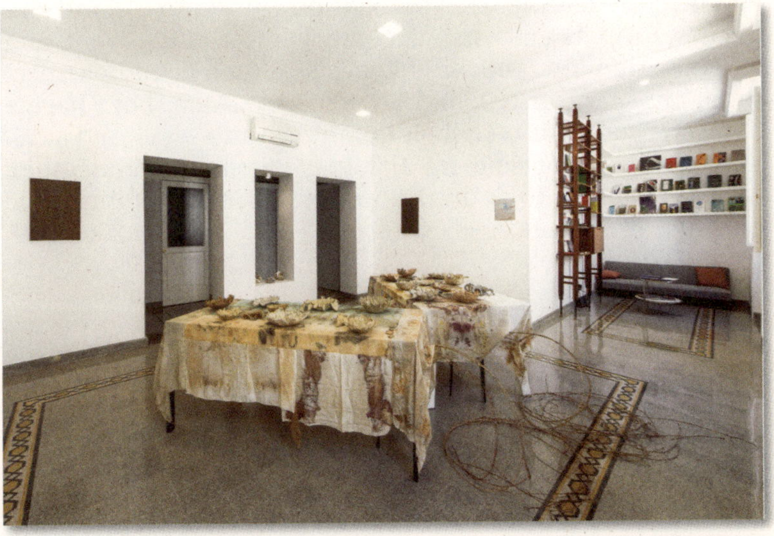

Gorge, Bloom, Foliage. World Above, World Below. And Small Creatures. Chiara Camoni with Michele Tocca, exhibition view, IUNO, Rome, 2022, photo by Sebastiano Luciano.

the spaces we've been practicing, represent places where the world can be examined through the lens of art.

The university is one of these spaces, too. Your courses always have a specific approach, making academic research and artistic practices resonate together. You worked on exhibitions with your students past and present, fostering networks, emphasizing how aesthetic movements underlie political choices. This approach to your role seemed to me as if you were trying to deconstruct academic logic, welcoming in the havoc of independent artistic practices. It's like when you open the window to get some air into a room.

You recently felt the need to focus on a new project, imagining new formats that can overcome the logic of the event, and welcome different pathways, types of research, and perspectives. My space, IUNO, and your space, CALM, both have a domestic connotation (albeit not in the same way), and a call to create space for time, for dialogue, for encountering other, and once again I don't think it's a coincidence that this is the place we've reached.

With love,
Cecilia

Lausanne, Switzerland, 14 June 2023

Dear Cecilia,

Today I read the essay you and Francesco Ventrella dedicated to Anna Banti: "From Art History to Life Writing: Anna Banti's Feminist Resonance." One of the things you discuss is how stories have become invisible because they are left untold.

It's June 14 and Lausanne has been flooded with purple—red and blue mixed together—with twenty-thousand people here for the third feminist strike. For two days, six police officers have been in court charged with killing Mike Ben Peter, a fellow Lausanne citizen from Nigeria who died on 28 February 2018. I'm dwelling on it, while I read about how you and Francesco eloquently explain resonance. I notice how you are careful not to portray Anna Banti as feminist, a position she didn't identify with, while still inviting her to tackle the history she was living through. Reading your words brings to mind Banti's novel *Artemisia,* in which she confronts Artemisia Gentileschi with the ruins of post-war Florence, removing her from the 1631 eruption of Vesuvius, which she experienced when she was in Naples. This is maybe a means of protecting their interwoven voices from the overwhelming noise of history and retaining the dialogic nature of this novel where an art historian—the writer—listens to the voice of an artist attempting to transcribe rather than interpret. Banti fulfils this desire we both felt to meet a subject of study we have loved so much, to listen and trace in documents what Anna Banti calls the "truly unspeakable." A familiarity with the documents and awareness that we're reading them in the present underpins our correspondence—our two letters from 2023 and the broader correspondence represent our affinity for one another and our parallel studies over many years.

In our calls and emails before these letters we came up with the words our dialogue on knowledge-sharing would be centered on. One of these words was time, which we consider necessary to build relationships and which is at the heart of our reflections and our needs at this time in our lives. The time dedicated to making, the freedom not to say yes to everything for contingent and material reasons, but instead giving yourself the space to make things differently and sometimes, ecologically, less.

Another word we settled on was correspondence, which to me means an exchange that may not be regular but is frequent and allows us, even when not actually together, to think-together. Correspondence is also a type of resonance and I think it is an aspect of the way we've kept our dialogue going from when we first met all those years ago. It's a sort of reciprocal expectation: expecting that at some point our closeness will once again help us to come across a subject to examine. And we've found ourselves at more or less the same time opening independent spaces when we're almost fifty, and laughing together at the fatigue—a joyful fatigue, to be sure—that it takes. I underlined part of the text by Chiara Zamboni that you sent me, the part where she talks about the "coming and going between institutional and self-organized spaces" which is part of Italian feminism, but which to me also feels a bit like our story.[3] Maybe we're slowing down and we are letting thoughts settle and close gaps in a specific place, like IUNO. Since June 2022, I've been living in La Meute, a cooperative in Lausanne, which wanted to make room for an art space. That space, CALM, now exists. The name is an acronym, attenuating with a bit of irony, the aloof name Centre d'art La Meute. The house and spaces are led by sound artist Stéphane Vecchione, theater director Patrick de Rham, and architect David Vessaz. CALM is on the ground floor and has door windows that connect it with the exterior. This reminds us that the eco-district we dwell in has a complex story, and that our building isn't purely private because inevitably our cooperative is

3 Chiara Zamboni, "Amicizia e amicizia politica nel pensiero femminile", *Segni e comprensione*, n. 90, (2016).

complicit of the property market and contributes to the gentrification the area. We knew this before we moved, but it became all the clearer in November 2022 when we learned that the Lausanne authorities were considering clearing a squat called Porno Diesel to make space for a participatory horticulture project. You live in a neighborhood and, therefore, you create a community, which brings values, and then for some political reason you are forced to move, as if the act of living somewhere is a purely private matter and not political. Living here makes me instead feel like I'm both a host and a guest, quite fitting for a house that is aware of its public dimension, as you and Louise Garrett remind me with your project on radical, unconditional hospitality. Our exhibition space is partly financed by the rent we all pay. I'm starting with economics because we know all too well that the problem independent spaces have is their longevity, what the demands of life do to the collective dedication such spaces require, financing and being able to live off your work, links with the communities who visit these spaces and which are also changing all the time. The top-down funding model envisioned by the cooperative in our case intercepted participatory planning by a group of individuals who wanted to live together in a different way, taking a different approach. This isn't the kind of thing you can plan for: it just happens. I think the risk of wanting to become an example is offset when we don't use models but rather methods, trying to play slyly in the creases within institutions. I think methods have an innate open-source potential. In this sense, they're open to kinds of collective rewriting that rigid, vertical models don't allow for. When we started the long process that ended in us building a property we don't even own—we rent it—we decided to earmark a third of it for public use. There are twelve students (student rents are high here, too), an artist residence managed by curator Gina Bini for the EPFL, a refugee center run by EVAM, a local NGO, currently home to sixteen unaccompanied minors, a non-profit bar, and a workshop. And then we have CALM, a non-profit, focused on culture.[4] Our first exhibition was a reenactment of Group Material's show *The People's Choice*.[5] Everyone living in the building chose an object dear to them and put it into this exhibition. It was a sort of affidavit framing modern art as a common endeavor rather than an inaccessible language. It promoted community dialogue and exchange, starting with the staging—everyone took part in that—and sharing stories and memories associated with each of the objects in the exhibition. Samuel Schellenberg collated those stories and put them in writing. Some people brought drawings done by their children, unpinning them from their bedroom walls; some brought their hand-embroidered wedding dress; some brought the family camera or sand collection, or even the bike they got when they arrived in Lausanne—hard to use in a city that's nothing but hills.

I think we keep inventing spaces because we reach a point at which we miss conviviality and that we start from the conversation as a practice that sometime can foster the emergence of ideas and events that become public and contaminate the public sphere. Of course, this leaves open the question of accessing these public spaces. Who are they open to? When? For how long? Who runs them? What sort of autonomy can they have? How can we exist in these spaces and ensure they are not over-governed, so they can be shared? That's the work you and Ilaria Gianni do for IUNO—making space for research, allowing the time to read bell hooks' writing in collaboration with an independent bookstore, and all that living together centered on an artistic practice taking place in a space for art within a circular economy. Maybe this need arises right

4 CALM was founded in 2021 and is managed by an association currently made up of choreographer Ruth Childs, artists Maria Iorio and Raphaël Cuomo, director of Arsenic Patrick de Rham, choreographer Sonja Jokiniemi, accountant Yves Mabillard, cultural journalist Samuel Schellenberg, and sound artist Stéphanie Vecchione.

5 *The People's Choice* is a 1981 project from New York. To open their space, the collective Group Material invited their neighbors to lend them something of sentimental value, which didn't have to be artistic. This transient collection was presented to the public as part of an exhibition.

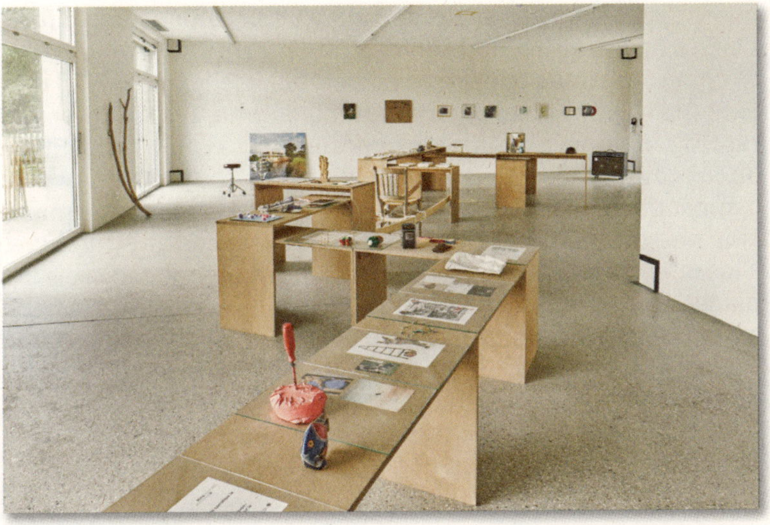

Du CALM, exhibition view, Centre d'art La Meute, Lausanne, 2022, photo by Raphaël Cuomo.

at the point when we reach a certain institutional space, we try to exist there in a certain way but the institution can only yield so much. The world of art schools and cultural institutions we both practice in is incredibly open compared with the wider world at the moment, however fragile it is and how much better it could be. There too I feel like a guest, engaged and empathetic but still distant enough to be able to criticize and be criticized. I'm not neutral towards the public institution. I wish it were more welcoming, and better at welcoming, while recognizing that it welcomes more than other places. Defending it and giving constructive criticism is like shoveling the driveway while it's still snowing. In Zurich there's a bookstore called La Libreria Italiana, the Italian Bookstore. Lisetta and Sandro Rodoni, migrants from Italy, blue collar workers and trade unionists turned booksellers, opened it in 1961. Its slogan? "La Libreria Italiana is where to go when it's raining outside." Working in parallel is a type of resistance and recalcitrance—to borrow a phrase from Paul Goodwin—against the type of language and the time institutions demand is a way to hold back time and space for cultural practices. This lateral move relates to sharing knowledge, and also to the places where feminine thought flourishes, where, as Zamboni says, you can do something else that can't be done elsewhere. Practices can be rooted—a sort of permaculture, biodynamic culture: taking and giving to the land—but linking places together too. After all, what I'm doing here may well have a knock-on effect elsewhere.

With love,
Federica

↘ Cecilia Canziani

is an independent curator and professor at Accademia di Belle Arti of L'Aquila. Her practice focuses on the analysis of the structures and rituals that determine the production and reception of art from a gendered perspective, contemporary art practice as an interrogation of cultural space and its context with a particular interest in memory and history, and the exploration of speculative and collaborative exhibition formats. Canziani's recent projects include *Rome, a portrait*, Palazzo delle Esposizioni, Rome (May—July 2023); *Io dico io*, Galleria Nazionaledi Arte Moderna, Rome (with Lara Conte and Paola Ugolini, February- May 2021). She is the co-founder with Ilaria Gianni of the independent space IUNO, Rome, and with Chiara Camoni of the project *The right measure*.

↘ Federica Martini

is an associate professor and head of the CCC Critical Curatorial Cybermedia Master's programme at HEAD—Geneva, HES-SO. Her research focuses on the history and geopolitics of exhibitions and (in) visibilities in contemporary art practices. Martini worked at the Castello di Rivoli Museo d'arte contemporanea (Rivoli-Turin), the MCBA (Lausanne), and the EDHEA (Sierre). Her publications include *At Your Earliest Convenience: Geopolitics and Aesthetics of the Gift at the Palais des Nations* (with Petra Köhler, Nicolas Vermot-Petit-Outhenin Georg Rutishauser, 2023), *On Words—Isabelle Cornaro, Silvie Defraoui, Latifa Echakhch* (with Sarah Burkhalter and Julie Enckell, 2023), and *Feminist Exposure: Pratiques féministes de l'exposition et de l'archive* (with J. Taramarcaz, 2023).

ON HEXAGONAL ROOMS AND OTHER SPACES

NOTES OF
AN ACCOMPLICE
FRIDA CARAZZATO

This note starts with a question the narrator surprises the reader with. It's from *The Library of Babel*, a story by Jorge Luis Borges. Written in 1941, it was published posthumously in the collection *Ficciones*. The narrator in this infinite library says it will outlive humanity before turning directly to the reader and asking: "You who read me, are You sure you understand my language?"

This is quite jarring for the reader trying to imagine the spaces of the infinite library from the description. It's a question for a reader who isn't in the space described at the time it's asked, but in asking it the questioner signals a change of direction and places the reader into the space in which the narrator's voice is speaking. They share it.

Indeed, Borges's opening sentence "the universe (which others call the Library)" is nothing other than an endless, infinitely-repeating architectural space. The library then is a place which contains every possible combination of every book. It contains all knowledge. Borges writes that in the library are men who have traveled there and

↘Frida Carazzato
is a research curator at Museion—Museum for Modern and Contemporary Art in Bolzano and a member and co-founder of the Lungomare Cooperative. In the last decade, her curatorial practice focused on the production of interdisciplinary art projects that can connect the museum with the public and urban space. She oversees the research projects for the Museion collection and their development through research-based exhibitions and public programs. *Albert Mayr Time* aspects and *Lucia Marcucci Poesie e no*, are the latest solo exhibitions dedicated to the artists of the Museion collection she curated. Carazzato is currently in charge for the development of academic collaborations.

librarians,[1] but reading the story again, we find no trace of their dialogues. I can't help but wonder then who the *humanitas* of this library are? What are the books in the library passing down? How? Being infinite, the library's books will never all be read, I think, and it's also unlikely that the librarians know all the books the library holds. Maybe the knowledge grows corridor by corridor, but at the same time, so does the awareness that the library's mysteries also keep growing.

The question comes up again: "Are you certain you understand my language?" The thing that's most shared between people is language.[2] We exist within language, and it's through language that we exist in the world. It's through language that we create relationships and place ourselves in relation to others. The concepts underpinning classical Western thought show that dialogue is dia-*logue*, from *logos* (word). Words give structure to our relationships. But translating it into the historic period we're in now, it shows even more clearly that the time of static, one-way, sectarian visions has passed. Our home planet is bound up and interdependent. No type of expression, no human action, is isolated because every dimension, every angle, is part of countless worlds of experience. "The landscape of your word is the world's landscape. But its frontier is open."[3]

1 Translation by Andrew Hurley in Jorge Luis Borges, *Collected Fictions* (New York: Viking Press, 1998).

2 "[...]language, the most intimate but also the most shared thing we have; that a language, insofar as it governs our relationship to the other and to the world, and whose law tears us away from a kind of silence [...]," Jacques Derrida, A. Dufourmantelle "Of Hospitality", *The documenta 14 Reader* (Munich: Prestel Verlag, 2017).

3 Édouard Glissant, *Poetica della Relazione: Poetica III* (Macerata: Quodlibet, 2007).

Imagining the dialogues not included in *The Library of Babel*, this question would echo throughout them all, through the corridors joining the hexagonal rooms Borges describes, a multiverse of relationships starting from the intimacy of that question. Right there, where knowledge speaks.

If the infinite nature of this Babel could be translated into a space and into a practice here today, it would be a space accessible to any traveler, which creates awareness because it facilitates conviviality, living "with" one another and sharing the same space which, in time which becomes shared between one's own presence and the presence of others. A space which is free because it's occupied by those who can speak in that space with their own geographies, starting from their own past, their own present, their own wants. A space which becomes a place for democratic practice, a collective creative act of deinstitutionalized knowledge, through sharing experiences, untold stories, and intergenerational knowledge.

The title of the chapter *Sharing Knowledge* links different dialogues and refers to Lungomare as a practice arising from the need to translate this spatial experience into various projects and figures which created relationships and communities over the years by sharing their own perspectives and experiences.

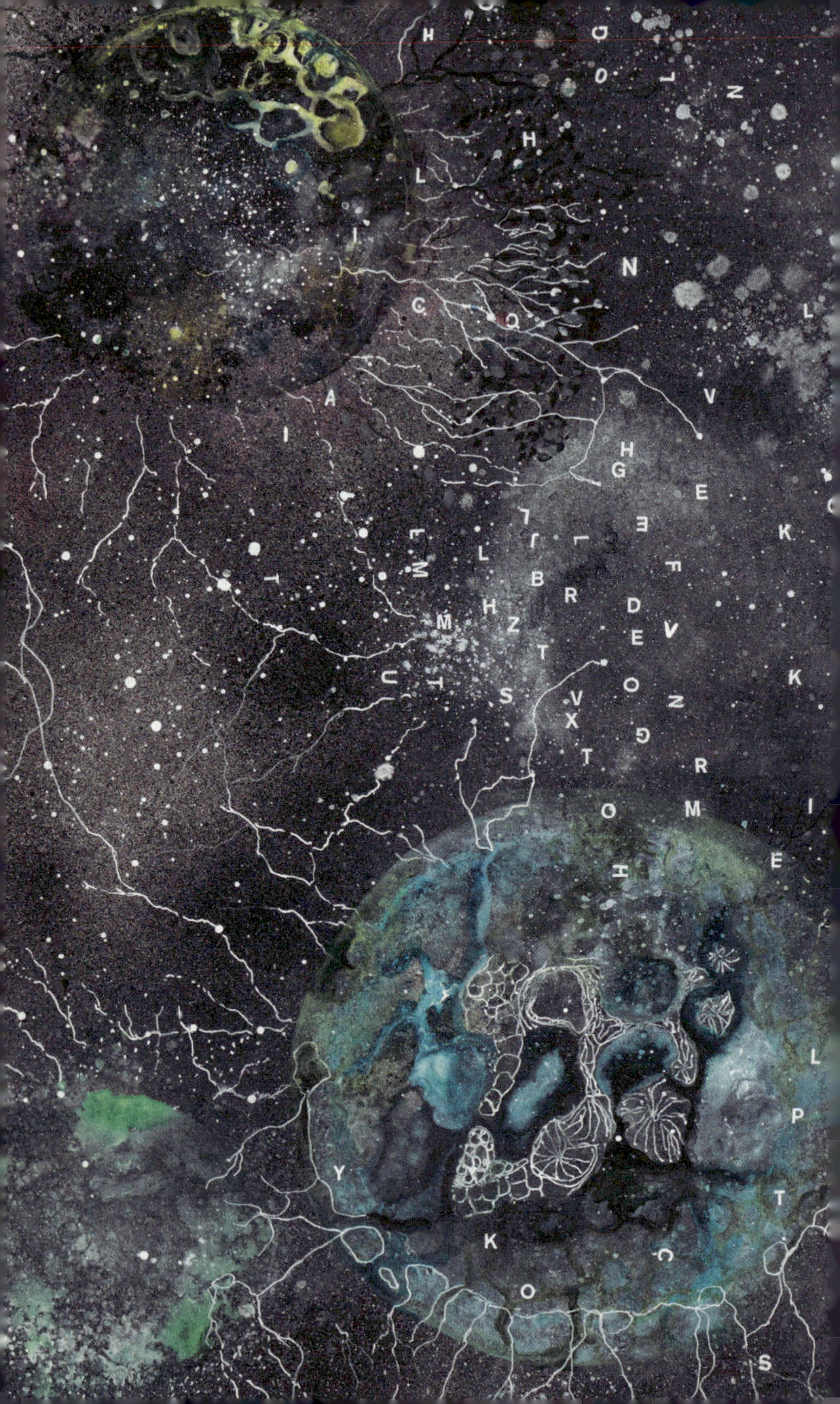

CHAPTER 4

SENSE OF BELONGING

DIALOGUES

↘ Sophie Krier AND Stéphane Verlet-Bottéro IN CONVERSATION WITH Sandro Mezzadra

↘ Wissal Houbabi IN CONVERSATION WITH Bayo Akomolafe

↘ Binta Diaw IN CONVERSATION WITH Justin Thompson

↘ Maxi Obexer IN CONVERSATION WITH Natalka Sniadanko

NOTES OF AN ACCOMPLICE

↘ Marion Oberhofer

OVERTIME AS METHOD

↘ Sophie Krier AND Stéphane Verlet-Bottéro
IN CONVERSATION WITH Sandro Mezzadra

On May 25, 2019, thirty-five people gathered on a high mountain pasture in South Tyrol to reenact Allan Kaprow's Overtime: A Happening. *The reinvention formed the final chapter of the yearlong program* School of Verticality[1] *and was a joint effort between artist-in-residence Sophie Krier, artist-curator Stéphane Verlet-Bottéro, and Lungomare. Four years later, we look back at this work through the lens of Sandro Mezzadra's research on borders.*

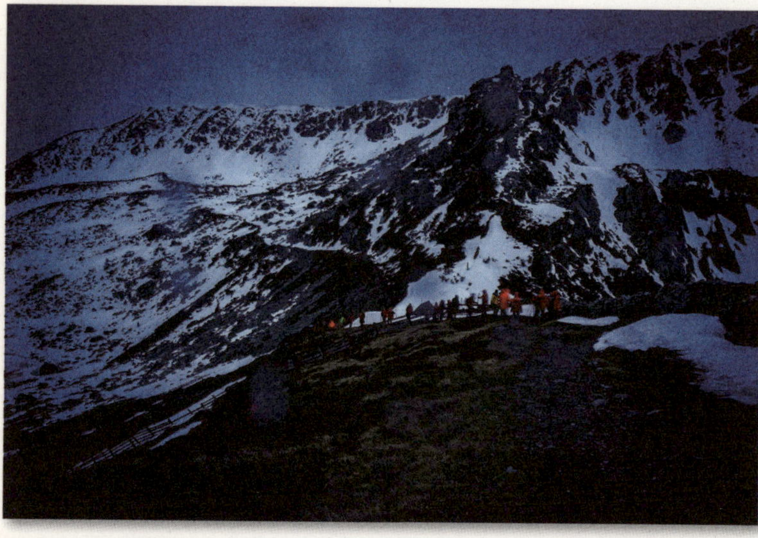

OVERTIME, happening, Alpe di Villandro, 2019, photo by Jörg Oschmann. Courtesy of the artists and Lungomare.

1 *School of Verticality* (2018–ongoing) is a public program about listening and learning with situated ways of knowing. Its first iterations were developed by Sophie Krier during a long term residency at Lungomare (*Weaving Gardens, Seeding Stories, Breaking Bread*). The verticality of the title refers to an in-depth investigation that crosses different layers of society and phenomena.

STÉPHANE VERLET BOTTÉRO The most famous happenings by Allan Kaprow are *Sweet Wall* or *Fluids*. Their narratives are quite literal—the wall ends up collapsing. In contrast, *Overtime* is not well known at all. It was never reinvented. It involves a softer, subtler action. Paradoxically, the wall becomes a link between the participants. In *Overtime*, people have to move a fence together. This implies inclusion, aggregation of differences, the notion of desire, and learning how to play with the border.

SOPHIE KRIER We reinvented *Overtime* in 2019 in South Tyrol, on Villanderer Alm/Alpe di Villandro, in the valley towards Brennero. We went up there because these alpine pastures (Almende) were commons that have become commodified for leisure, tourism, all that. The site has other interesting border connotations. It's a linguistic border. It's a geo-biological border. In ancient times there were offering places for sacrifices to goddesses: frontiers with the otherworld... Our research materials are compiled in *OVERTIME PAPERS*,[2] a four-part critical reader that puts Kaprow's work in dialogue with the local context.
I'll just show you some pictures. Here we start to make the line. And this is when we are lighting the flares. Every fifty meters, there is that light protocol. We also did these assemblies to discuss the instructions, make amendments if it was necessary. We used a snow fence, made of light material. We were moving a lightweight line, but it was still very difficult. And we were stopped by a rainstorm around 1 a.m. We had to go down.

2 Sophie Krier, Stéphane Verlet-Bottéro (eds.), *OVERTIME PAPERS* (Bolzano: Lungomare, 2019).

SANDRO MEZZADRA Must have been cold.

SK It became dangerous as it was very dark.

SVB Last year we went back and showed the film in the Villanders mine (*Bergwerk*).[3]

SM Is the mine still active?

SVB No, it peaked during the sixteenth. It was related to the Fugger family and proto-capitalism. The whole area is quite a charged space, with the 1919 partition of course, the internal colonization… Moving the fence was like conjuring all those ghosts from history that make the mountain a borderscape.

Another interesting point for our conversation is the title, *Overtime*. We believe that Kaprow was thinking about the relation between labor and art, playing with the idea of "Overtime hours," additional work time. He did the happening with his students, as if he wanted to question what is work, what is leisure, what is art. Is studying already working? In a way, he was anticipating the blurring of labor boundaries in post-fordism.

SM I find the idea of a moving fence very interesting, because it foreshadows the externalization of borders. Today, perhaps even more than when we wrote *Border as Method*[4] with Brett Neilson, there is a tension between processes of militarization of borders that aim to transform them into walls, and processes of externalization that make the geography of borders more elusive.

3 In 2022, Sophie Krier and Stéphane Verlet-Bottéro screened the film based on the happening reinvention in an ephemeral *Bergwerk-Kino*, a cinema-in-a-mine.

4 Sandro Mezzadra, Brett Neilson, *Border as Method, Or, the Multiplication of Labour* (Durham: Duke University Press, 2013).

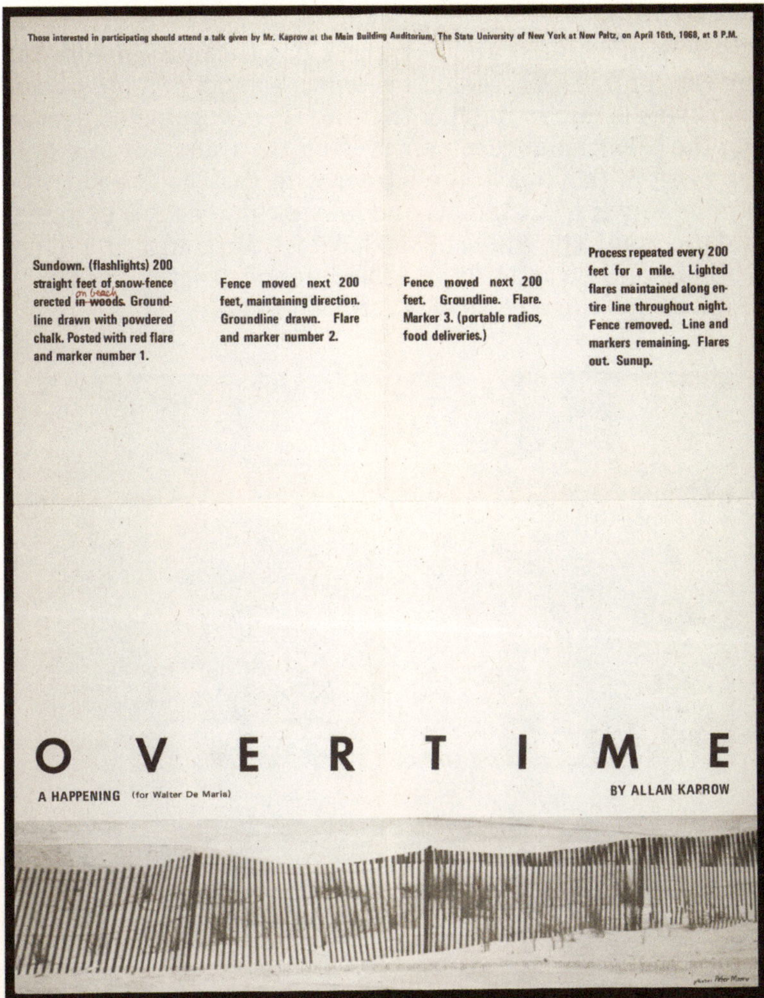

Allan Kaprow, *Overtime*, poster, 1968. Courtesy of Allan Kaprow Foundation and Getty Research Institute.

Take the great book by Gloria Anzaldúa, *Borderland / La Frontera*.[5] In the mid-1980s, at the time of her writing, the northern Mexican border was the hotspot of migration. Today, there are still a lot of conflicts and tensions along the northern border, but the southern border has become a hotspot of migration as well. This is due to the fact that the US government is pushing the Mexican government to stop the transit of migrants long before they reach the border with the US. Crossing the border between Guatemala and Mexico has become extremely dangerous. The whole of Mexico has been transformed into a borderland, so activists and scholars speak of the country in terms of a *frontera vertical*, a vertical border.

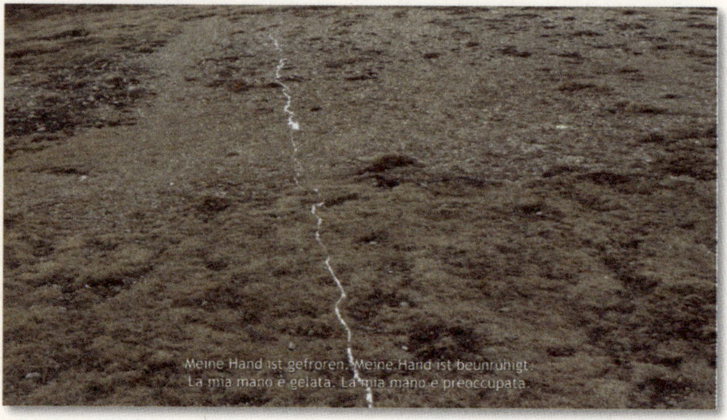

Sophie Krier, Stéphane Verlet-Bottéro, *OVERTIME*, 2023, film still.
Courtesy of the artists and Lungomare.

SK So the whole country has become a wall. Is this what they mean?

SM Not necessarily a wall: a border. Say you have crossed the border between Guatemala and Mexico. You want to get to the border between the US and Mexico. You have to confront

5 Gloria Anzaldúa, *Borderlands: La Frontera: The New Mestiza* (San Francisco: Aunt Lute Books, 2012).

typical border control devices that are operative not only along the literal border, but across the whole territory. In Europe, migrants who confront the European border regime in the Mediterranean or along the Balkan route, actually encountered this border regime long before, maybe in Turkey, in Libya, in Mali.

In critical border studies and border activism, there is a focus on the image of the wall, so we tend to think that borders really are lines. Of course, there is a proliferation of walls in the world, and we must take this into account. But at the same time, we must look at the processes that make borders mobile. This becoming mobile of borders means that the experience of borders shapes biographies even after people crossed an international border.

There is a very good book by Shahram Khosravi titled *"Illegal" Traveller: An Auto-Ethnography of Borders.*[6] For once, I like the Italian title very much: *Io sono confine,*[7] "I am border". It is a very effective work on the multiple ways in which the experience of the border can shape a biography.

SVB This is an idea that was very acute in the experience we developed, because *OVERTIME* was about strangers coming together with their individual experience of the border, through that gesture of moving the wall. Different people coming from different communities, met for the happening. There was the Lungomare team, local farmers, researchers, artists, a person who had come to Italy in exile, someone working with female victims of domestic violence... Very different people. A collective "becoming" emerged. The following years, we went back to meet again, screen the film, share meals.

SM There is a process.

SVB Yes, a process in the sense that a new community was born out of this experience. That was really strong.

6 Shahram Khosravi, *"Illegal" Traveller: An Auto-Ethnography of Borders* (Basingstoke: Palgrave Macmillan, 2010).

7 Shahram Khosravi, *Io sono confine* (Milan: Elèuthera, 2019).

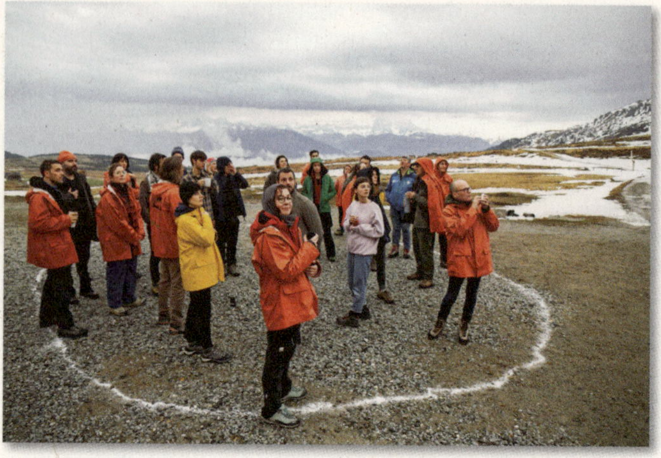

OVERTIME, happening, Alpe di Villandro, 2019, photo by Jörg Oschmann. Courtesy of the artist and Lungomare.

S M I have spoken about space and geography, but we can also look at the same processes from the angle of time. Borders do not only stop the movement of people—they also slow movement down, and spread the temporality of waiting across different spaces. I was talking last week with a very good Palestinian friend, Ruba Salih, who is doing ethnographic work in the camps where Palestinian refugees live, in Jordan and Lebanon. She said that ever since the Oslo agreements, diplomacy and the Palestinian authority have coalesced around the sidelining of the right of return and they took it off the agenda. So waiting became the new mode of life, and camps have become cities. Refugees still see the right of return as a sacred project but have also began to develop novel horizons beyond the failed and mutilated nation state project.

Another important point is that the imagination of borders, even in critical studies, is almost solely focused on exclusion. With Brett, we are convinced of the need to articulate this with the inclusionary function performed by borders. We borrow the concept of articulation from Stuart Hall. For example, it is clear that the processes of illegalization of migration project their shadows on the patterns of recruitment of migrant workers. In this sense we speak of differential inclusion. Thousands upon thousands of migrants die in the central Mediterranean: i never forget this, ever since I became interested in the issue of borders twenty-five years ago or more, out of indignation. But I don't think that we can really succeed in making sense of this if we focus only on the central Mediterranean and do not look at the border regime as a whole, which is also a migration regime. We need to "articulate" it with the way in which those entrepreneurs of construction and agriculture want to recruit migrant workers, and shape patterns of seasonal labor, circular migration, etc.

SVB In South Tyrol, we understood that alongside exclusionary forces, such multi-scalar processes of hierarchical inclusion are affecting diverse agents. For example, mountain farmers became differentially included throughout modernity, while, as you know, the commons were getting enclosed or privatized by capital. Privately owned land got concentrated while common pastures shrank while capital reshaped the mountain landscape to multiply labor power. Othering processes continue to reorganize the mountain space as the alpine border regime is now determining the movement of non-white bodies escaping war and dispossession. So the same forces of capitalist accumulation are forcing people out of Africa through the Alps, and pushing the ecological habitat of birds or plants upwards by climatic effects. It is a space characterized by the fleeing of many bodies—humans, animals.

SK There is South Tyrol with its specific border regime. There is Kaprow and *Overtime* in San Diego (US), which is also a specific take on the border. And there is your own experience, as we meet today in Bologna. We're interested to see whether we can draw some connections between these three sites: South Tyrol, San Diego and Bologna. You mentioned before we started recording that you were born in Genoa and just told us that you became interested in the subject of borders twenty-five years ago. How would you situate yourself in relation to this interest in borders since the 1990s?

SM When I moved back from Savona to Genoa in 1981, I already had a background as an autonomist militant, and thus joined the autonomous movement there, although it had been radically weakened by the wave of arrests of 1979. My political and intellectual training was shaped by the autonomist movement as well as the so-called workerism or autonomist Marxism, since the end of the 1970s through the early 1980s. So, in Genoa, I was politically active besides being a philosophy student. I used to say that the city in which I grew up and studied in the 1980s was a white city. In the early 1990s, we discovered that the city was not white anymore. At first, we tried to intervene to support the migrants, but we didn't have the tools. The issue of racism was totally outside our political and intellectual horizon. We learned by meeting and making friends with newcomers from Senegal or Morocco. We created an association. In the following years, my life became a full-time engagement with struggles that were quite successful. What was at stake in those years was the legitimacy of the migrant presence in the city. Our Senegalese friends told us about their border crossing, but they also taught us to discern the operation of borders within the city.

This is when I really discovered the issue of border. I say "discovered" because, again, borders were completely outside my academic horizon. In the 1980s, it was the Cold War. Borders appeared to us in Europe as frozen. It did not seem like an interesting issue. I was doing my PhD on completely different topics. Then after a few years of full-time engagement, I placed migration and borders at the center of my research agenda, and in 2002 I met Brett, moved to Bologna, and started making international connections to understand globalization from the angle of border and migration.

SVB I see another interesting connection with your work, in the way we approached the reinvention of the happening as an artistic inquiry that operates back and forth between the "fieldwork" on the territory, and the knowledge that we try to elaborate on those categories of border-making processes. Your idea of method too is a kind of folding together of theory and experience.

SM That's a very important question and also a quite difficult one because the question of theory and practice—let's put it so—is often framed in terms of the relation between theoretical work and empirical work. This is something we do not accept. We try to work toward a different way to make sense of that relation. Usually, people have a theory, then comes empirical work, then comes reframing or verifying, and so on—which is okay, but we don't do that. We rather emphasize the gap between the two. We think that only by emphasizing the gap, it is possible to be creative in theory and, at the same time, understand something in concrete contexts.

We have provisional tools like what we call the research platform. For instance, we worked quite extensively on the port of Piraeus in Greece that has been overtaken by COSCO, the state shipping company of China. We didn't simply organize a workshop in Athens with all the project partners. Instead, we opened a platform during several months: people were able to stay and exchange with Greek researchers, artists were invited to participate, then we had workshops with everyone involved, so it was a continuous flow of experiences.

SK At some point in the book you mentioned that a possible definition of labor could be "life-engendering life."

SM That's a definition by Marx in the 1844 manuscript.

SOPHIE KRIER It sounds very autonomous. Dictated by life rather than money. Like giving birth.

SVB From the point of view of engendering commons, I remember how one of the participants, Heidi Oberkofler, was telling us: " I work with a group of women who suffered abuse, violence. In order to heal, to do the emotional labor, the first step for them is to say: I need to set my boundary." So if border is the method of capital, what counter-method can we develop to engender care, to engender solidarity?

SM It's a question that we got a couple of times: who uses borders? It is clear that capital has an interest in the existence of borders, which it negotiates in a very different way from the state. This is another original point of *Border as Method*: critical border studies usually look at states and political borders, we try to articulate that with an analysis of what we call

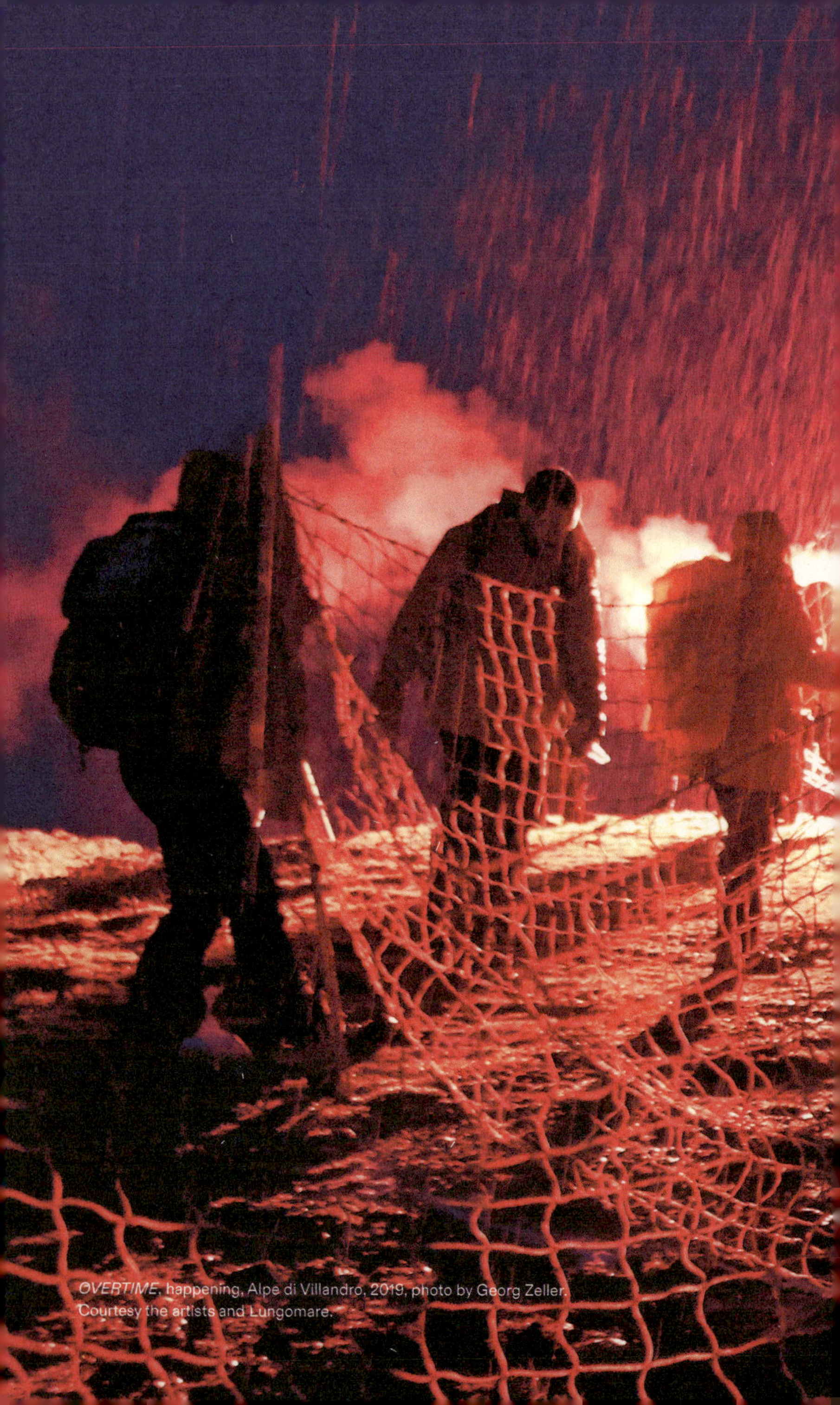

OVERTIME, happening, Alpe di Villandro, 2019, photo by Georg Zeller. Courtesy the artists and Lungomare.

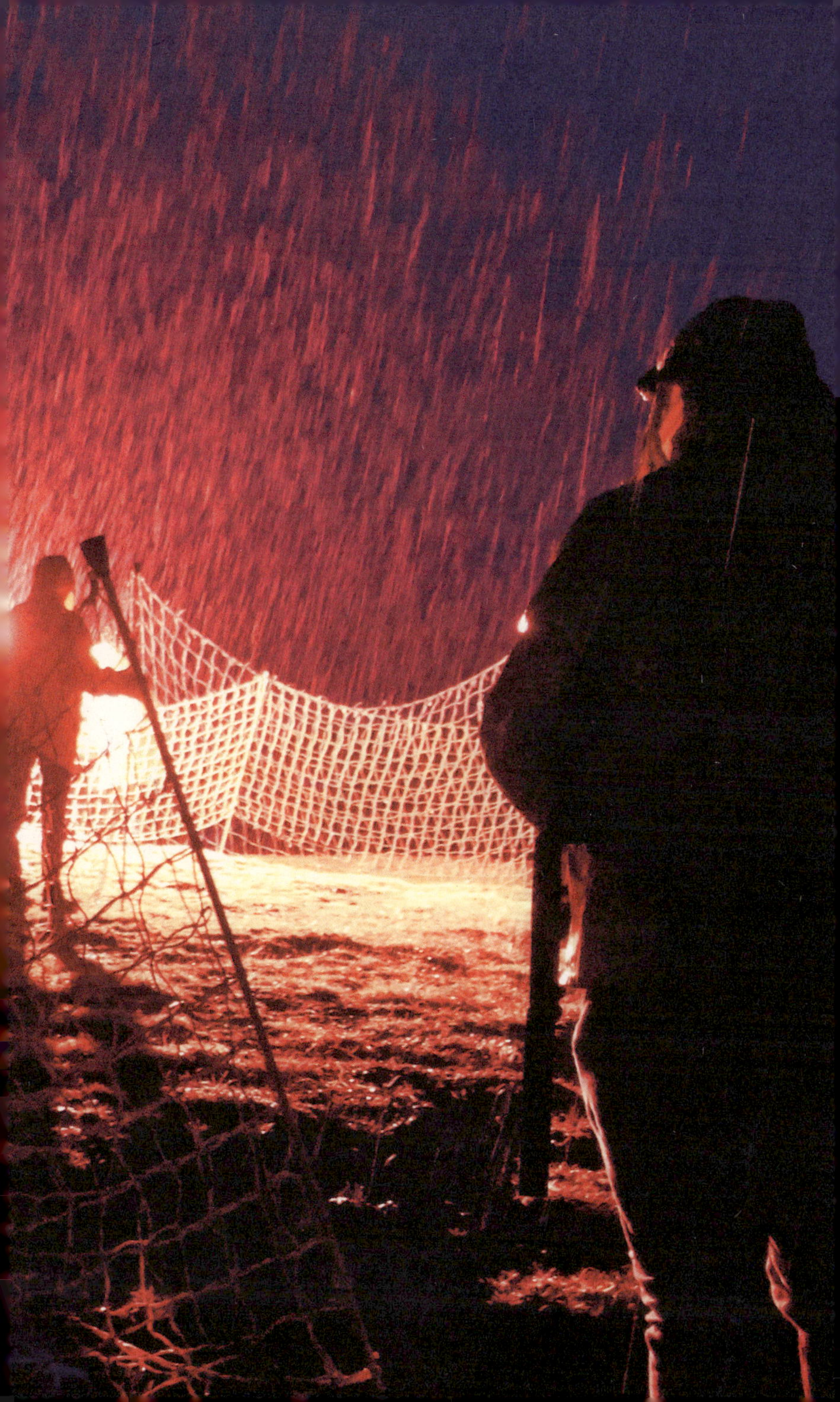

"the expanding frontiers of capital"—going back in history to the seventeenth century and the enclosures. Today capital continues to have an interest in the existence of borders, in order to have different tax regimes or labor regimes, but it also transgresses borders through the circulation of commodities and so on. Capital produces its own spaces whose boundaries do not necessarily coincide with political borders.

From our point of view, we must fight these hierarchizing effects of bordering processes. And at the same time, we also need to imagine situations in which someone, or a community, are able to develop their own bordering processes and their own ways of managing bordering processes.

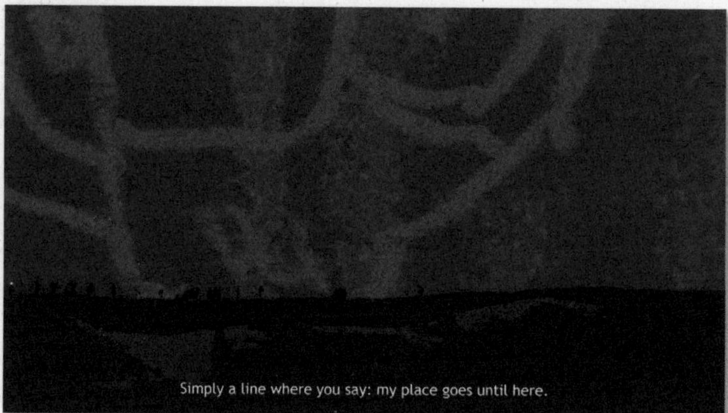

Sophie Krier and Stéphane Verlet-Bottéro, *OVERTIME*, 2023, film still.
Courtesy of the artists and Lungomare.

SVB As in *Governing the commons*.[8] It's interesting that Elinor Ostrom used the term "governing." Her position is radically opposite to state governmentality, but this doesn't mean that there's no governing at all.

8 Elinor Ostrom, *Governing the Commons: The Evolution of Institutions for Collective Action* (*Political Economy of Institutions and Decisions*), (Cambridge: Cambridge University Press, 1992).

SM Indeed, because otherwise it would be the tragedy of the commons...! Anyway, it's not an easy issue. I also dream of a world without borders—abolitionism. But to imagine a world without borders is difficult. There is a form of "border fetishism" that sees the border only as a wall, as a thing—without the social relations. There are borders in processes at stake among the three of us right now. These kinds of processes have to do with the production of differences and distinctions, that also lay the ground for communication between us... Working with an expanded notion of borders, it is very difficult to abolish them, and I wouldn't go for their abolition. But this is very different from the border in the central Mediterranean that kills people every day.

SBV It also comes back to the question of translatability. Abolition thinking comes from the US. How can we use it or translate it in other contexts?

SM Several people are trying to do that. I also wrote an essay titled "Abolitionist Vistas of the Human."[9] In the US, abolition refers to the struggle against slavery. W.E.B. Du Bois famously wrote about "abolition democracy:"[10] after the abolition of slavery during the Civil War, he saw the possibility of the abolitionist coalition as a more general factor of democratization of the South. Angela Davis of course has written about such "abolition beyond abolition,"[11] but also Ruth Benedict, and many others. This is challenging because we need conceptual translation to make it productive in a different situation, like the European one.

9 Sandro Mezzadra, "Abolitionist Vistas of the Human. Border Struggles, Migration and Freedom of Movement," *Citizenship Studies 24*, n. 4, (2020).

10 W. E. B. Du Bois, *Black Reconstruction: an Essay toward a History of the Part Which Black Folk Played in the Attempt to Reconstruct Democracy in America* (New York: Harcourt, Brace and Company, 1935).

11 Angela Davis, *Abolition Democracy: Beyond Empire Prisons and Torture* (New York: Seven Stories Press, 2005).

SK In a sense, *OVERTIME* is also about translating. Allowing different modes of knowing to coexist. Cohabiting in difference. As we explored in our editorial series *OVERTIME PAPERS* Kaprow wanted to dissolve boundaries between life and art, and challenge Western modernity's habit of framing actions and thoughts in normative ways. The happening allowed us to apprehend these ideas through a collective embodied experience that activated non-linear assemblages of temporalities and sensitivities.

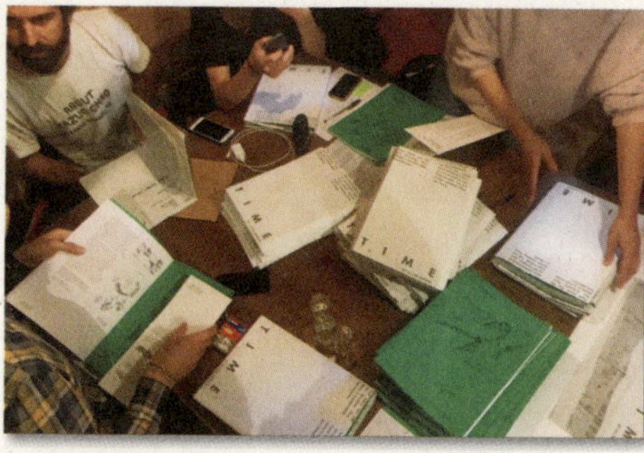

Sophie Krier and Stéphane Verlet-Bottéro, *OVERTIME PAPERS*, 2019. Courtesy of the artists and Lungomare.

SM Yes! There is that wonderful passage by Audre Lorde where she says that one of the most difficult tasks of our life is to experience differences as bridges, not as barriers between us.[12] Once we are not unilaterally focused on walls, borders can also become bridges. Most of the time they are both walls and bridges.

12 Audre Lorde, "The Transformation of Silence into Language and Action" (1977), *Sister Outsider* (Berkeley: Crossing Press, 1984).

↘Sophie Krier

is an artist and researcher, who interweaves biographies of beings and places by conceiving situations for shared reflection. *Undisciplined spaces of learning* conceived over the years include the book series *Field Essays* (2008-ongoing), which aims to make room for listening pauses between practitioners and thinkers; *School of Verticality* (2018-ongoing), a program focussing on "acupuncture of place" that Krier developed in the context of a research residency hosted by Lungomare; and the *Travelling Academy* podcast series and exhibition *In Search of the Pluriverse* (2020-2022) commissioned by Het Nieuwe Instituut and co-curated with Erik Wong. Krier is currently researching presence in soil-based, equine and buddhist practice.

↘Stéphane Verlet-Bottéro

(he/him) is an artist working at the intersection of social practice, installation, writing, gardening and cooking. He is interested in the entanglements of community, materiality, body and place. Based on site-specific research and durational interventions, his practice explores pedagogies of repairing. He co-initiated the collaborative platform *School of Mutants* in Dakar in 2018. Bottéro's work has been exhibited at biennales, museums, and festivals, including ZKM, Karlsruhe; Centre Pompidou Metz; 12th Berlin Biennale; 14th Dakar Biennale; RAW Material Company, Dakar; 12th Taipei Biennial; 7th Oslo Triennale; Le Lieu Unique, Nantes; Het Nieuwe Instituut, Rotterdam; Sheffield DocFest.

↘Sandro Mezzadra

teaches political theory at the University of Bologna and is an adjunct research fellow at the Institute for Culture and Society of Western Sydney University. In the last decade, his work has particularly centered on the relations between globalization, migration, and political processes, on contemporary capitalism, as well as on postcolonial theory and criticism. He is an active participant in the "post-workerist" debates and one of the founders of the website Euronomade (www.euronomade.info). With Brett Neilson, he is the author of *Border as Method, or, the Multiplication of Labor* (Duke University Press, 2013) and *The Politics of Operations. Excavating Contemporary Capitalism* (Duke University Press, 2019). He is currently coordinating the Horizon 2020 project PLUS ("Platforms, Labor, Urban Spaces").

FLUIDS, ORALITIES, SPORES

↘ Wissal Houbabi
IN CONVERSATION WITH Bayo Akomolafe

I like talking about shit, periods, mold, and misery, coming up with cultured, intellectual language, I ape and simulate this kind of speech for the fun of it—even though I don't even have an undergraduate degree. I have a very dirty mouth. Shit, fuck, ass, for fuck's sake, balls, fuck off, screw you, I don't give a shit, all of that, I say it every single day. Writing often involves filtering one's everyday experiences. When writing and analysis reaches the level of pure abstraction, it can become so inorganic that it seems almost like it's been automatically generated. Are humans more technology rather than animals experiencing things? And if so, how can we filter words to create thought?

It feels as though Bayo Akomolafe sees the world the way it presents itself. Even the shape dialogue takes means it's less filtered than writing, which is why I couldn't wait to sit down with someone who not only managed to turn organic complexity into an intellectual reflection but into a veritable living experiment.

WISSAL HOUBABI We now speak of young people as an oppressed category, without considering the even more dramatic position of whoever happens to be a child of the diaspora. It has been said that we're markedly poorer than our parents, with the majority of people facing unaffordable living costs. The climate crisis is making us inadequate to the world. Not only are we terrified of floods, earthquakes, and sweltering heat, we're also stuck with unbearably high prices: in a lot of cities having your own room is becoming a luxury, more and more people have at least two jobs, and being hyper-specialized in something is no shield against poverty. They tell us "the population is aging, have kids," the age at which you're no longer considered a young person goes up every year, justifying exploitation and precarious employment.

The world we know is probably dying, or maybe it's already dead and what we're seeing is it starting to rot. It seems that studying only human history made us forget how intricately connected we are to everything else, even colonial history tells us this.

I come from a town in Morocco that was built after the French found a huge phosphate mine. My grandmother was from around there but she lived in the countryside in Middle Atlas, while my grandfather moved there from the south to find work. My dad says he was born in a *nouvelle construction* district. My grandfather's generation died early because phosphate toxins contaminated the water. Kidney cancer was the most common cause of death. My dad's generation is famous for having black teeth—everyone in Khouribga, where my grandparents lived, does.

My people are children of the diaspora.

Talking about these nuances is hard when migration is described as being "economic" or for "international protection," and it's hard when we don't take the long view of migration. How can we combat political and institutional narratives that funnel all the complexities and pain of the world into an assiduously imperialist view?

[At the conference] yesterday you were talking about viruses, and I was reflecting on what Diaspora means. In the West, we're thought of as a contamination, something to be afraid of. People use words like "invasion" and "ethnic replacement," but sometimes thank us for our perspectives because we can look beyond their blind spots. We're not, and we won't ever be, "normal": We're exceptional or we're monsters, we're foreign bodies "attacking" the West...

BAYO AKOMOLAFE There's a sense in which the nation-state, the Westphalian order and its passive aggressive semi-permeable borders, the presumption of a free market and the paradigm of the neoliberal individual are flailing in the turbulence of material worlding events. Just like you say, younger people today are living in times of spending cuts, the atrophy of safety nets, the vilification of migrancy, and the consolidation of power in corporations. It's increasingly difficult to make a living under these circumstances. It's even more difficult when you're an immigrant living in centers of power that depend on extractive relationships with your homelands. The pressure to fit in, to be included, to present a friendly face, to deny the losses that are threaded through your flesh, and to move on and make a life, might feel overwhelming.

Giorgio Agamben popularly noticed how the modern State is dependent on the ironic sustenance of "bare life," which it aims to transform into the "good life," the extraction of which provides the justification for the continuance of Statehood. Ursula K. le Guin's story[1] of the depraved child living beneath the utopian Omelas is yet another way to frame this painful cyclicity of minefields and exploded bodies. As the gates of our global system tremble in the face of fierce upheavals, I expect that some operations will "brace" up, dig in further to protect their senses of the familiar, and keep churning the war machines that blacken our teeth and silence our songs.

1 Ursula K. Le Guin, "The Ones Who Walk Away from Omelas," *New Dimensions*, vol. 3, (1973).

In this way, our modern order depends on these losses to feed itself. Even a politics of inclusion seems like a violent reinstatement of the conditions that produce irradiated, appropriated, displaced bodies. What we might need then is a different kind of politics—one that knows how to cultivate loss as one cultivates delicacies from pathogens.

WH I started thinking about what orality means. Often, written history betrays the nuances of perspectives—it's written by the winners, so the losers and the disarmed miss out. I started writing poetry in Italian because I gave this part of my experience to writing and to literature. I started to need to express some ideas that could only come out in my mother tongue, so embraced its exotic appeal and then began thinking again, wondering whether this was something I actually like? Where am I? I thought people who write poems should reflect on the language they use, especially if they embody many languages, and they should analyze and manipulate the linguistic substance. Get to know the secrets of phonetics and return to music. In poems, I fit Italian words into the structure of Moroccan grammar. A close friend of mine told suggested Moroccan because the oral dialect is always in tension and in motion across time. That's why he call it a dialect, rather an incredibly modern language (in a good way). It's a language that swallows up just about anything, and doesn't seem to have a way to express the idea of "coining" new terms because it doesn't actually have a fixed vocabulary.

I recently read that the alphabet was imported by colonizers into lots of languages in Africa. The colonizers wanted to dominate the local language so they could manipulate the local population as much as possible. Not only was the Bible the only book translated into languages which had never even been written down before (which is quite an interesting thing in and of itself, if you ask me), but they tried to work closely with the local intellectual elite to mediate not just language but deeper meaning as much as they could.

Allow me to quote two articles I found in the Italian National library at the ISIAO archive:[2]

> [...] *just as civil institutions gradually come to reach the most primitive populations, the most barbaric languages farthest removed from the Western world gradually evolve following contact with European languages. The history of civilization can be thought of as the history of the evolution of language: everywhere the creation of new ideas goes hand in hand with the creation of new ways of expressing oneself.*
>
> *Lots of African languages have already been changed. This began when languages which had only ever been transmitted orally, shifting as each generation passed, were given an alphabet by the Europeans.* [...] *giving a language an alphabet doesn't just mean recording it, it means making it become fixed, and therefore means carrying out an action on the language.*
>
> Vol. 1 - *Evoluzione dei linguaggi indigeni a contatto della civiltà* by Martino Mario Moreno (Turin 1892 - Rome 1964), Italian diplomat and orientalist.
>
> *Colonizing Africa ramped up the military and political power of the dominating country, contributed to its economic wellbeing and gave an outlet—as in our case—for the healthy fruitfulness of the bloodline, and was also a supremely Christian civilizing mission, for which we bear responsibility before God and before history. Now, to influence the life and soul of the natives, to redeem them from the low state in which many of them find themselves, to lead them to progress, understanding them, getting a clear idea of their psyche which is far more complex than we think, is vital; and to do this it is first necessary to know their languages, which are the*

2 ISIAO - l'Istituto Italiano per l'Africa e l'Oriente (Italian Institute for Africa and the Orient).

true, genuine, deep expression of the soul. Without this knowledge, as those who have experience of it know, a gulf will stand between our officials, staff, and our missionaries and their subjects, they would hold no sway over them, could not give rise to any of the intimate motions which gradually bring the native masses closer to their rulers, create discipline, make them diligent, make them glad of the new civilized life brought to them.

Vol. 2 - *Funzione sociale e politica dei linguaggi*
by Francesco Beguinot (Paliano 1879 - Naples 1953)
Italian orientalist and Berberologist.

I think this is an under-examined perspective, the blending of language—we reflect on thought a lot, but not on language. How can we create thoughts that truly stand outside any paradigm if we focus increasingly on semantically clean, pure, intellectual, Western languages that are internationally recognized? A language that's less organic, less accented, less recognizable to local communities, unable to contradict itself? I started to think of Italian and Moroccan as a toxic relationship, in which my mother tongue brought me care, family, domesticity, but not productivity. Whereas Italian, to me, felt like my father tongue, something I can use to leave my home, use to sit an interview, use to bring money home, and helps me to think logically and use reason.

Why is it that even in Italy, decolonial thought tends to favor imperialist languages? Why is it that even decolonial thought is a Western product? How does decolonial thought relate to our original spoken languages?

BA I grew up in a Yoruba household and culture that straddled tense lines (or rather electrical wires!) between the functional respectability of the English tongue and the vernacularity of our local languages. Yoruba is a very tonal language; it finds its rhythms in how a word is sung, much less in how it is written. We had oral narratives and complex systems that enabled storytellers like *griots* and the *gangan* drummers to thrive. If you've ever seen the Yoruba talking drum being played, you might begin to understand the marvelous traditions that were once the technologies of our homemaking rituals.

However, language is a post-humanist phenomenon. We speak "with-in;" we speak like our environments and our environments become shaped by our languages in return. As our worlds become marked, tracked, scorched, flattened, inflamed, boxed in, archived, assembled, and surveilled, our gestures change as well—and language becomes a very hard and gritty thing, useful for pointillist purposes... for affirming how separate and sovereign we are in our modern subjectivities.

I remember being taught—whether explicitly or implicitly—that my language was no good, that to be sophisticated was to abandon the local and desire the far-away. I remember learning "Received Pronunciation," the standardized British way of speaking English. We watched BBC newscasters speak their language, endlessly fascinated by them, and slowly distanced from the mercuriality of the Yoruba language and its rich oralities.

Coloniality is the persistence of a grammar of being that works by seeking to subsume other logics into its own rationality. It's a parenthetical remark pretending to be the full sentence. It's not as totalizing as it seems. This is the reason why I believe that in seeking to upend a violent regime of control, one risks plenty in the attempt to overthrow it. One risks plenty in trying to win. One risks plenty in trying to make a point. Points don't do much except perforate the page. The thing to do is to trace out wandering lines of flight, to sing, to tremble, to experiment with speaking that does not collapse at the gilded feet of intelligibility, to travel.

WH I was thinking about a book I came across a few years ago which talked about human evolution and about how, often, opposable thumbs are used to prove evolution. However, few people see menstruations as something just as important to mark evolutional watersheds, maybe due to the fact history is often narrated from a male perspective. They say that not only was menstruation the first way of recognizing a cycle and therefore of establishing a place in time, but it also has the huge power to make visible how humans are interdependent: when women spend time together, their menstrual cycles line up. Our body purifies itself by shedding blood. It's not only bound up with our reproductive cycle, but also a ritual the body does for its own ends. When we realized this cycle was linked to fertility, or rather that blood can represent power, men started to "simulate" this bloodletting. Therefore, it seems that a man's need to produce blood originates from the unresolved powerlessness he feels towards nature.

It's incredible that blood is associated with values caused by fear and powerlessness: the one drop rule, how a single drop of blood was enough to identify Blackness and require segregation, or blood purity being used to justify hunting Moors in Spain, blood requiring to be "Christian." It seems crazy, but this still goes on. *Jus Sanguinis* is how people are branded "natives" by birth, automatically entitling them to civil and political rights and social privileges. Blood is fluid so I can't help but wonder why it's fluid blood that we use as a tool for crystallization and oppression, rather than one of the more solid organs.

BA Modernity is defined by fixed identitarian particularities. Its fetish is the individual, the dissociated individual who is cut off from ecological flows and events. This is how it lives—by situating the citizen as a thing apart. By reducing becoming to identity. By refusing to see in terms of the monster and its errant multiplicities instead of as a thing to be discarded or benevolently rehabilitated. As such, fluid processes are encoded as propertied features one has: the impurity of blood, the hue of one's skin tone; the size of one's nose.

What modernity tries to exteriorize is the possibility that identity is fugitive; what it does with borders and walls is to assert its right to surveillance. The hope for a different world rests in our becoming opaque.

Conclusion

Wrapping up, Bayo Akomolafe using the term "opacity" is meaningful. It's an intellectual lens that keeps expanding[3] thanks in part to the crucial observation of Édouard Glissant[4]: transparency as a founding value keystone value of Western modernity creates standards, categories, ranges, and verdicts. It's as though the West's strongest poison is really its need to know and to control everything. And maybe by "civilization" we mean its exact opposite.

3 *Museo delle Opacità* (Roma: Museo delle Civiltà, 2023). https://www.paesesera.toscana.it/museo-delle-civilta-museo-delle-opacita-bertina-lopes-dal-6-giugno-2023/, accessed 22 April 2023.

4 See: For Opacity, Édouard Glissant, https://www.jackie-inhalt.net/reh/bilder/edouard-glissant-for-opacity.pdf, accessed 18 April 2023.

↘ Bayo Akomolafe

is a philosopher, transnational intellectual, and poet born of Yoruba parents in Western Nigeria. In 2021, he received the New Thought Walden Prize, intended for young thinkers who offer surprising new insights into the global crisis. He teaches at Pacifica Graduate Institute, California, and the University of Vermont, Burlington, USA. In July 2022, he was appointed Global Senior Fellow of the Othering and Belonging Institute at the University of California, Berkeley, where he acts as a "resident provocateur." Also in 2022, Akomolafe became a Senior Fellow of the New Institute in Hamburg, Germany. He lives in Chennai, India, with Ej, his life partner and their children Alethea Aanya and Kyah Jayden Abayomi.

↘ Wissal Houbabi

is an artist, performer and independent writer born in Khouribga, Morocco. Through her work, Houbabi explores various fields: from researching hip-hop feminism to writing short stories that explore the condition of diasporic culture. Poetry for her is a field for experimentation, she tries to break the meshes of linguistics and poetic language and interrogate the relationship between languages and dialects, sounds and meanings by using words as clay. Among her performances is *La Muta* with Vittorio Zollo. She has created workshops, paths, and poetry projects with various cultural and artistic institutions, including IUAV, Mudec, and ERT. Houbabi is the author of the installation *phonomuseum_rome* at Museo delle Civiltà (Rome) and part of the exhibition *L'Offesa* on Lucia Marcucci at Ar/Ge Kunst (Bolzano).

TO NO ONE BUT US

↘Binta Diaw
IN CONVERSATION WITH Justin Randolph Thompson

The following letter with artist Binta Diaw is a first gesture towards positioning and fixing the current moment within a continuous exchange. I have been in dialogue with Diaw since the end of 2019 as a friend, a mentor, and peer. When she asked that I write to her about my own understanding of the word and concept of belonging, I thought that it was apt that I take some time teasing out the meaning of this word on a personal level. It became apparent from the outset that this could not be done without additionally paying attention to its meaning as deployed through the context of DEI (Diversity, Equity, Inclusion) initiatives where the desire for belonging is troubled by the many articulations of self congratulating in relation to doing what intends to be normative work. It was also evident that I could not address these ideas without grounding them in my experience as shaped by being born into US society, with all of its insularity. Crucial, however, as well, was to speak to the parallels, contrasts, and contradictions provided by spending more than half of my life (all of my adult life) in Italy.

Florence, Italy, 23 March 2023

Dear Binta,

In order to begin, the following passage from Aimé Césaire on diasporic perceptions of homeland and the unpaved routes of return is intended to set the tone about collective responsibility.

> *The singularity of our history, constructed out of terrible misfortunes that belong to no one else.* [...] *What else can be the result of this but that our paths toward the future—all our paths, political as well as cultural—are not yet charted? That they are yet to be discovered, and that the responsibility for this discovery belongs to no one but us?*[1]

I was born and raised, shaped perhaps, within one context of racialized surround[2] only to spend my formative years of adult life in another separate, yet mutually informed, entrapment of forced cultural estrangement. Moten's reflection on the surround is anchored in a rendering visible all of those forms of coloniality employed to deter fugitivity while feigning a sense of protection. As someone highly critical of the violence inherent in careless use of ideas that reproduce seemingly innocuous, or even worse, benevolent facades of social value, I am constantly troubled by, and concerned with, the

1 Aimé Césaire, Clayton Eshleman, Annette Smith, *Notebook of a Return to the Native Land* (Middletown, CT: Wesleyan University Press, 2001).

2 Stefano Harney, Fred Moten, *The Undercommons: Fugitive Planning & Black Study* (Wivenhoe: Minor Compositions, 2013).

actual meaning embedded in the words we choose to speak, or to write. The precariousness of fixity in the written word, appearing at first glance to blanket all, to provide a streamlined and simplified perception, to posit easily obtainable shortcuts, guides me towards an ambiguity that is necessary if any conversation is to be had beyond the oft gratuitous and self-gratifying surface. In leaning towards ambiguity as a means for unmooring tired or overused meaning, it is crucial to be aware of what writer Ralph Ellison eloquently, yet bluntly alludes to, stating that "some things are just too unjust for words, and too ambiguous for either speech or ideas." It is in observance of such things that I turn to art, seeking approaches to articulation that have the capacity to prevaricate speech itself and the formation of ideas. It is grounded in this positioning that I have shaped my reflections on belonging. It does feel that the responsibility of conjuring and holding the true meaning, or what this word might be able to provide us within dialogue, belongs to no one but us.

I have always looked with concern at notions of "belonging" when they are positioned as objectives. I am brought to reflect upon all of the work, violence, and epistemicide that have been so key to historical and art historical marginalization and exclusion. Against this carefully constructed backdrop of non belonging, a space has been carved out that is a perpetual liminal site of inequity. From this vantage point, the articulation of this word and the deployment of its subverted power, place its meaning typically as voiced by some hypothetical "in" group to which those strategically positioned beyond its borders are understood as seeking access. This transforms belonging, when sought after, into a seeking of something that you have simply been told is not yours. What does it mean to pursue belonging? Who is tasked with this? Who is positioned in a way to not have to reflect upon this at all?

Can it be said that any sense of belonging necessitates the formation of borders, limitations, pre-requisites or assumptions? I believe that the surround that raised and shaped me, much like the entrapment that forms my current reality, are carriers of these borders, providing a sense of belonging through the familiarity that they represent, yet keeping tabs on what it means to truly fit.

Beyond these considerations I have a great appreciation for what associate professor of classical literature at Princeton University, Dan El Padilla Peralto, posits as a crucial question in relation to notions of citizenship and belonging. Rooted in his critical work that problematizes the premise of the study of "the Classics" and, perhaps more centrally in relation to his own biography as someone who experienced being "undocumented" in the US, he asks if there is a framework for citizenship that is not predicated on exclusion? Is citizenship, which oft alludes to nationally constructed ideas of belonging, by nature a practice of exclusion? Padilla Peralto, in a lecture delivered at the YBCA (Yerba Buena Center for the Arts) 100 Summit in 2016, dedicated to art and activism, reflects upon the nature of paperwork determining the outcome, safety and well being of individuals in the world and their mobility. Conscious of the privileges of citizenship, it is still important to think about the ways in which this acceptance on behalf of the state fails to protect many of us from the forms of estrangement that are generative of different classes of citizens even within the same nation. If a national framework of belonging is one within which many who have been systematically excluded seek belonging, then perhaps the perpetuity of this cycle of exclusion is a prerequisite for the safety and security that the state says it provides to its citizens.

I offer all of these considerations to you in response to your invitation to dialogue with you about belonging in hopes that it may be a helpful point of departure for our ongoing exchange. I am quite aware of the ways in which my perspective has been informed by my upbringing as a citizen of the United States of America who was free to move into the Italian context free from many of the legal limitations that are faced by many. It is my hope that the words written above are reflective of this position, critical of all of the things that have contributed to my own vision or rejection of belonging, and truthful to the realities shared by us as well as those which can never be mutual.

With gratitude,
Justin

The following words are my response to my dear friend and mentor Justin, who kindly accepted my invitation to share thoughts and personal experiences on the notion of belonging. One of the reasons why I asked to Justin to join me in the conversation is because of his fascinating way of letting people, especially black people, feel always at home and listened to.

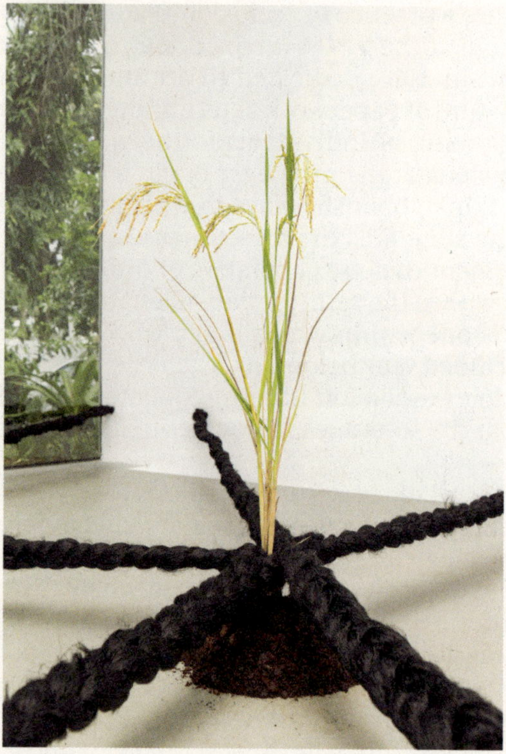

Binta Diaw, *Dïà s p o r a*, 2021 (detail), extension hair, iron wires, soil, rice plants and seeds, site-specific installation. Courtesy of the artist and Galerie Cécile Fakhoury, photo by Issam Zejly.

Dakar, Senegal, 14 April 2023

Dear Justin,

How are you?

I am writing to you in response to your intense letter of reflection. Unlike you, I start by saying that what I am about to write to you will be contextualized between Europe and Africa from a diasporic perspective. My biography and practice as an artist has always tried to open up a window or a reflection on belonging. During the last year, I needed to reconnect to my motherland. Senegal has always had an attractive energy that was calling me. It is about a call.

When you grow up, as a black woman, in a European context, you are in a systemic identity conflict. Who am I? Where do I come from? Where can I be myself? All of these questions followed me from my childhood to now. Today, I have finally anchored myself somewhere. This somewhere can be understood as a place, a smell, or a person. I can be and feel who I am wherever I am. It is no longer about where... it is more about movement. Stuart Hall affirmed:

> *I knew both England and Jamaica well, but I belonged to neither. This is precisely the experience of the diaspora, far enough from the sense of exile and loss and close enough to be able to understand the enigma of an always deferred attainment.* [3]

3 Stuart Hall, *Il soggetto e la differenza. Per un'archeologia degli studi culturali e postcoloniali* (Rome: Meltemi, 2006).

Binta Diaw, *Paysage Corporel V*, chalk on cotton paper, 2019-ongoing. Courtesy of the artist and Galerie Cécile Fakhoury.

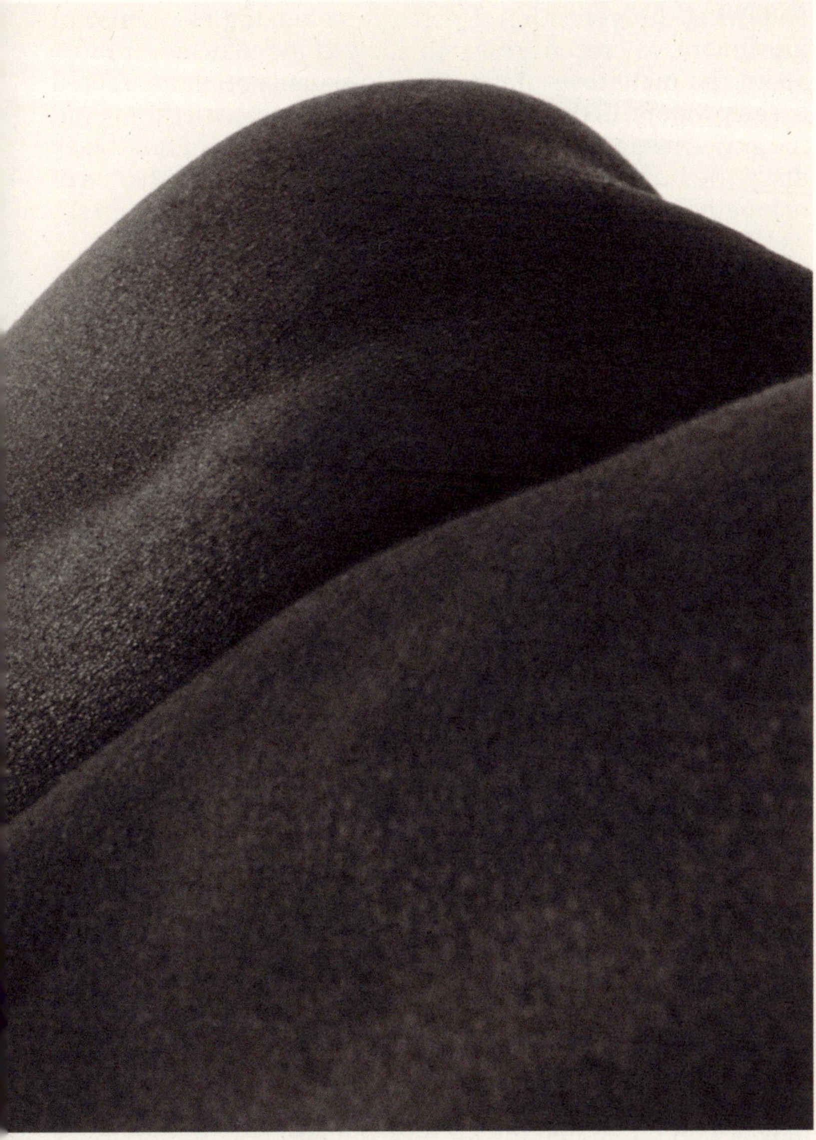

Following this reflection, I perceive belonging as a sense of movement. My recent research allowed me to discover more about the mangroves: immense ecosystems of plants rooted in salty waters, in the soil and in strict contact with the air and the sky. This physical state of Being reminds me of how black diasporic bodies today face the possibility and the chance of belonging to different strata of our contemporary human societies and communities.

Through these plants, I opened up some reflections about the possibility of being rooted despite the movement, or rather, thanks to it. This sense of being rooted is the security of being part of somewhere or someone. This security can be associated with how we (as black diasporic bodies) can speak and communicate through different languages, pronunciations, sounds and gestures. Another aspect I found really interesting about mangroves is their capacities for solidarity in growing, breathing and changing themselves and the environment around them together. This sense of collectiveness can explain how minorities in Europe must strive to survive, to stay alive together.

Amongst the numerous Wolof sayings, I would like to share this: *Nit nitay garabam*. The human being is the cure for human beings. Let's analyze the word *garab*, which means both tree and medicine in Wolof. We can understand how this language's complexity and visual poetics, like many other African or Aborigine languages, can relate humans to Nature and vice versa.

This primordial relation between the human world and the natural one reminds me of some readings from my project *Collective Practices: A Living Experience of Feeling Listened* at Lungomare in Bolzano. I remember being very confused and curious about this city and its territories. From some exchanges and meetings, I heard about an important political and controversial figure: Alexander Langer. He was a change maker who fascinated me for his vanguard positioning in his complicated and fragmented society and community, the Südtirol, today known as South Tyrol (Alto Adige in Italian), the most northern Province of Italy and as Trentino-Alto Adige one of the twenty regions in Italy. He is one of the first who denounced the difficulties of accepting human diversity on different levels in Italy and posed the question of the notion of *Heimat* within new meanings: no longer a refuge in terms of ethnicity, but a place of participation and sharing of environmental, economic and social choices. From this perspective, there is no doubt that the legacy of Langer's thought is still today a precious resource in any discourse on autonomy, belonging and coexistence.

Returning to some of your words, I've been attracted by two in particular: marginalization and exclusion. I think it is clear that I connect the notion of belonging to a collective form of being and existing. Still, I think reflecting on how belonging can bring a sense of marginalization and alienation is essential. Reconsidering my thoughts, I acknowledge how belonging can be difficult to find or not accessible. So, from here, why is it necessary to define or give a written definition of a word that can sound different for each of us?

I end my thoughts with this question and the necessity to understand belonging as movement, and movement as an act of liberation.

Here my reflections, written in one take.

I am glad you joined me.
Yours,
Binta

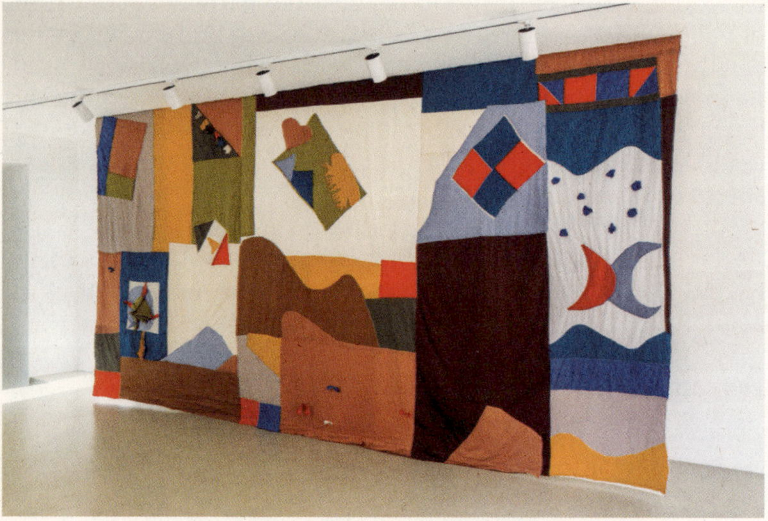

Binta Diaw, *Collective Practices: A Living Experience of Feeling Listened*, 2021, photo by Luca Guadagnini. Courtesy of the artist and Lungomare.

↘ Binta Diaw

is a visual artist based in Milan, Italy, originally from Senegal. Cherishing intersectional interpretation of strictly framed narratives, Diaw dedicates piratical and theoretical resources to challenge artistic legitimacy and reimagine social belonging, to open up modes of displaying and unravelling colonial outcomes. Gesturing to these premises, Diaw slips history in *(her)* stories. She studied fine arts at Brera Academy of Fine Arts in Milan and at ÉSAD in Grenoble. Her work has been exhibited internationally in institutions and galleries such as the Liverpool Biennale; the 12th Berlin Biennal; Magasin CNAC in Grenoble; Galerie Cécile Fakhoury in Paris, France and Abidjan, Côte d'Ivoire; and the 13th Rencontres de Bamako—African Biennale of Photography in Mali. Diaw has received numerous awards such as the Prix Carta Bianca (2022), the PART-Rimini Award (2022) and the Bourse arts plastiques de la ville de Grenoble (2020).

↘ Justin Randolph Thompson

is an artist, cultural facilitator, and educator who works between Italy and the USA. His life and work seek to deepen the discussions around socio-cultural stratification and the arrogance of permanence by fostering projects that connect academic discourse, social activism, and DIY networking strategies. Since 2016, Thompson has been a co-founder and director of Black History Month Florence and of the research center The Recovery Plan, both existing as a multi-faceted exploration of Black histories and cultures in the context of Italy. He is a recipient of a Creative Capital Award (2022), an Italian Council Research Fellowship (2020), and The Louis Comfort Tiffany Award amongst others. His work and performances have been exhibited widely in institutions, including The Whitney Museum of American Art; Centro de Arte Reina Sofia; The American Academy in Rome; and the Museo MADRE in Naples.

BELONGING: A PERSONAL AND POLITICAL CHOICE

↘ Maxi Obexer
IN CONVERSATION WITH Natalka Sniadanko

The political history of the country you're born in leaves its mark. When I was twenty, I rejected that concept, but then I began to understand how true it is. It makes a difference if I'm born into a swaggering, powerful country which prefers to suppress its misdeeds and feeling of shame for said misdeeds. Or if I'm part of what we call a minority which has to, one way or another, defend its cultural belonging within itself. Or if I come from a borderland which has never and can never reclaim its sense of its own political and cultural belonging, though this ambiguity can also become its strength and its skill. Considering that contemporary Europe recognizes pluralist societies and recognizes freedom of movement and migration as an obvious reality, the experiences people have in complicated borderlands should be appreciated as trailblazing for the future. The more Europe overcomes national exclusionary policies, the stronger it becomes. The European Union's political model was once regionalism, not nationalism. In some ways this has been forgotten, though in other ways, this is still promoted.

Does the mark left by your background also determine your sense of belonging, or even your national or cultural identity? I don't think so.

Familiarity with the landscape into which you are born leaves its mark on your body and mind. Being a child looking up and seeing mountains, working on steep slopes, looking out over hills and valleys, adapting to mountainous landscapes as my ancestors did, has left a mark. Yet questions of landscape and geography are not nation-specific. There are connections between places across the world where people pick grapes, or work delicately in rough conditions to grow plants and fruits, or raise animals on steep mountainsides. So why do we get attached to our familiarity with a specific piece of land or mountain, or even talk about people belonging to a place-specific community?

We feel kinship with people with similar backgrounds, in our linguistic, communicative, social interactions. I understand people with the same background as me. I know them. I get them. But I don't feel connected to all of them. I feel a sense of belonging with people I'm "connected to," whatever their background. Shared connections to the spiritual universe we live in, literature, music, theater—these matter. Who I feel kinship with is still a personal decision. Especially if I understand this decision as one that I'm free to make.

South Tyrol is a borderland in Italy inhabited by a cultural minority whose identity was once contested. Its language, culture—and through these, its people—were supposed to be dislodged from the country by Mussolini's policy and canceled entirely. Those days are gone now and today, after decades of struggle, its cultural identity is no longer disputed. This means we're also free to question it—or even to cast doubt as to whether it is the identity we've longed for.

> *Everyone seems to agree that we have an identity, or even that we're always looking for an identity. Are we, though? If we are to recognize identity by means of our logic, we must treat difference in the same way. When we're searching, are we searching for differences, or do we just want to keep moving forward and growing?*[1]

French philosopher François Jullien[2] proposes replacing the concept of identity with that of "resource," which he uses to mean fertility. And instead of difference and distinction, he advocates for distance—distance, remoteness and, above all, the liminal. The concept of identity tends to entail fixed ideas and compartmentalization, and it has a hard time keeping visible the simultaneous interconnections between many things,

1 Maxi Obexer, "Europa von den Rändern her denken," Vortrag, Greifswald 2019 (Athens: inter alia, "Kulturelemente" 2020).

2 Francois Jullien, *Es gibt keine kulturelle Identität* (Berlin: Edition Suhrkamp, 2017).

which in my view makes it unusable as a concept. The identitarian movement recently has also made it a problematic concept. I lean more in favor of the idea of responsibility and derive that feeling from the sense of belonging that I freely chose. I feel responsible for the country I feel an affinity to: the country I'm from, but it's also the country I was raised in. I can feel a sense of responsibility for multiple countries, care about them, engage with them. People born in a country and people who've moved there can both take on a sense of responsibility. The sense of belonging is a decision which follows on from responsibility.

Natalka Sniadanko is an author whose works refer to a reality we in Western Europe are largely blind to. The invasion of Ukraine reveals not only the abyss that large-scale imperialist thirst for power and annihilation shows us, but also the blind spots in Western European attitudes.

Natalka Sniadanko has a background in Ukrainian Studies, a subject virtually ignored until recently; even other countries in Europe aren't too familiar with Ukraine as a cultural unit, which suited Russia just fine. They were happy to reinforce that view. Natalka Sniadanko has been working on that topic for many years. She currently lives with her two children in Marbach; her husband is fighting in the war.

At the *Summer School Südtirol*—an interdisciplinary forum—she read from her novel *The First Investigation of the Empress*.[3] The novel is a whistle-stop tour through the political systems of the last two hundred years, highlighting the deep connections across Europe and, incidentally, also describing how Ukraine was founded by Archduke Wilhelm of Austria. He was a dazzling, extravagant, thoroughly queer figure who was also driven by a strong desire for independence.

MAXI OBEXER Natalka, how would you describe your sense of belonging to Ukraine today, in light of the Russian invasion? Has the war changed anything?

NATALKA SNIADANKO I don't think anything has changed in that regard. The war has destroyed other things, like our sense of safety, security, trust in others. The closer war comes, the more deeply you feel it. You can't tell yourself it's happening somewhere else, that it's not happening to you where you are. I believe now that it can happen again anywhere, any time.

MO Now, finally, with Putin's war against Ukraine ongoing, the West sees what is at stake. It's becoming clear that it's not just territorial integrity on the line, but the defense of a country that wants to be free, and that seeks its freedom in its devotion to European rule of law and democracy. Russia is brutally stamping out Ukraine's freedom and independence,

3 Natalka Sniadanko, *The First Investigation of the Empress* (Перше слідство імператриці) (Lviv: Vydavnyt͡stvo Staroho Leva, 2021).

seeking to eliminate Ukrainian culture—which is a European culture. They want to flatten Ukraine completely, following a logic which you believe has a long tradition—the idea that Ukraine should be an agricultural hinterland subordinate to Big Brother Russia. This narrative has had success in the West, too. That's a topic you engage with extensively. What about it is false?

NS Absolutely everything about Russia's post-imperial historical narrative is false. Russia has been trying to eliminate Ukraine as an independent country with its own culture and traditions for centuries. First they banned our language, then tried to shape a primitive folk culture, and then took the more direct route of brutal violence and war, like the one we're going through now. For as long as the West sees Ukraine through a Russian lens—which it still does—this will continue, and other countries will also be at risk. They were silent when the Chechen war broke out, and again when it came to Karabakh, to Georgia, Moldova, and in 2014.

MO Violently suppressing a country using culture and history means the situation for Ukrainians is existential and creates a very different sense of belonging and identification with the country's destiny. Given Putin's attempts to eliminate Ukraine as an independent nation, would you now defend the country's national and cultural identity more strongly?

NS The concept of national identity isn't tainted in Ukraine compared with other countries where it's often led to strong nationalist movements. Which is why its national and cultural identity must be protected. That's always been the case. In terms of the information war, the intellectual sphere, nothing has changed. This war has been going on for centuries and we have to defend ourselves. At the start of the war the Ukrainian president's motto was "it doesn't matter what language you speak." He doesn't say that any more, though—he only speaks Ukrainian now. Ukraine's national and cultural identity used to only be protected by a small circle of Ukrainian intellectuals. The rest of society didn't really care all that much. Now far more people understand the importance of identity, and the language someone speaks absolutely does matter if you live in a country under threat and have an identity under threat.

M XI OBEXE R
A You recently told me your daughter asked you how someone becomes Ukrainian.

NS For many years we've been using the term "political nation" in Ukraine. For a long time, we tried to turn the different regional identities into a homogeneous national ideal, but it was difficult to define "national." The idea of a political nation is much more elastic, and isn't something that's necessarily determined from birth. You can grow up thinking of yourself as a Russian speaker and later think of yourself as Ukrainian, if that's how you feel. The important thing is for it to be a choice, unlike what's happening at the moment with Russian soldiers forcing people in the occupied areas to become Russian citizens.

MO What's changed since then? How connected to Ukrainians feel to their country now?

NS The Crimean Tatars are a good example of how things are going. They were initially in favor of being annexed by Russia and favored a referendum. They even changed their name! Now, they feel Ukrainian. I've heard more than once about Crimean Tatars who've fled and who refuse to speak Russian abroad, even when they can't speak any other languages. In Ukraine, Russian is now the language of the enemy. The killer. That feeling is probably here to stay.

MO You're a writer who grapples with big issues, topics that matter to Ukraine. Ukraine's place in Europe is a key part of that. You tell the story of how Ukrainian culture emerged from the heritage of European history. And you tell a different story while you do so, going beyond the familiar narrative. Tell us about your thinking behind that.

NS I did it because Russian propaganda disputes Ukraine's place as a European country. Its history was erased during the Soviet era and is regularly falsified even now. That's why working through it in literature matters. Russia's attempts to counter Ukraine's independence as a nation of European culture are nothing new—they follow a long tradition.

MO How did Russia do that? How is Putin doing that now?

NS Ukrainian First Lady Olena Zelenska is leading a project seeking out books containing Russian propaganda in the best public libraries across the globe, and they've found an alarming number of books already. Russia invests millions in promoting its propaganda. That's the reason why everyone in Germany knows the name of a Ukrainian nationalist like Bandera but hardly anyone knows the name of any other Ukrainian artists, historians, or politicians.

In the occupied parts of Ukraine, the schools are the first thing the Russians go for. Teachers have to collaborate, on pain of torture. Using Ukrainian in the classroom is banned and pupils have to relearn the whole curriculum, this time in Russian. The German view of Ukraine, too, is shaped by ignorance of the country's cultural and intellectual achievements. They're not invisible—we don't want to see them.

In public dialogue I often ask the audience to name ten Ukrainian artists. How many new books have been published since the war started? Are more historical books about Ukraine's cultural history going to be published now? The Goethe-Institut in Kyiv, incidentally, is managed centrally by the one in Moscow.

MO Your book questions many certainties. First of all, you describe nothing less than the emergence of Ukraine, in a turbulent ride through the political systems—through the monarchy of the Habsburg Empire, nation-building, and the Soviet Union.

For left-wing readers in the West, reading the founding myth of a nation might feel a bit strange—they may even suspect it supports right-wing identity politics. How do you handle that? At lectures and discussions?

NS Like I said, you need to know the context. Ukraine has never been led by a right-wing government. Right-wing parties aren't in Parliament in Ukraine, unlike in Germany. Identity politics in Ukraine is bound up with the struggle to survive, not with the right. We spent decades under a communist dictatorship that styled itself as left-wing, but advocated Russian nationalism—so was actually right-wing. Confusion about the meaning of words is hard to explain here, but it's a simple fact. You can call yourself a Ukrainian patriot even if you grew up speaking Russian—lots of people do. Ukraine isn't a titular nation, it's a political nation in which Ukrainians have equal rights for the first time.

MO You invite your readers to view the cultural emergence of a country as a process that all the movements in Europe were involved in. System change, resistance movements, protests, cultural and artistic movements, all of these played a role. Ideologies and odysseys, delusions of grandeur and downfalls, coincidences and, repeatedly, failure also permeate this process. You describe this historic flow through a daring visionary, who combines the liberation ideals of his time, the man, the Grand Duke, who fights for the foundation of Ukraine, who becomes the founding father for a short time, more by chance than by design, until he finally ends up languishing miserably in Russian prison. How did you come up with this character?

NS I first heard about him in the nineties, when information about him trickled through. After reading Timothy Snyder's book,[4] I couldn't help myself, I had to keep researching. I reached a point when I had to get rid of my obsession, and the way to do that was by writing a book. I simply couldn't miss out on using such great material.

4 Timothy Snyder, *The Red Prince. The Fall of a Dynasty and the Rise of Modern Europe* (London: Random House, 2009).

MO You describe Ukraine's cultural history from the perspective of women. Why? Women's perspective casts light on yet more realities. Do you think it also expresses a different kind of national belonging?

NS In the Soviet Union, patriarchy existed but was very different to the patriarchy in the West. Women had far more rights—they could vote, get an education, do any job and climb to the top of the professional ladder—but had to do all of the domestic work of rearing and caring for children, and looking after their husbands, on top of their professional work. They were invisible and subordinate, despite the rights they had. The patriarchal moral system ran deep. Even women who had successful careers never dared talk about it. I wanted to give them a voice at last. That's what I do in my other books, too.

↘Maxi Obexer

is a writer and playwright from South Tyrol, currently based in Berlin, Germany. Through her practice, she engages in comparative literature, politics, philosophy, and theatre. Obexer teaches dramatic writing at theatres and universities, among them at the Maxim Gorki Theater in Berlin, Literaturhaus Leipzig, Berlin University of the Arts and Dartmouth College, USA. In 2014, with Sasha Marianna Salzmann, she co-founded the New Institute for Dramatic Writing (NIDS) in Berlin, which aims at bringing the social importance of dramatic art to the public consciousness and strengthening diversity within the theatre industry. Some of her plays, such as *Illegale Helfer*, *Gehen und Bleiben*, *Wenn wir lieben*, and *Das Geistershieff* have been publicly acknowledged and translated into English. Her work has been awarded with Robert Geisendörfer Prize, Eurodram Prize, as well as Potsdam Theater Prize and Alice Salomon Poetics Prize.

↘Natalka Sniadanko

is a Ukrainian poet, writer, journalist, and translator. In 2001, Sniadanko published her debut novel, *Collection of Passions*. She has since written seven novels, including *Frau Müller Does Not Wish to Pay More*, which was nominated for the BBC Ukraine's Book of the Year. Her works have been translated into eleven languages, with individual books published in German, Polish, Hungarian, Czech, and Russian. Sniadanko's writing has garnered support from culture and arts foundations in Poland, Germany, Austria, and Hungary through fellowships and grants, such as the Joseph Conrad Korzeniowski Literary Prize. Alongside her literary pursuits, she has worked extensively as a journalist and translated over a dozen books from Polish and German. Her essays and stories have appeared in prominent publications like *The New York Times*, *The Guardian*, and *The New Republic*.

ON SEDIMENTS AND LONGINGS

NOTES OF AN ACCOMPLICE

MARION OBERHOFER

Writing about the sense of "belonging". Ambivalent, to say the least. My word cloud immediately fills up with concepts such as homeland, nation, and "that's how we do things here." And they spark emotions such as disquiet, sorrow, anger, and a feeling of powerlessness. As if that weren't enough, the public narrative on "belonging" is dominated by national and right-wing populist thoughts, while the European Union continues expanding its murderous border-based regime: Who belongs within them, who needs to leave or, rather, who won't we allow in the first place?

When thinking of belonging and the feelings associated with it, I can say the latter aren't easy. It's better to mistrust them—that's my gut reaction. And yet to feel as though you belong and are accepted is a core human need. Being the social creatures that we are, people seek confirmation and yearn for relationships based on trust. To create a coveted or even necessary "feeling of identity," we need social recognition and, well, belonging. Linda Martín Alcoff, a philosopher, claimed that identities constantly contain "ways of life," shared values within a community, links to places, traditions, and historical events, cultural expressions and, ultimately, familial structures.

↘ Marion Oberhofer
works as a curator at the intersection of art and science and is a member of the Lungomare Cooperative. As part of the curatorial team at the Vienna Museum of Science and Technology, she is currently involved in the conception and implementation of the new permanent exhibition on the climate crisis. She also works as an assistant at the /ecm postgraduate Master's Program in Exhibition Theory and Practice at the University of Applied Arts Vienna, focusing on curatorial research and critical theory. As a freelance cultural mediator, she realises projects with various accomplices inside and outside institutional spaces.

In other words, identities aren't concepts set in stone. Rather, identities are defined by the flow of history, change and are changed by this flow, and are threaded in the sociocultural negotiations which sediment in a sense of belonging.

> *In South Tyrol, identity—yet again conceived in ethnic terms—is one of the supreme immaterial values. This is not disputed and hardly a public event goes by (...) without this claim being solemnly stated. So often and so solemnly that the doubt may arise that, sometimes, what are being brandished are "identity prostheses."* [1]

At the heart of Lungomare's curatorial activities lies the task to uncover, dig over, and rethink the sediments in the borderland that is South Tyrol in a critical manner. Art creates a forum conducive to social interactions, joint experiences, dialogues, and cooperation—art offers opportunities to get involved and to create a link with other people, to question cultural and ethnic categories, and to imagine types of belonging, which acknowledge our differences and allow for a divergence of opinions. Art as a testimony to common humanity shows that despite differences, we all experience joy, sadness, love and longing. These experiences can be shared in community-based artistic process in which bodily, local, partial and chronologically anchored knowledge can be activated.

> *Living in the borderlands produces knowledge by being within a system while also retaining the knowledge of an outsider who comes from outside the system. [...] The basic concept involves the ability to hold multiple*

1 Alexander Langer, Siegfried Baur, Giorgio Mezzalira, *Südtirol ABC Sudtirolo* (Merano: Alpha Beta, 2015).

social perspectives while simultaneously maintaining a center that revolves around fighting against concrete material forms of oppression.[2]

I was born in South Tyrol and I was afforded numerous privileges which engendered a sense of "belonging" to this wealthy borderland characterized by its linguistically and culturally diverse landscape. However, what unites me today to so many people working in culture and the arts, ties which go beyond geographical and political borders, is a life which is increasingly more precarious. The resulting feeling? Fear. Fear of precarious working and living conditions, how much we depend on resources granted in the context of projects and government aid, and the often-resulting feeling of being completely overwhelmed. The louder the neoliberal demand for self-responsibility roars, the stronger the feeling of social isolation. Philosopher Judith Butler postulates in her *Notes Toward a Performative Theory of Assembly* that common actions can stand against these painful experiences of individual vulnerability by creating an ethos of solidarity.

Communities should be seen as a verb, meaning that we should practice a sense of community by taking care of one another and acknowledging mutual dependences. An artistic practice which although may only create temporary communities, represents a place of belonging for me, a place where the tangible possibilities of belonging can be explored and tested.

2 Gloria Anzaldúa, *Borderlands: La Frontera: The New Mestiza* (San Francisco: Aunt Lute Books, 2012).

AS IF
16 Dialogues on Sheep,
Black Holes, and Movement

A Lungomare Reader

Edited by
Angelika Burtscher, Daniele Lupo

With an artistic intervention by
Marzia Migliora and Martino Gamper
for the special edition

Graphic design
Lungomare (Chiara Cesaretti)

Translation
ExLibris

Copyediting and proofreading
Sophia Holland

Production assistant
Elisa Del Prete, Kseniia Obukhova

Printing and lithography
Longo, Bolzano

Published by
Spector Books
Harkortstraße 10 04107 Leipzig
www.spectorbooks.com

Distribution
Germany, Austria: GVA, Gemeinsame Verlagsauslieferung Göttingen GmbH&Co. KG, www.gva-verlage.de

Switzerland: AVA Verlagsauslieferung AG, www.ava.ch

France, Belgium: Interart Paris, www.interart.fr

UK: Central Books Ltd, www.centralbooks.com

USA, Canada, Central and South America, Africa: ARTBOOK/ D.A.P., www.artbook.com

South Korea: The Book Society, www.thebooksociety.org

Japan: twelvebooks, www.twelve-books.com

Australia, New Zealand: Perimeter Distribution, www.perimeterdistribution.com

© 2023, authors, editors, Lungomare and Spector Books, Leipzig

First edition: 2023
Printed in Italy
ISBN 978-3-95905-752-3

Project supported by
Directorate-General for Contemporary Creativity by Italian Ministry of Culture, under the Italian Council program (2022)

italianCouncil
Bringing our Contemporary Art to the World

Direzione Generale
Creatività Contemporanea

Autonome Provinz Bozen-Südtirol, Kulturabteilungen / Provincia Autonoma Bolzano-Alto Adige, Uffici Cultura

AUTONOME PROVINZ BOZEN SÜDTIROL
PROVINCIA AUTONOMA DI BOLZANO ALTO ADIGE
PROVINZIA AUTONOMA DE BULSAN SÜDTIROL

Thanks
We thank Frida Carazzato, Marion Oberhofer and Georg Zeller for the collective thinking and sharing of the book idea. Veronika Hackl and Veronika Tauber were wonderful partners for discussing the introduction lines together. The collaboration with Chiara Cesaretti and Elisa Del Prete was very inspiring and supportive. It was a great pleasure to meander the book title together with Amy Francheschini and Lode Vranken.

And a big thank you to all our friends, colleagues and collaborators for this beautiful 20-year journey.
Let's continue this journey together!

IMAGE SELECTION OF PROJECTS CURATED AND PRODUCED BY LUNGOMARE BETWEEN 2003-2023.

IMAGES ON P. 1–11

Olaf Nicolai, *Chartreuse Jeune*, 2010, photo by Andreas Marini.

Can Altay, *Such Claims on Territory, (Studio Virgolo First Fragments)*, 2015, photo by Daniel Mazza. Courtesy ar/ge kunst and Lungomare.

orizzontale, *Public Acts – En plein air*, 2020, photo by Claudia Corrent.

Luna Maurer, **Roel Wouters**, *Proposals for change*, 2018, photo by Ivo Corrà.

Luigi Coppola, *Masses & Motets*, 2013, photo by Daniel Mazza.

Futurefarmers, *A Meander – Act II: (Com)positions with the river*, 2022, photo by Anna Michelotti.

construct lab, *Lungomare Gasthaus*, 2013, photo by Daniel Mazza.

Rosalyn D'Mello, 2021, photo by Lungomare.

Åbäke, **Martino Gamper**, **Alex Rich**, *Trattoria Circolare*, 2013, photo by Daniel Mazza.

Johanna Dehio & **Johanna Padge**, *Fiumicina*, 2022, photo by Elisa Cappellari.

Herwig Turk, *Space for Rivers*, 2023, photo by Elisa Cappellari.

FLUX Fragments, Exhibition, 2023, photo by Elisa Cappellari.

Maruša Sagadin, *City Twin Leiter*, 2013, photo by Daniel Mazza.

Binta Diaw, *Collective Practices: A Living Experience of Feeling Listened*, 2021, photo by Luca Guadagnini.

Can Altay, *Radical Hospitality, Studio Virgolo Second and Third Fragments*, 2014, photo by Daniel Mazza. Courtesy ar/ge kunst and Lungomare.

orizzontale, *Public Acts – En plein air*, 2020, photo by Claudia Corrent.

Ei Arakawa, **Nikolas Gambaroff**, *FI VE SH IL LI NG SF OR AF UR CO AT*, 2009, photo by Christian Fusco.

Shilpa Gupta, *Don't see Don't hear Don't speak*, 2009, photo by Christian Fusco.

Can Altay, *Split Horizon*, 2014, photo by Daniel Mazza. Courtesy ar/ge kunst and Lungomare.

Utopia Europa, 2016, photo by Daniel Mazza.

IMAGES ON P. 296–304

Sophie Krier, *School of Verticality – Weaving Gardens*, 2018, photo by Jörg Oschmann.

Sophie Krier, *School of Verticality – Breaking Bread*, 2018, photo by Jörg Oschmann.

Johanna Dehio & **Johanna Padge**, *Fiumicina*, 2022, photo by Elisa Cappellari.

Sööt/Zeyringer, *Semiotics of the River*, 2022, photo by Elisa Cappellari.

Beatrice Catanzaro, **Kolar Aparna**, *You are but you are not*, 2017, photo by Ivo Corrà.

orizzontale, *Co-Carts*, 2020, photo by Claudia Corrent.

Luigi Coppola, *Masses & Motets*, 2013, photo by Daniel Mazza.

etwas läuft falsch / qualcosa non va, 2021, photo by Daniel Mazza.

Nikolay Oleynikov, *Learning Mural*, 2013, photo by Daniel Mazza.

Sophie Krier, **Stéphane Verlet-Bottéro**, 2022, *OVERTIME Screening*, photo by Elisa Cappellari

etwas läuft falsch / qualcosa non va, 2021, photo by Daniel Mazza.

Futurefarmers, *A Meander – Act III: Sound-Festival for the Elephant*, 2023, photo Elisa Cappellari.

Symbolic Actions for our Present, 2011, photo by Lungomare.

Johanna Dehio & **Marjolein Houben**, *Fiumicina*, 2022, photo by Elisa Cappellari.

Luna Maurer, **Roel Wouters**, *Proposals for change*, 2018, photo by Ivo Corrà.

Courtesy of all photos:
the artists and Lungomare

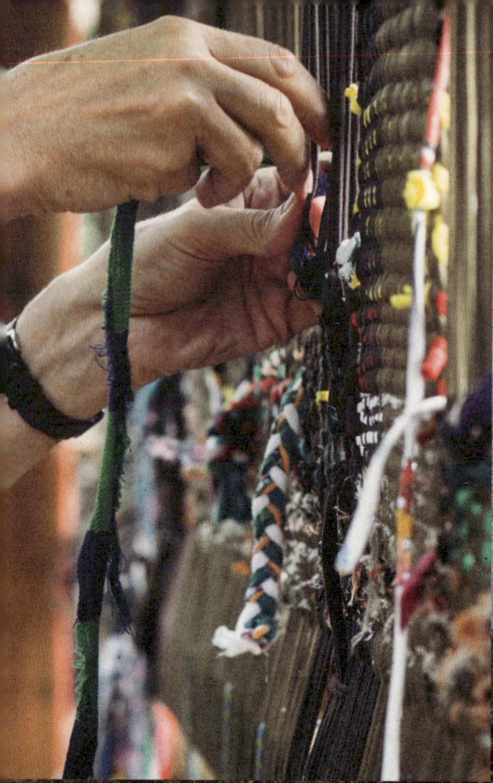
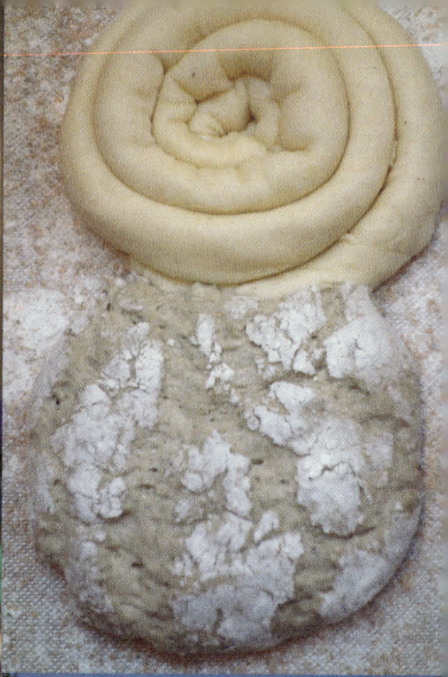
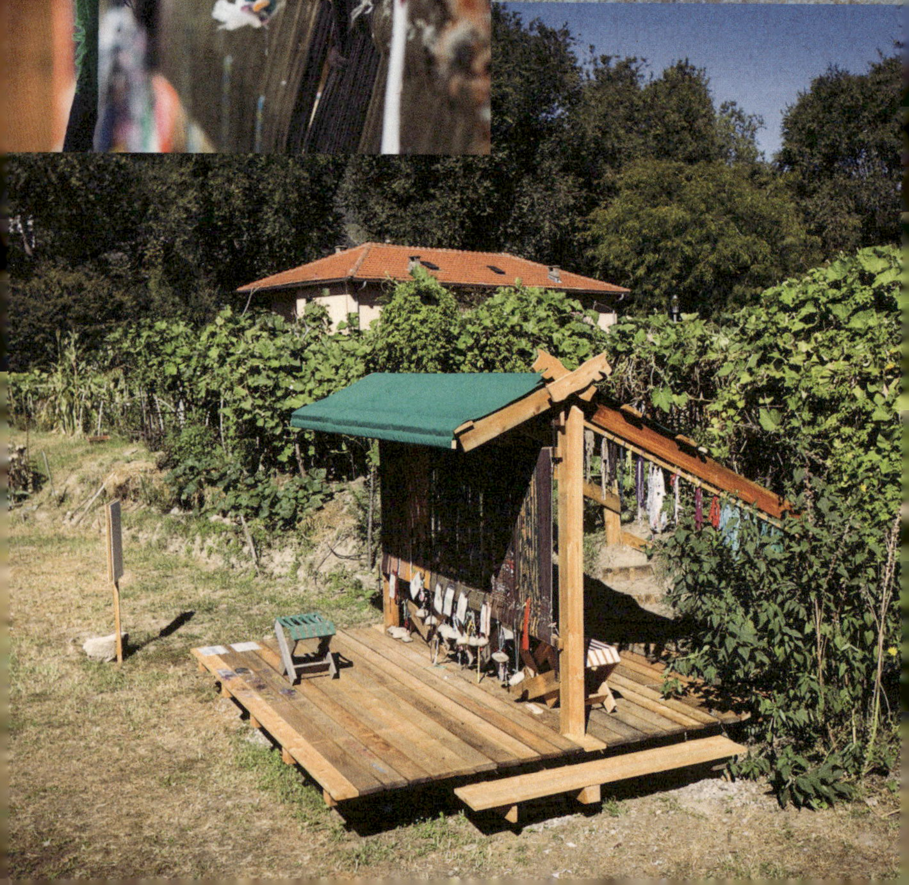

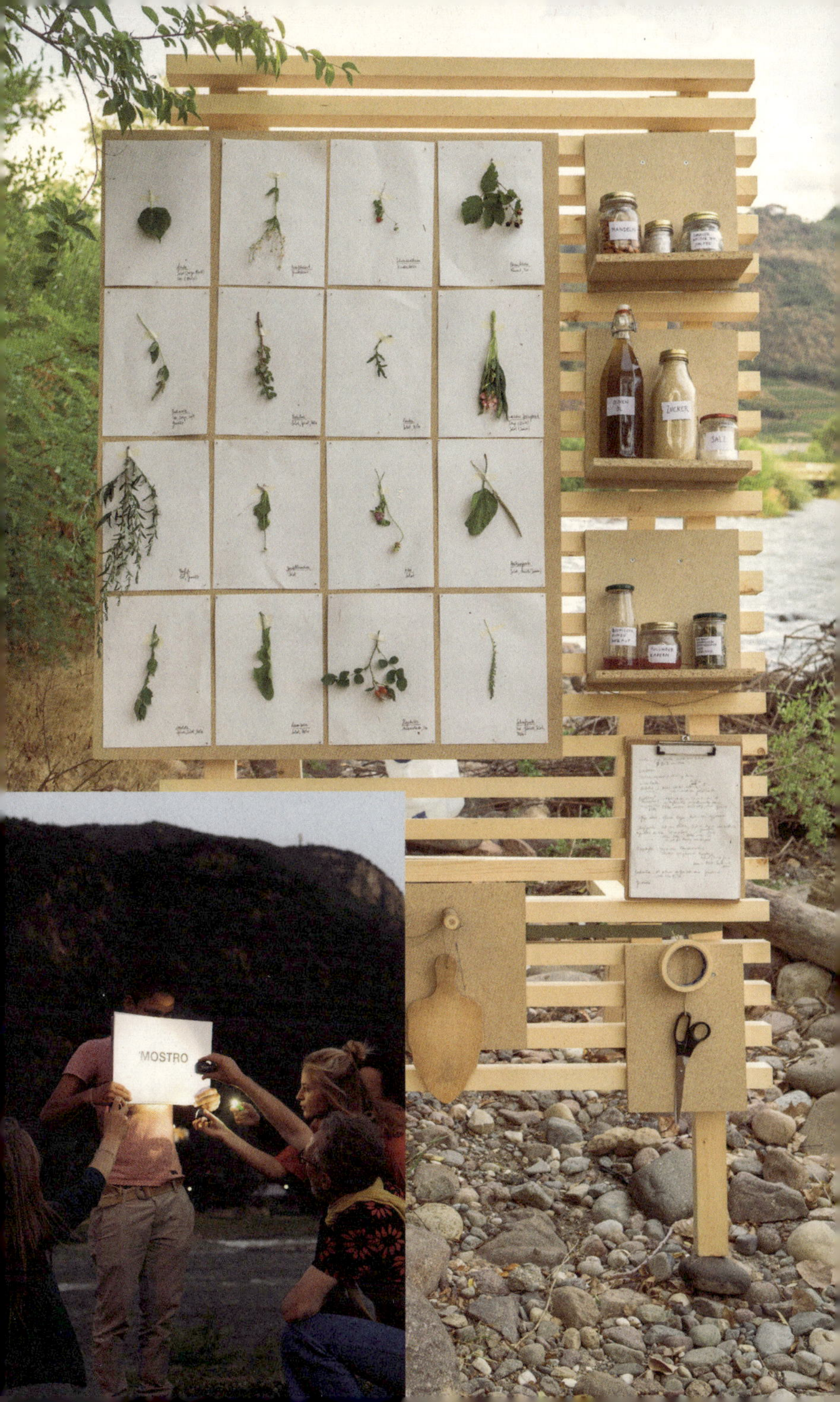
MANDELN
ZUCKER
MOSTRO

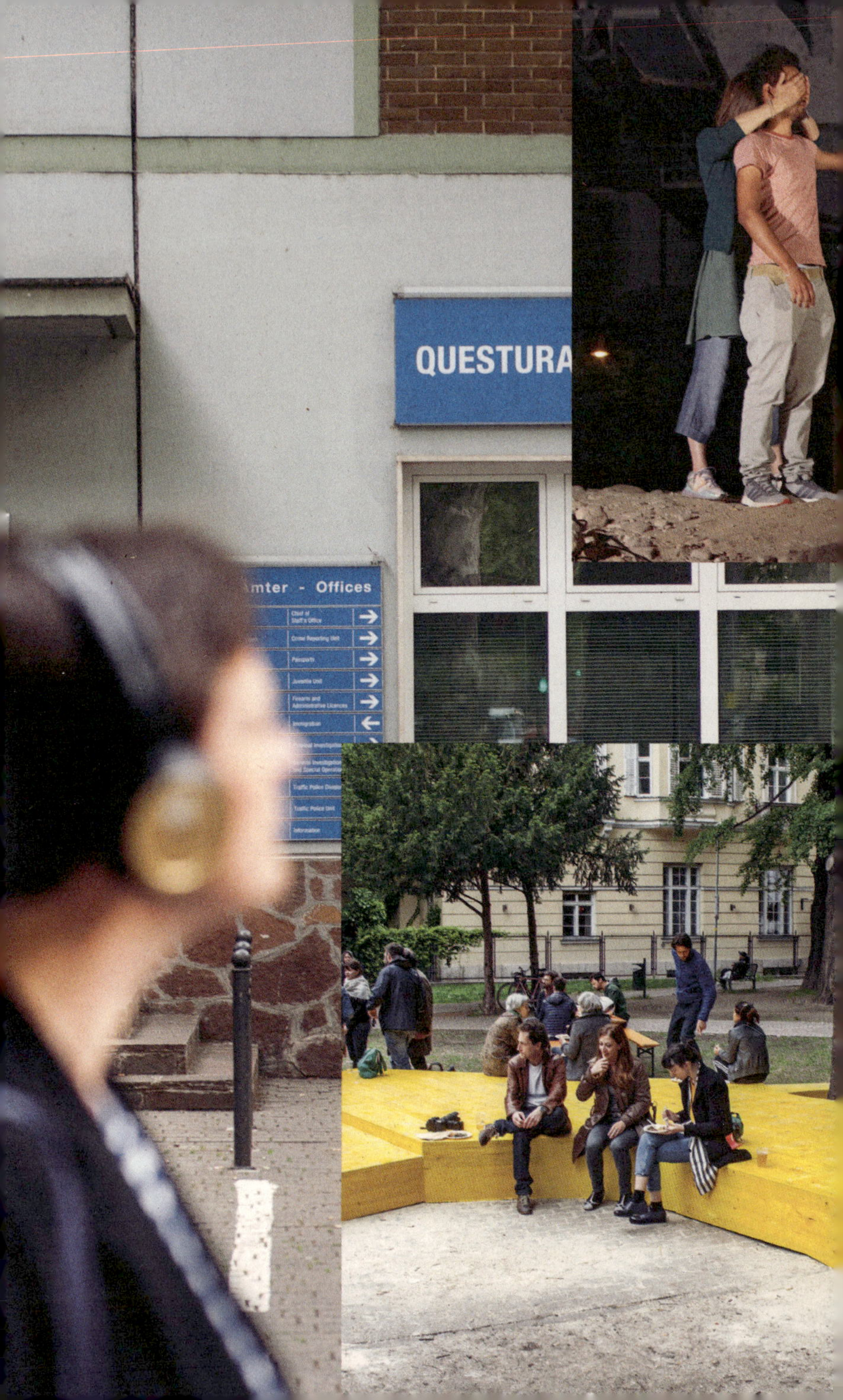
QUESTURA
mter - Offices

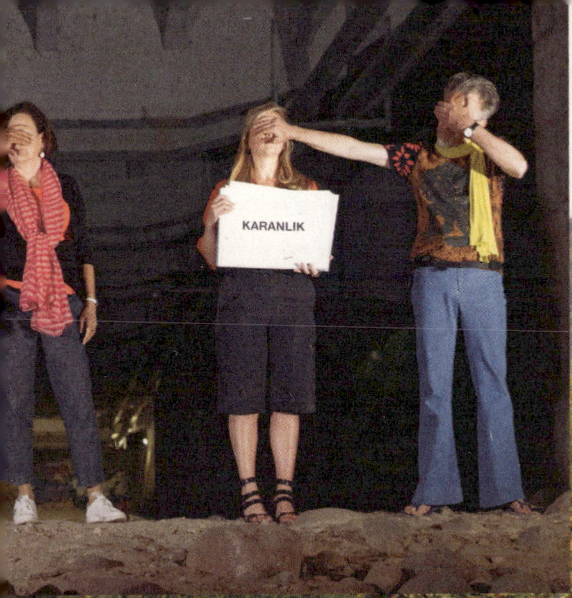
KARANLIK

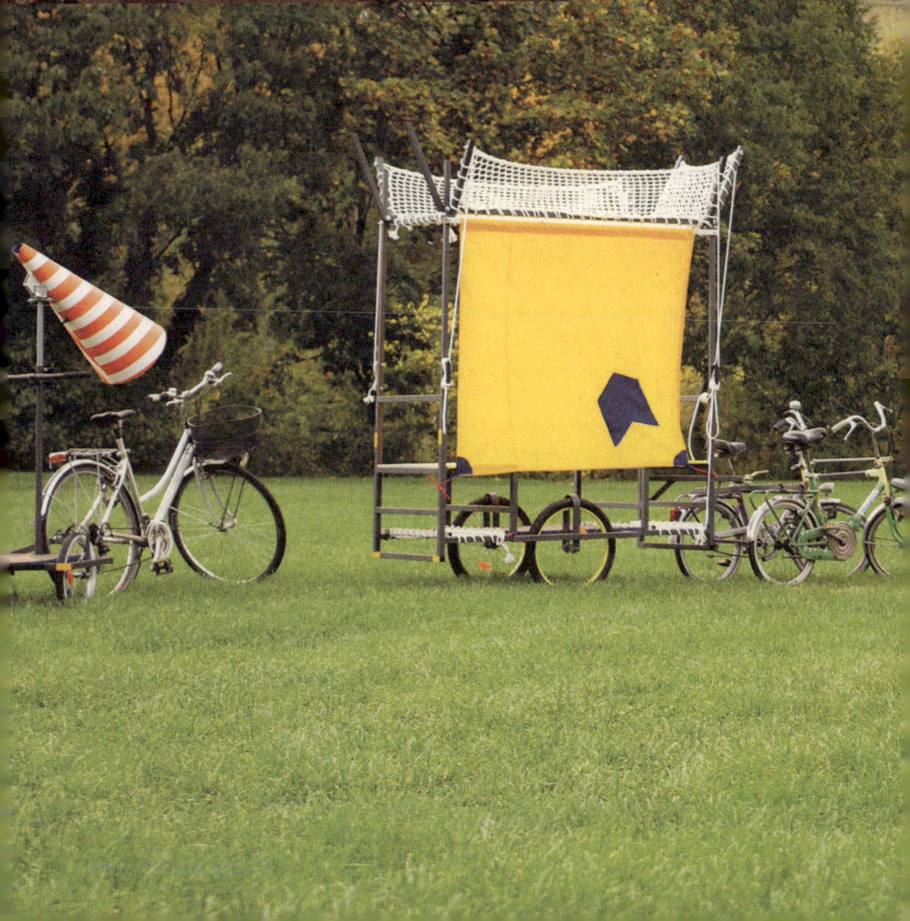

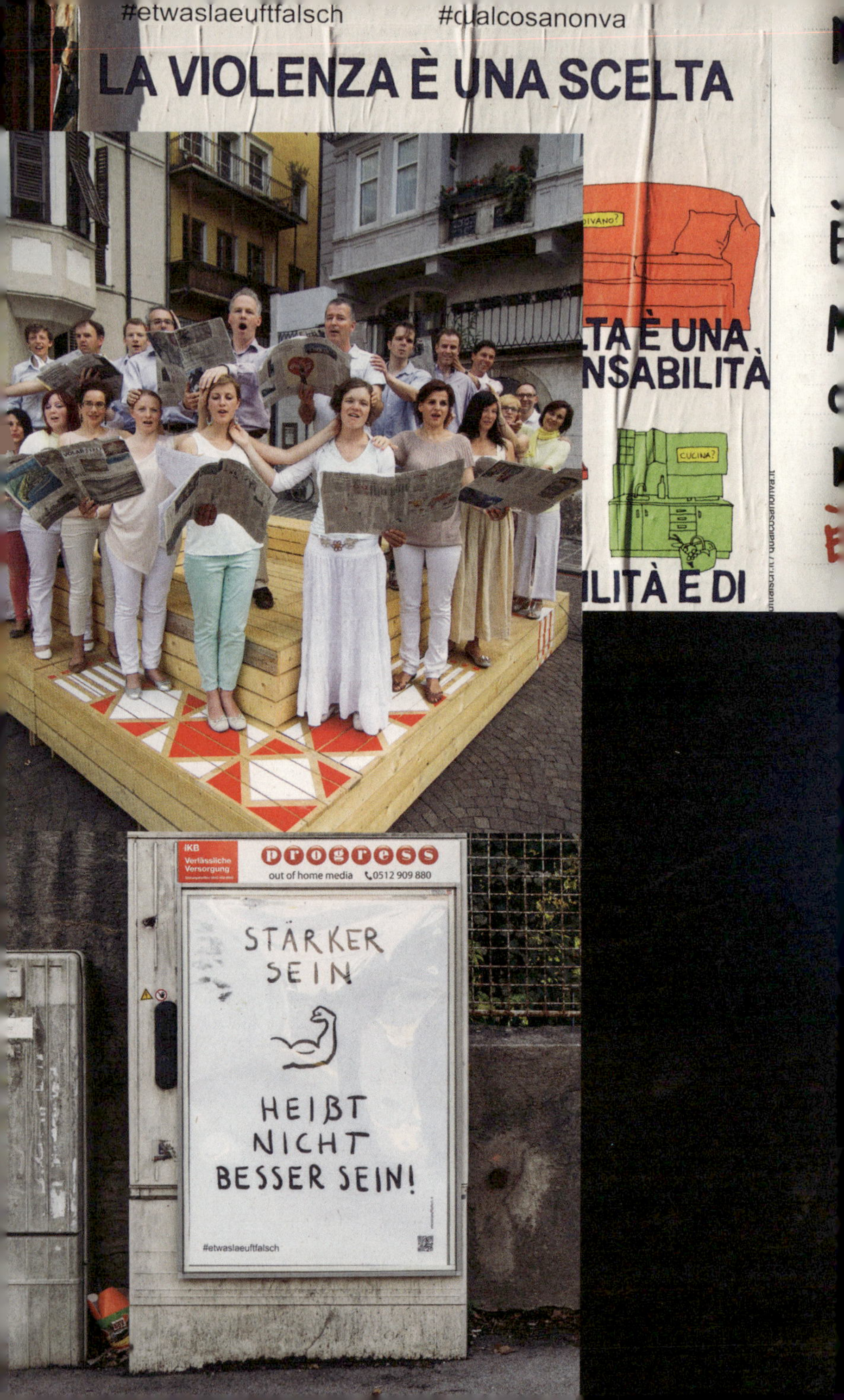
#etwaslaeuftfalsch
#qualcosanonva
LA VIOLENZA È UNA SCELTA
DIVANO?
LTA È UNA
NSABILITÀ
CUCINA?
ILITÀ E DI
iKB
Verlässliche Versorgung
progress
out of home media
0512 909 880
STÄRKER SEIN
HEIßT NICHT BESSER SEIN!
#etwaslaeuftfalsch

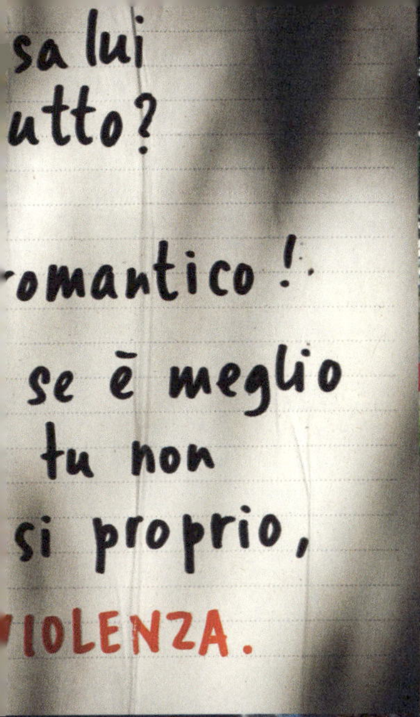
sa lui
utto?
romantico !
se è meglio
tu non
si proprio,
IOLENZA.

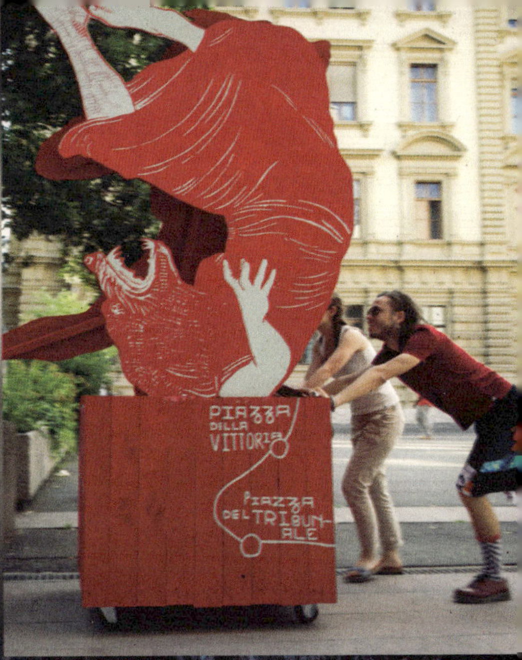
PIAZZA
VITTORIA
PIAZZA
DEL TRIBUN-
ALE

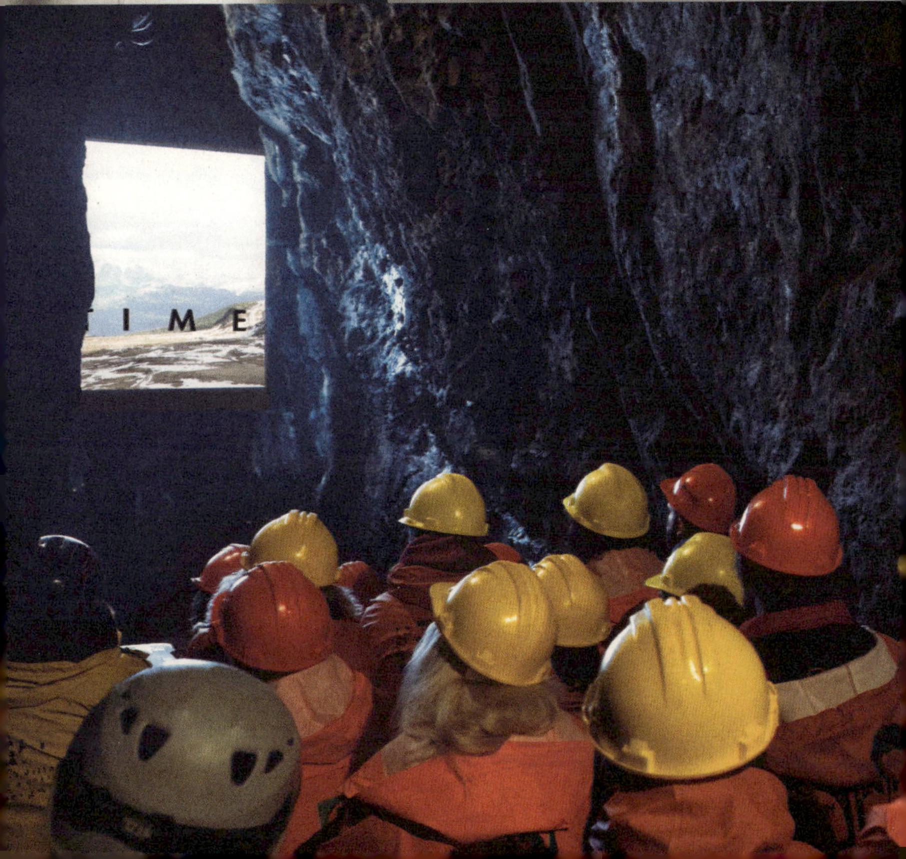
TIME

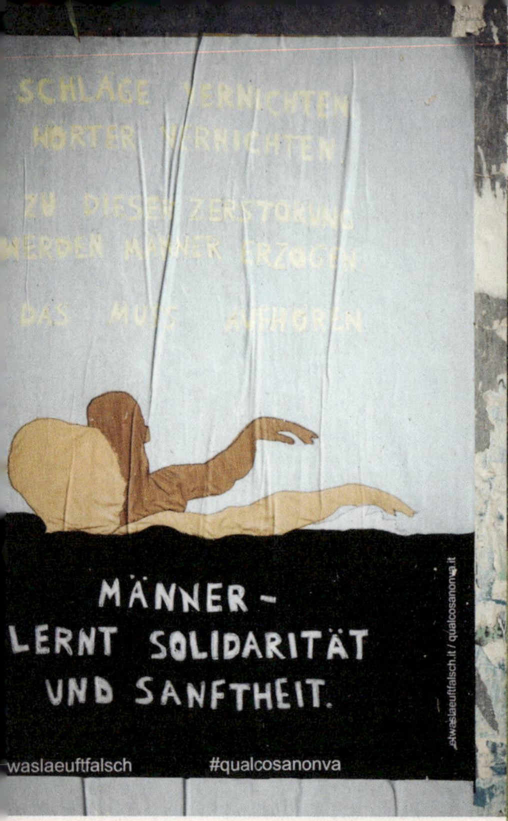
SCHLÄGE VERNICHTEN.
WÖRTER VERNICHTEN.
ZU DIESER ZERSTÖRUNG WERDEN MÄNNER ERZOGEN.
DAS MUSS AUFHÖREN
MÄNNER –
LERNT SOLIDARITÄT
UND SANFTHEIT.
waslaeuftfalsch.it / qualcosanonva.it
waslaeuftfalsch
#qualcosanonva

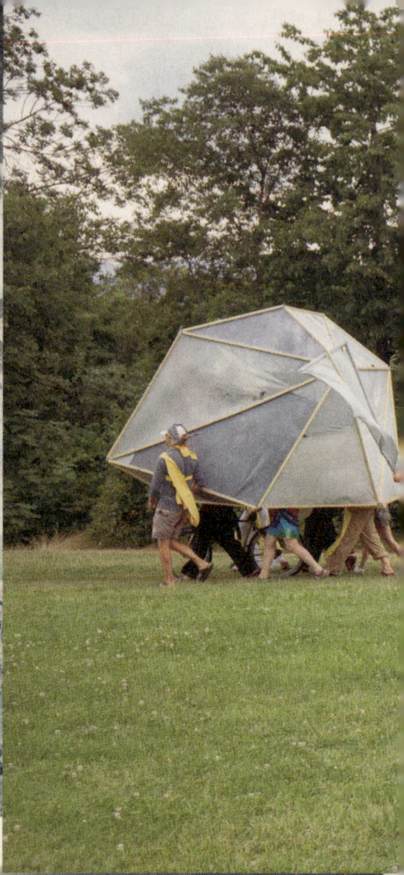

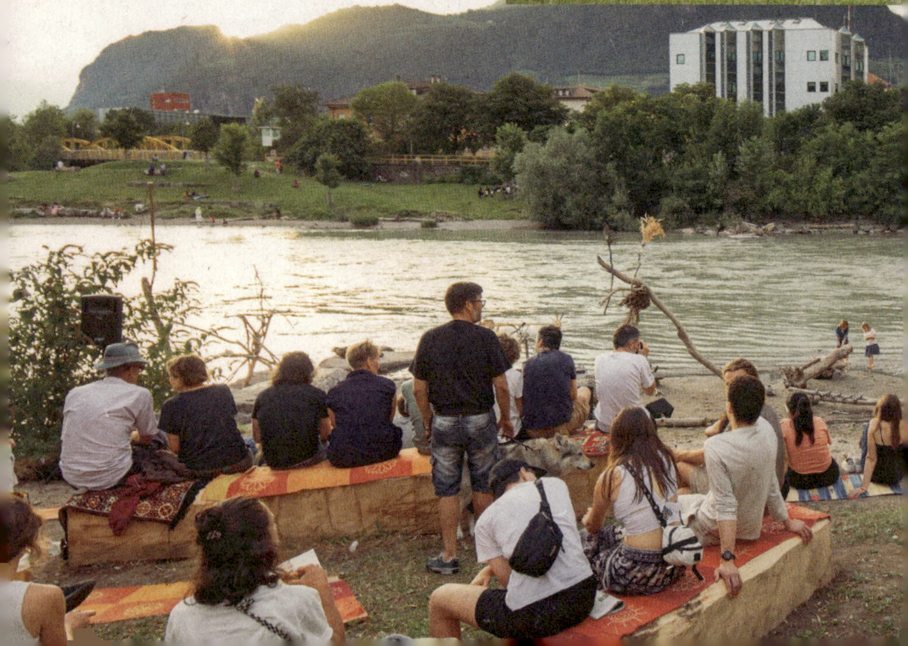

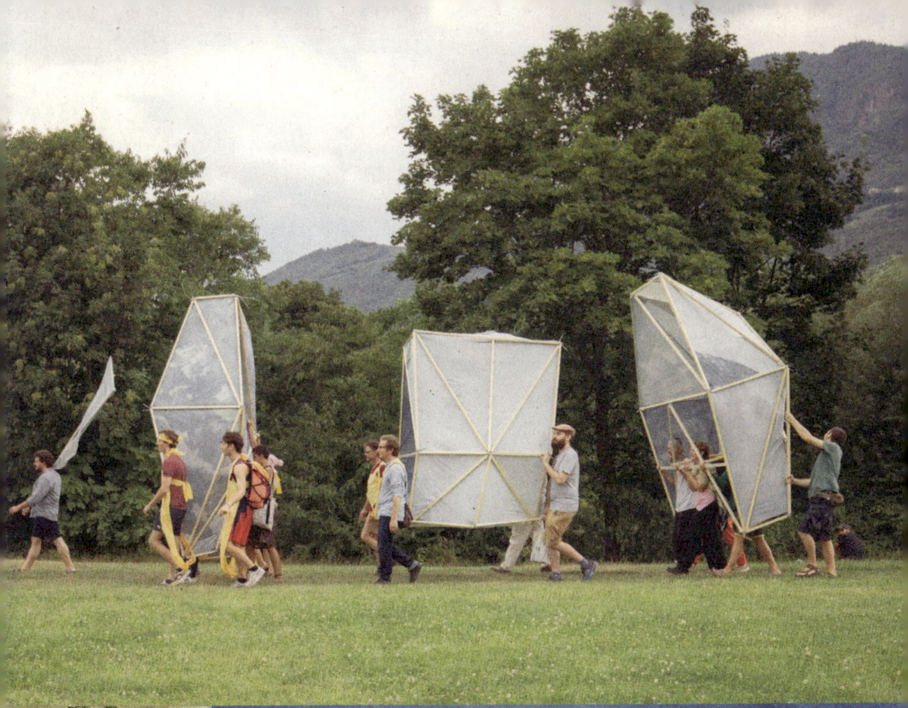

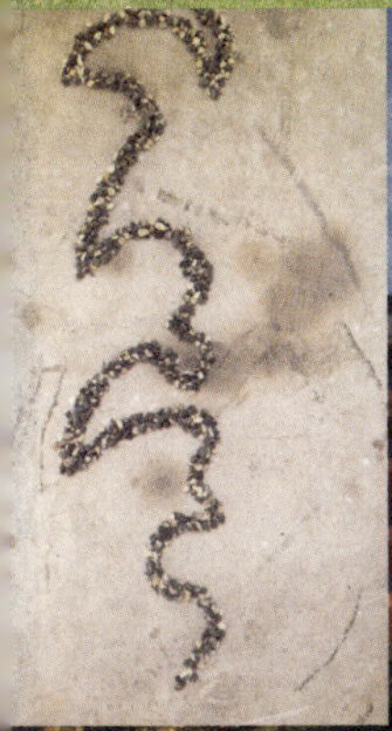

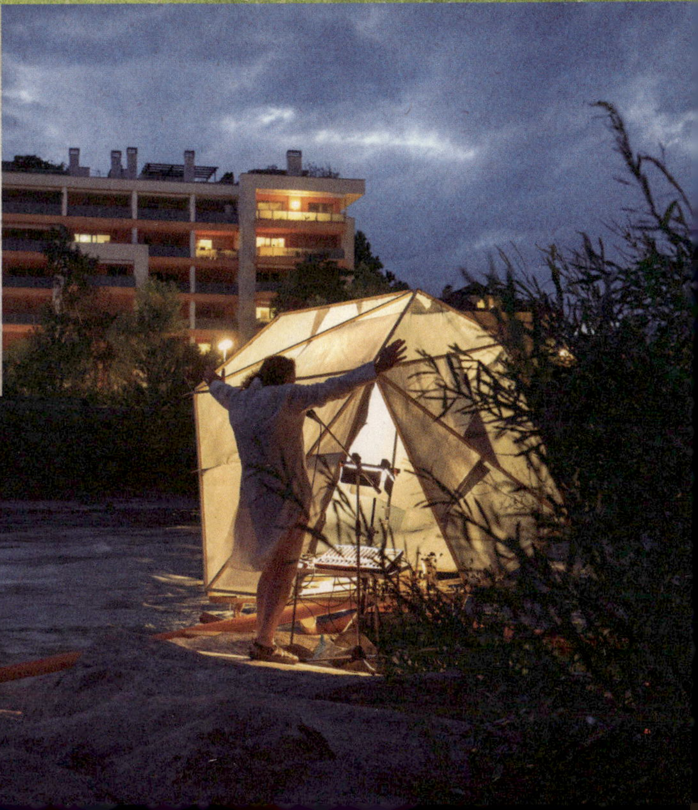

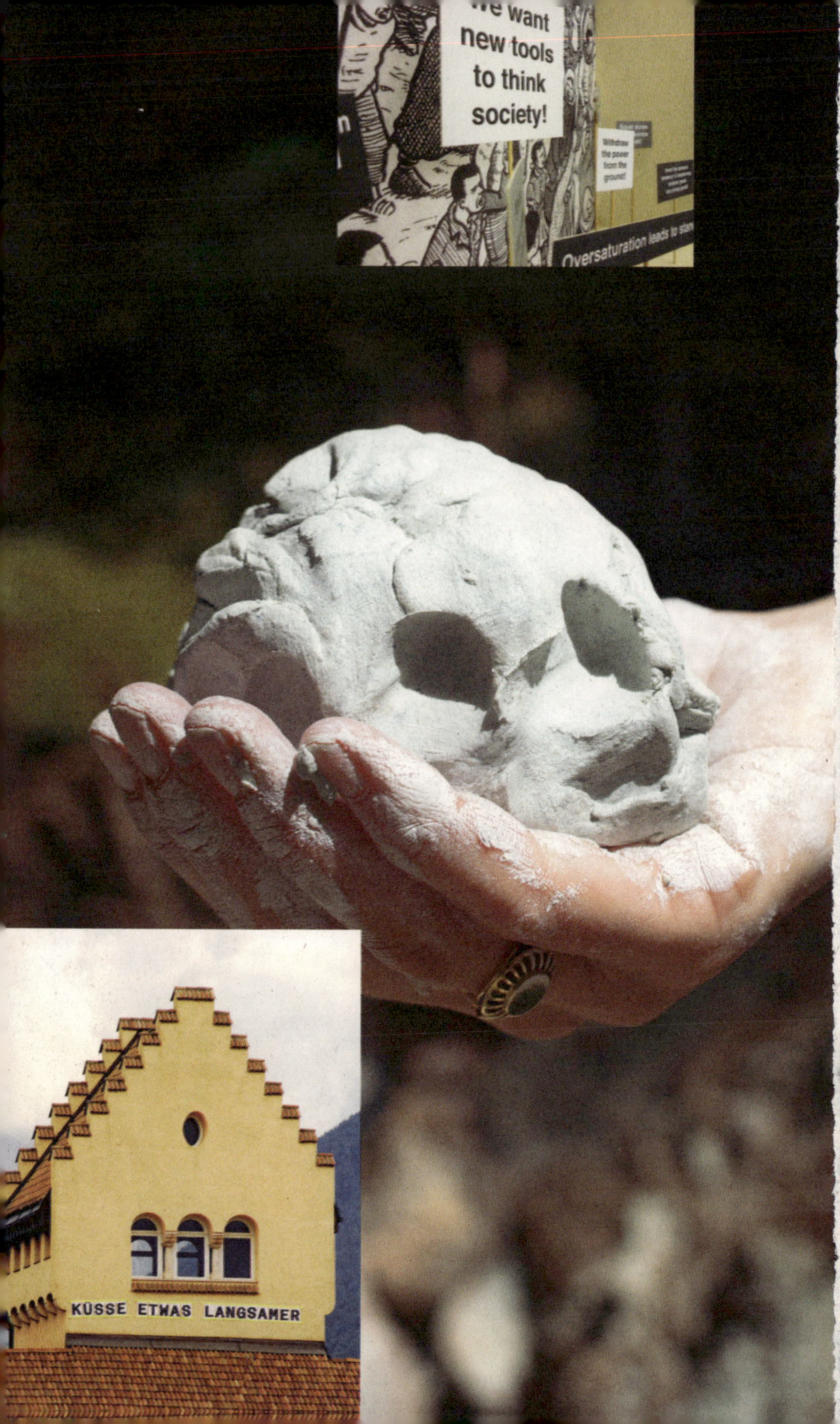
new tools
to think
society!
Withdraw
the power
from the
ground!
KÜSSE ETWAS LANGSAMER